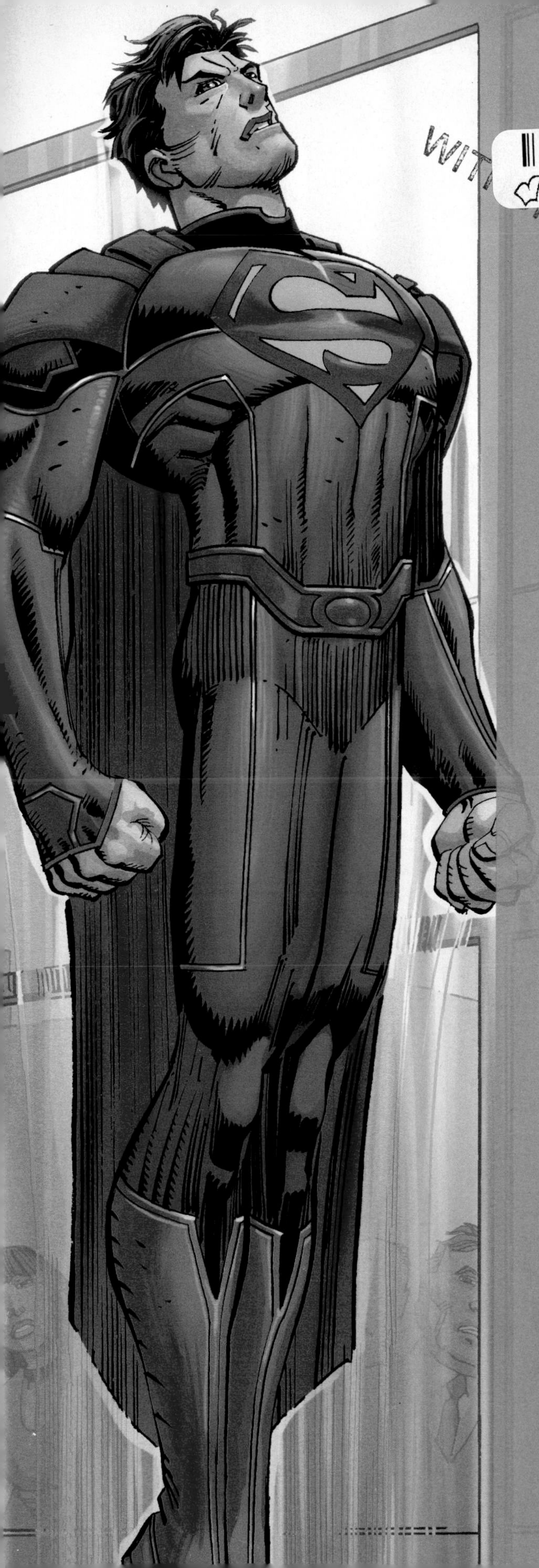

SUPERMAN ACTION COMICS

VOLUME 9
LAST RITES

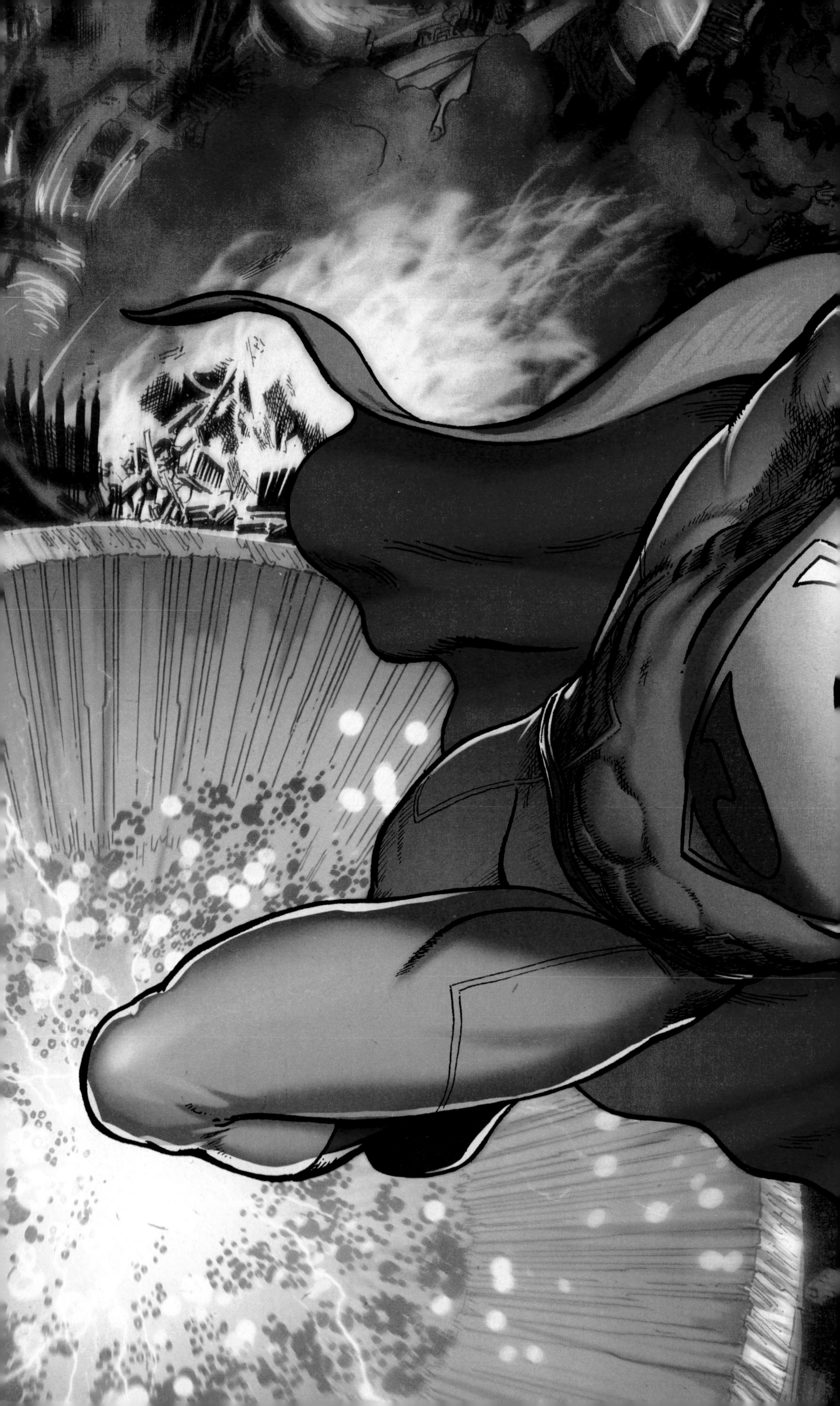

SUPERMAN ACTION COMICS

**VOLUME 9
LAST RITES**

WRITTEN BY
**GREG PAK
AARON KUDER
PETER J. TOMASI**

ART BY
**AARON KUDER
RAFA SANDOVAL
JORDI TARRAGONA
ARDIAN SYAF
JONATHAN GLAPION
SCOTT HANNA
SANDRA HOPE
DAVID MESSINA
JAVI FERNANDEZ
BRUNO REDONDO
VICENTE CIFUENTES
GAETANO CARLUCCI
JUAN ALBARRAN
PAUL PELLETIER
DALE EAGLESHAM
SCOT EATON
WAYNE FAUCHER**

COLOR BY
**TOMEU MOREY
WIL QUINTANA
ARIF PRIANTO**

LETTERS BY
**STEVE WANDS
ROB LEIGH**

COLLECTION COVER ART BY
AARON KUDER AND **TOMEU MOREY**

SUPERMAN CREATED BY
JERRY SIEGEL & JOE SHUSTER

SUPERGIRL BASED ON
CHARACTERS CREATED BY
JERRY SIEGEL & JOE SHUSTER

BY SPECIAL ARRANGEMENT
WITH THE JERRY SIEGEL FAMILY

EDDIE BERGANZA Editor – Original Series
ANDREW MARINO Assistant Editor – Original Series
JEB WOODARD Group Editor – Collected Editions
LIZ ERICKSON Editor – Collected Edition
STEVE COOK Design Director – Books
DAMIAN RYLAND Publication Design

BOB HARRAS Senior VP – Editor-in-Chief, DC Comics

DIANE NELSON President
DAN DiDIO Publisher
JIM LEE Publisher
GEOFF JOHNS President & Chief Creative Officer
AMIT DESAI Executive VP – Business & Marketing Strategy, Direct to Consumer & Global Franchise Management
SAM ADES Senior VP – Direct to Consumer
BOBBIE CHASE VP – Talent Development
MARK CHIARELLO Senior VP – Art, Design & Collected Editions
JOHN CUNNINGHAM Senior VP – Sales & Trade Marketing
ANNE DePIES Senior VP – Business Strategy, Finance & Administration
DON FALLETTI VP – Manufacturing Operations
LAWRENCE GANEM VP – Editorial Administration & Talent Relations
ALISON GILL Senior VP – Manufacturing & Operations
HANK KANALZ Senior VP – Editorial Strategy & Administration
JAY KOGAN VP – Legal Affairs
THOMAS LOFTUS VP – Business Affairs
JACK MAHAN VP – Business Affairs
NICK J. NAPOLITANO VP – Manufacturing Administration
EDDIE SCANNELL VP – Consumer Marketing
COURTNEY SIMMONS Senior VP – Publicity & Communications
JIM (SKI) SOKOLOWSKI VP – Comic Book Specialty Sales & Trade Marketing
NANCY SPEARS VP – Mass, Book, Digital Sales & Trade Marketing

SUPERMAN - ACTION COMICS VOLUME 9: LAST RITES

Published by DC Comics. Original compilation published Copyright © 2016 DC Comics. All Rights Reserved.

Originally published in single magazine form in ACTION COMICS 48-52 © 2016 DC Comics. All Rights Reserved.
All characters, their distinctive likenesses and related elements featured in this publication are trademarks of DC Comics.
The stories, characters and incidents featured in this publication are entirely fictional.
DC Comics does not read or accept unsolicited ideas, stories or artwork.

DC Comics, 2900 West Alameda Ave., Burbank, CA 91505
Printed by LSC Communications, Salem, VA, USA. 5/5/17. First Printing.
ISBN: 978-1-4012-7410-8

Library of Congress Cataloging-in-Publication Data is available.

PEFC Certified

Printed on paper from
sustainably managed
forests, controlled
sources

PEFC

PEFC/29-31-337   www.pefc.org

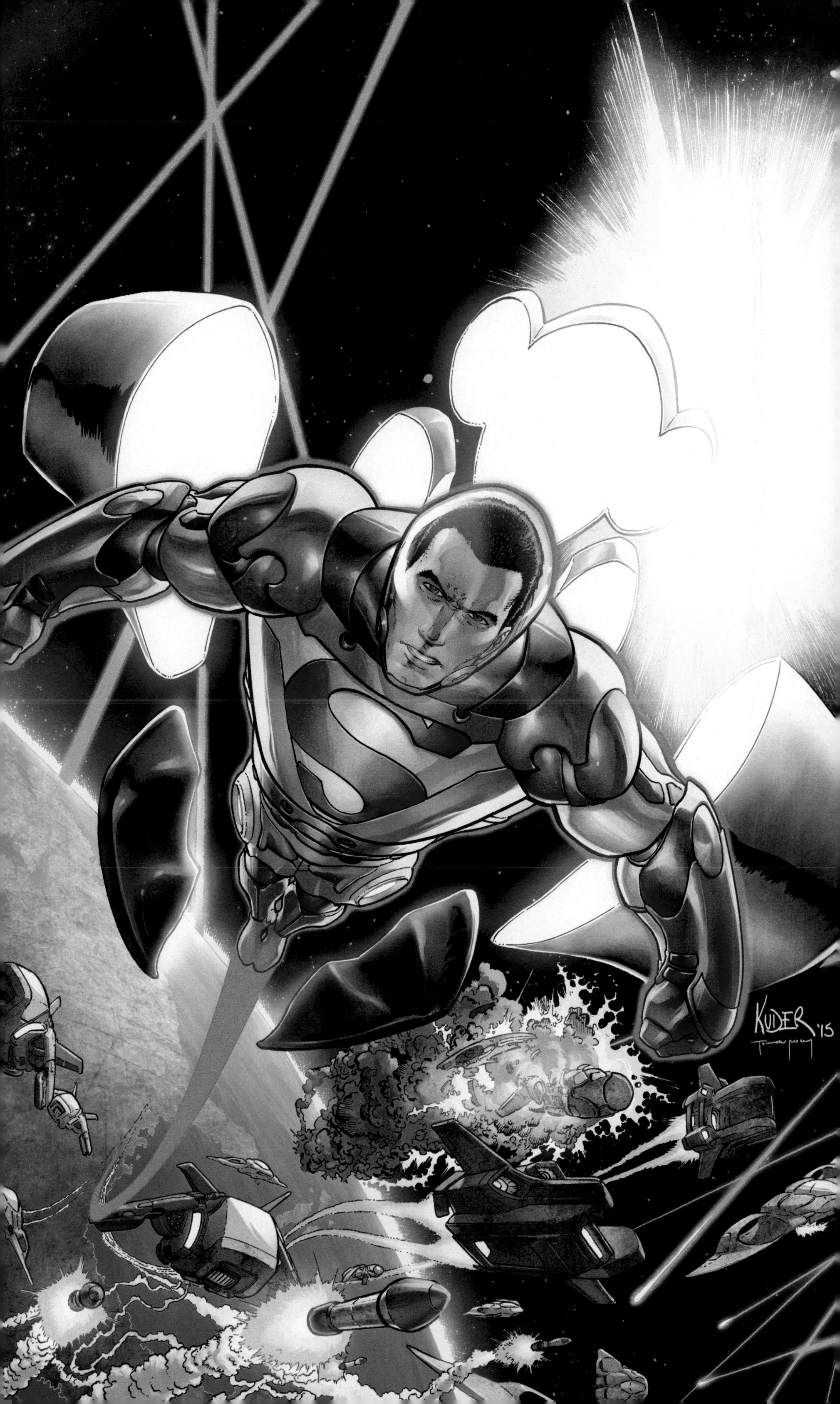
KUDER '15

Previously,
in SUPERMAN ANNUAL #3...

The immortal Vandal Savage has had one singular focus over the course of his impossibly long life. Over the centuries, every time the comet that granted him his abilities approached the Earth's orbit, Savage has tried to harness its powers once more. In Han Dynasty China, in Renaissance Rome, in WWII-era Germany...each time, Savage failed in his goal, but each time taught him more about the mysterious meteor...

In present-day Metropolis, a powerless and exposed Clark Kent struggles to adjust to normal life. Attempts by John Henry Irons to restore the Man of Steel to his former glory have come to nothing, so while the Justice League is called away to handle an emergency deep in space, Clark is forced to ask for help from the people of Metropolis just to keep a runaway oil tanker from careening off an overpass.

But when the Stormwatch Carrier, helmed by none other than Vandal Savage, appears in the sky over the city and destroys the Justice League Watchtower Satellite, it's the de-powered Superman alone who must stand and face him...

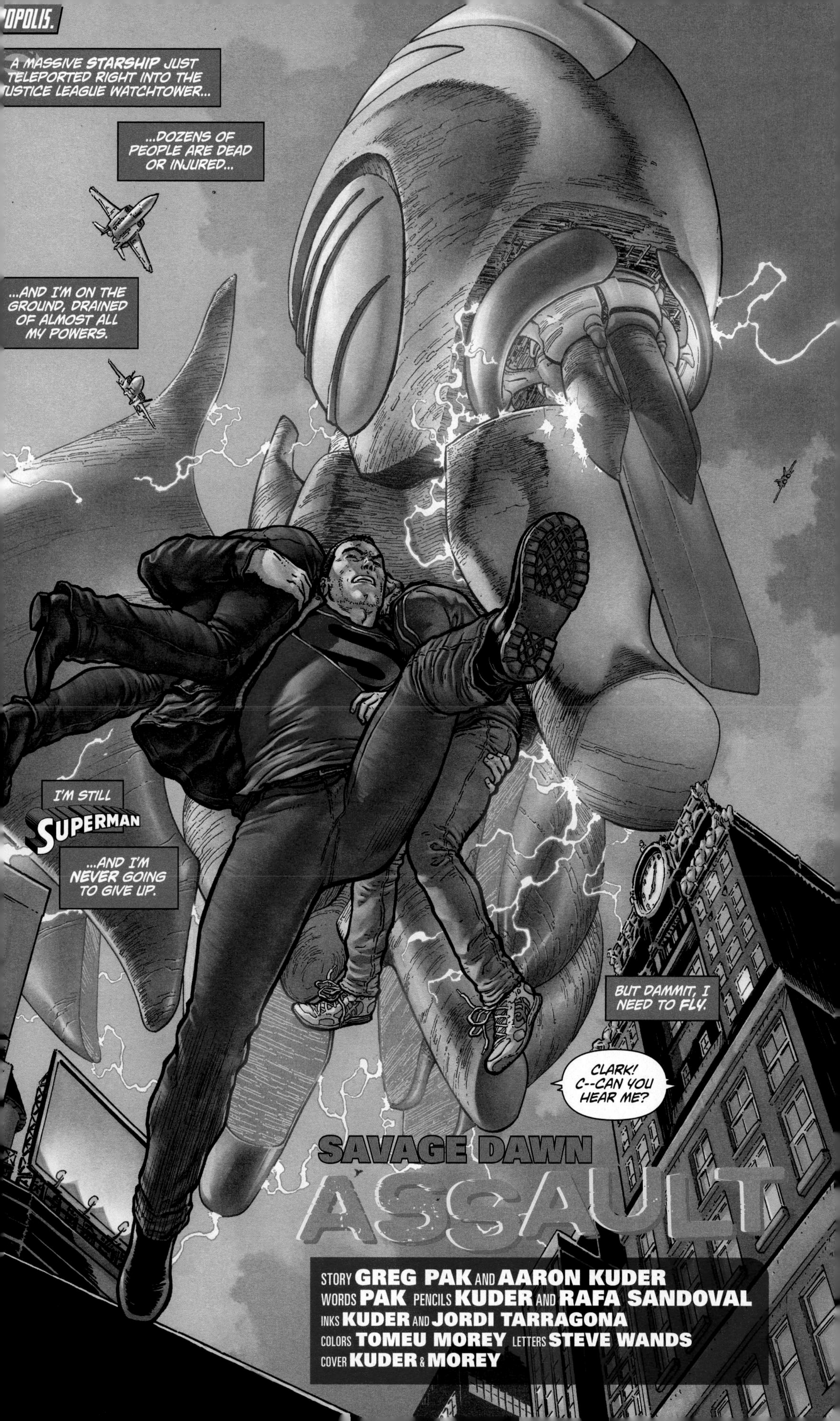
OPOLIS.
A MASSIVE STARSHIP JUST TELEPORTED RIGHT INTO THE USTICE LEAGUE WATCHTOWER...
...DOZENS OF PEOPLE ARE DEAD OR INJURED...
...AND I'M ON THE GROUND, DRAINED OF ALMOST ALL MY POWERS.
I'M STILL
SUPERMAN
...AND I'M NEVER GOING TO GIVE UP.
BUT DAMMIT, I NEED TO FLY.
CLARK! C--CAN YOU HEAR ME?
SAVAGE DAWN
ASSAULT
STORY GREG PAK AND AARON KUDER
WORDS PAK PENCILS KUDER AND RAFA SANDOVAL
INKS KUDER AND JORDI TARRAGONA
COLORS TOMEU MOREY LETTERS STEVE WANDS
COVER KUDER & MOREY

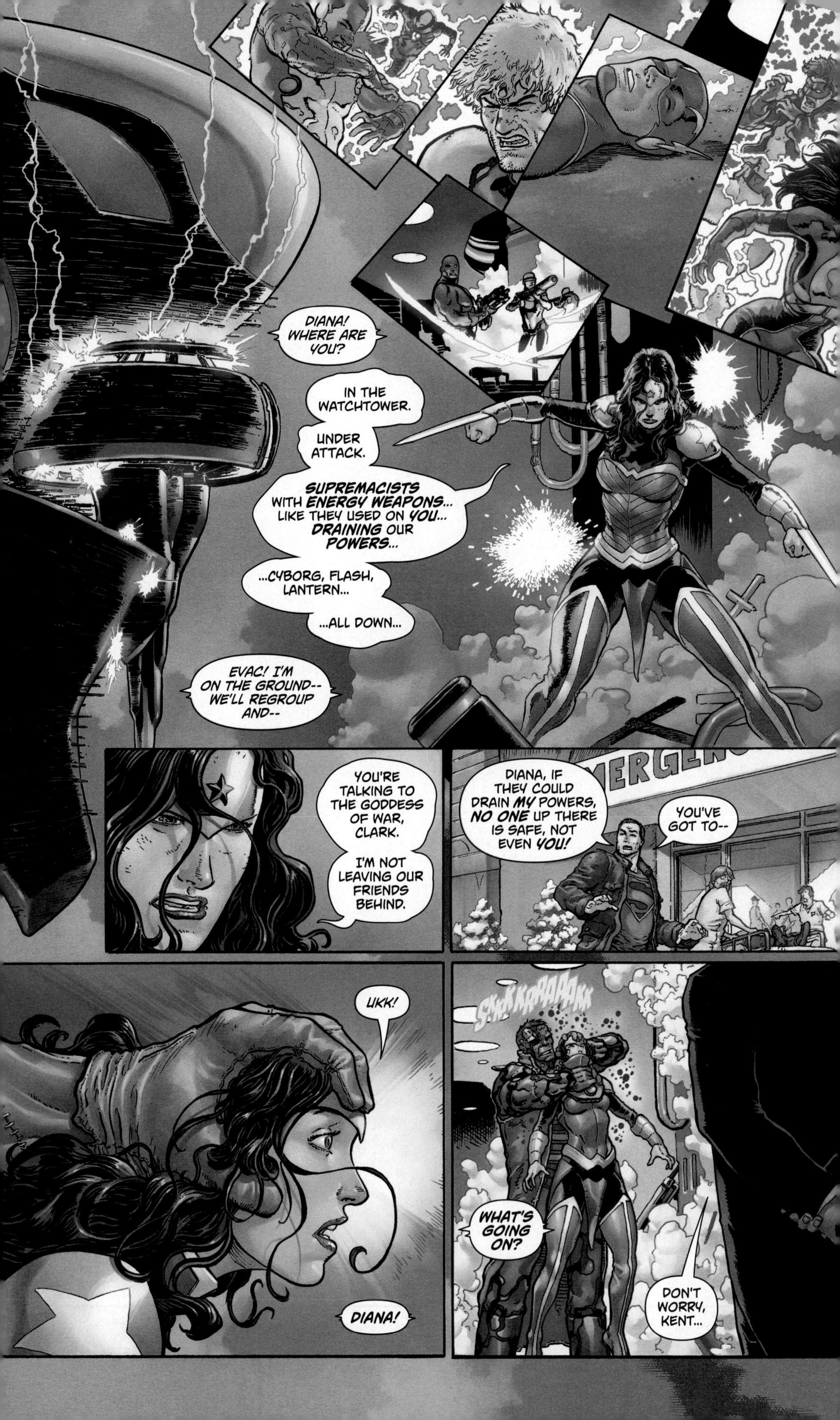
DIANA! WHERE ARE YOU?
IN THE WATCHTOWER.
UNDER ATTACK.
SUPREMACISTS WITH ENERGY WEAPONS... LIKE THEY USED ON YOU... DRAINING OUR POWERS...
...CYBORG, FLASH, LANTERN...
...ALL DOWN...
EVAC! I'M ON THE GROUND-- WE'LL REGROUP AND--
YOU'RE TALKING TO THE GODDESS OF WAR, CLARK.
I'M NOT LEAVING OUR FRIENDS BEHIND.
DIANA, IF THEY COULD DRAIN MY POWERS, NO ONE UP THERE IS SAFE, NOT EVEN YOU!
YOU'VE GOT TO--
UKK!
DIANA!
SKRAKKRAAAAKK
WHAT'S GOING ON?
DON'T WORRY, KENT...

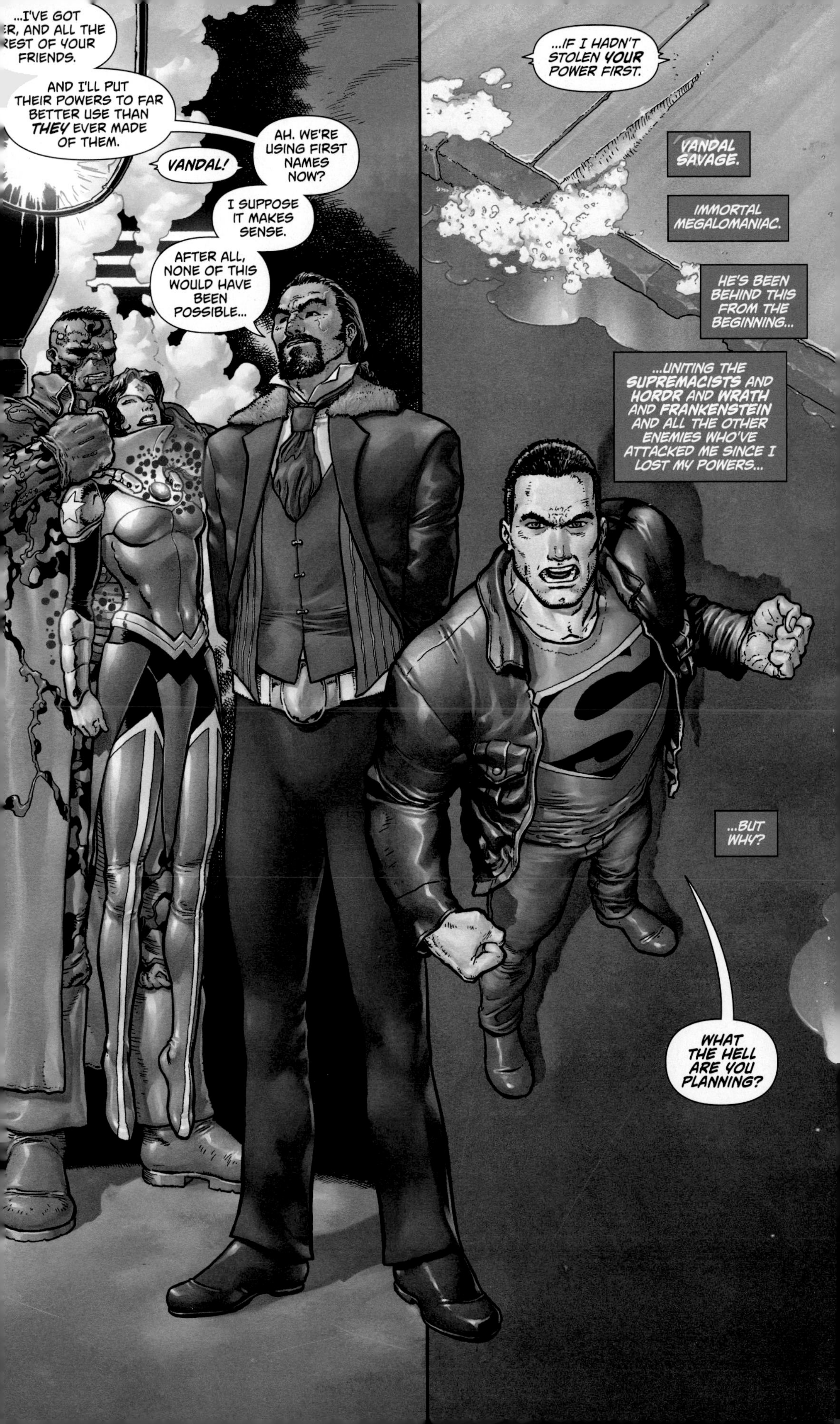

...I'VE GOT
ER, AND ALL THE
REST OF YOUR
FRIENDS.
AND I'LL PUT THEIR POWERS TO FAR BETTER USE THAN THEY EVER MADE OF THEM.
VANDAL!
AH. WE'RE USING FIRST NAMES NOW?
I SUPPOSE IT MAKES SENSE.
AFTER ALL, NONE OF THIS WOULD HAVE BEEN POSSIBLE...
...IF I HADN'T STOLEN YOUR POWER FIRST.
VANDAL SAVAGE.
IMMORTAL MEGALOMANIAC.
HE'S BEEN BEHIND THIS FROM THE BEGINNING...
...UNITING THE SUPREMACISTS AND HORDR AND WRATH AND FRANKENSTEIN AND ALL THE OTHER ENEMIES WHO'VE ATTACKED ME SINCE I LOST MY POWERS...
...BUT WHY?
WHAT THE HELL ARE YOU PLANNING?

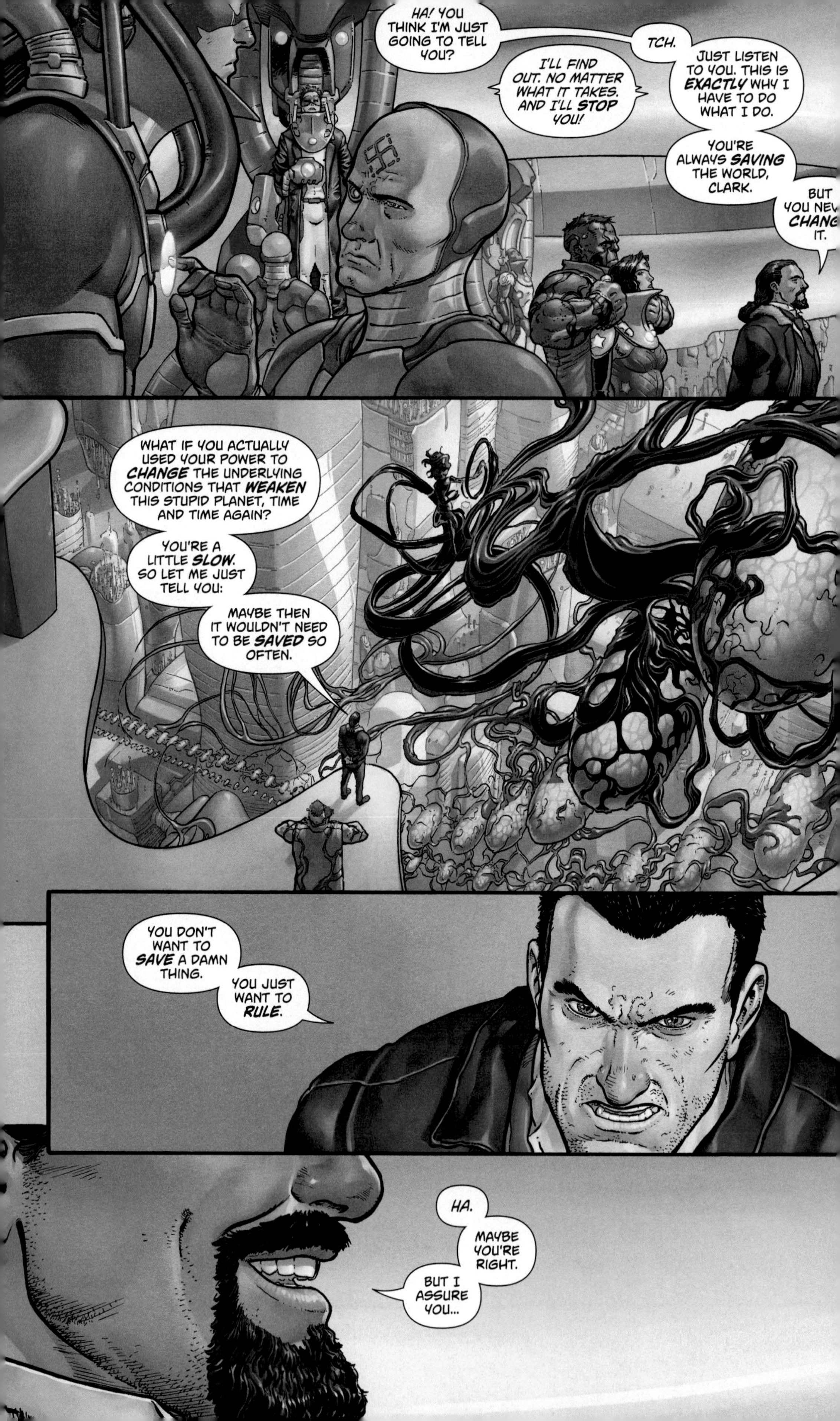
HA! YOU THINK I'M JUST GOING TO TELL YOU?
TCH.
I'LL FIND OUT. NO MATTER WHAT IT TAKES. AND I'LL STOP YOU!
JUST LISTEN TO YOU. THIS IS EXACTLY WHY I HAVE TO DO WHAT I DO.
YOU'RE ALWAYS SAVING THE WORLD, CLARK.
BUT YOU NEV CHANG IT.
WHAT IF YOU ACTUALLY USED YOUR POWER TO CHANGE THE UNDERLYING CONDITIONS THAT WEAKEN THIS STUPID PLANET, TIME AND TIME AGAIN?
YOU'RE A LITTLE SLOW. SO LET ME JUST TELL YOU:
MAYBE THEN IT WOULDN'T NEED TO BE SAVED SO OFTEN.
YOU DON'T WANT TO SAVE A DAMN THING.
YOU JUST WANT TO RULE.
HA.
MAYBE YOU'RE RIGHT.
BUT I ASSURE YOU...

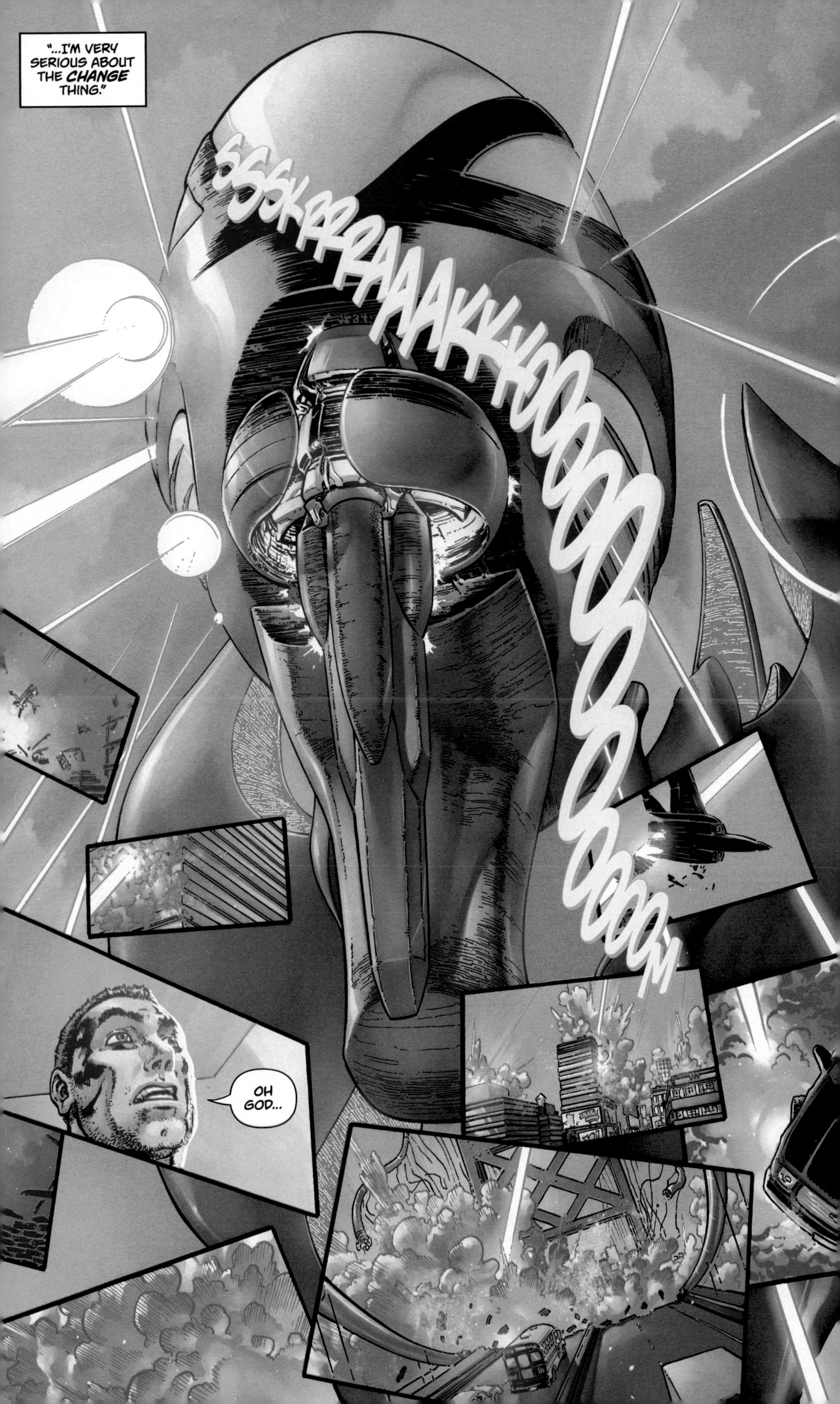
"...I'M VERY SERIOUS ABOUT THE *CHANGE* THING."
SSSKRRRAAAKKKOOOOOOOOOOOM
OH GOD...

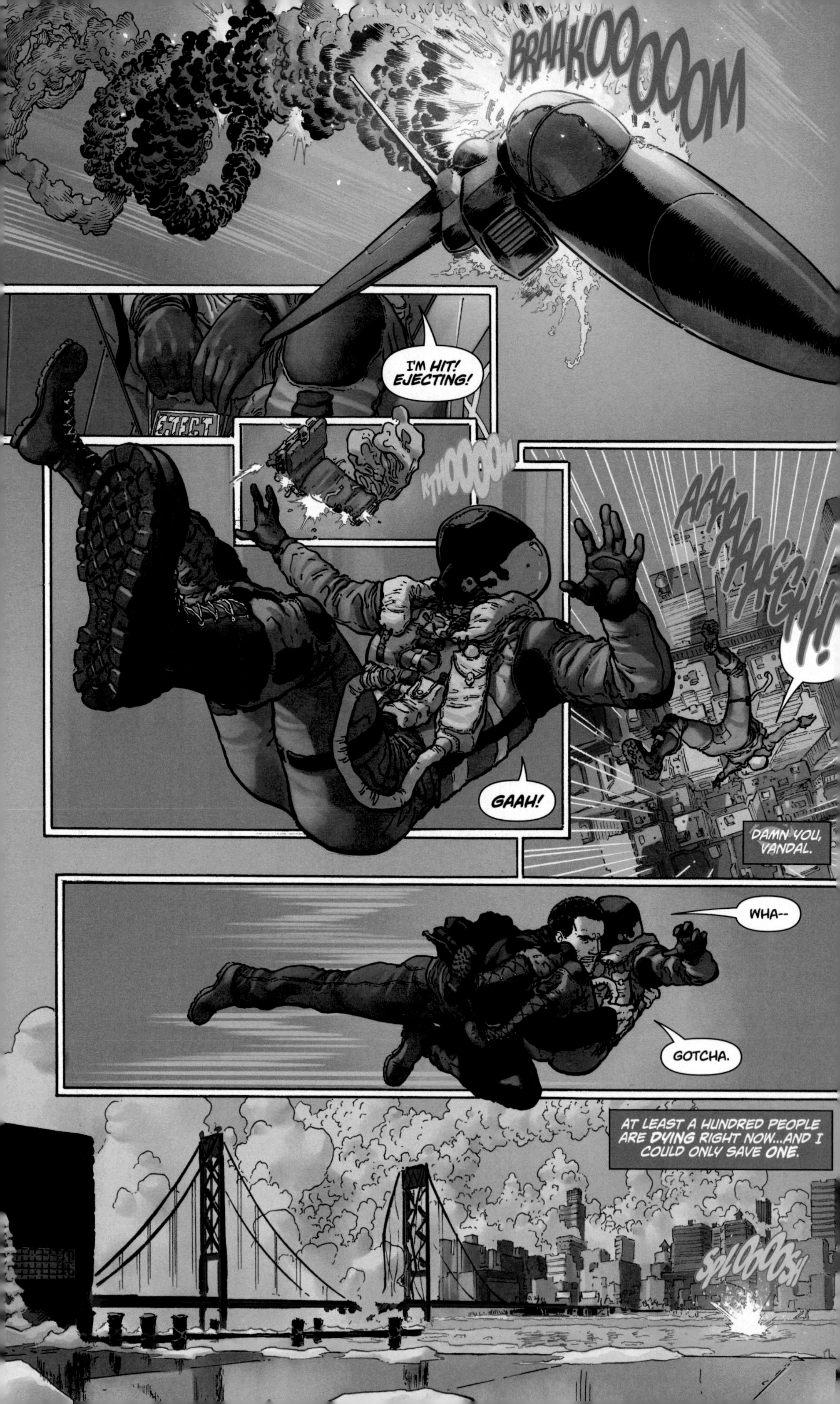
BRAAKOOOOOM
I'M HIT! EJECTING!
EJECT
KTHOOOOOM
GAAH!
AAAAAAAGGHH!
DAMN YOU, VANDAL.
WHA--
GOTCHA.
AT LEAST A HUNDRED PEOPLE ARE DYING RIGHT NOW...AND I COULD ONLY SAVE ONE.
SPLOOOOSH

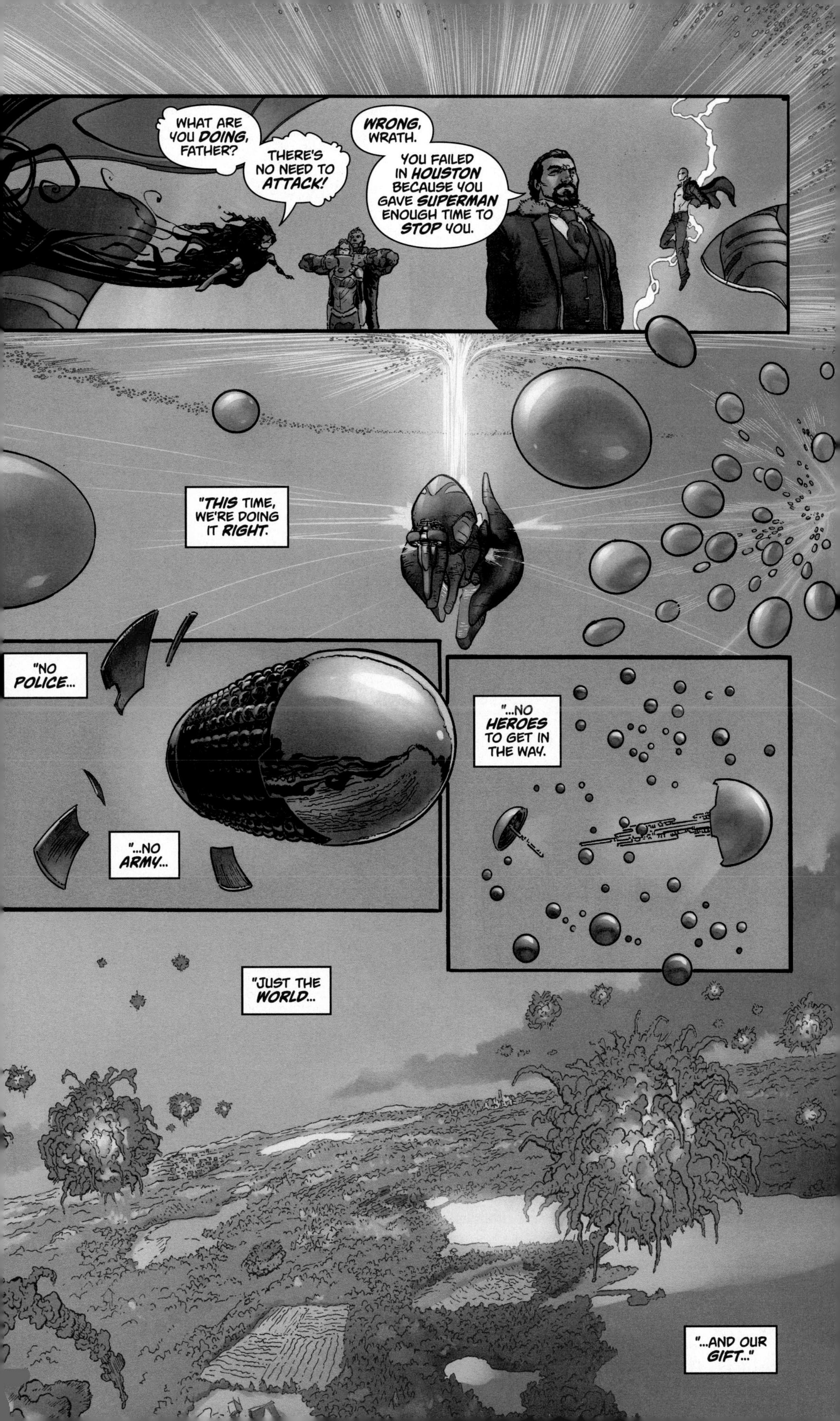

WHAT ARE YOU DOING, FATHER?
THERE'S NO NEED TO ATTACK!
WRONG, WRATH.
YOU FAILED IN HOUSTON BECAUSE YOU GAVE SUPERMAN ENOUGH TIME TO STOP YOU.
"THIS TIME, WE'RE DOING IT RIGHT.
"NO POLICE...
"...NO ARMY...
"...NO HEROES TO GET IN THE WAY.
"JUST THE WORLD...
"...AND OUR GIFT..."

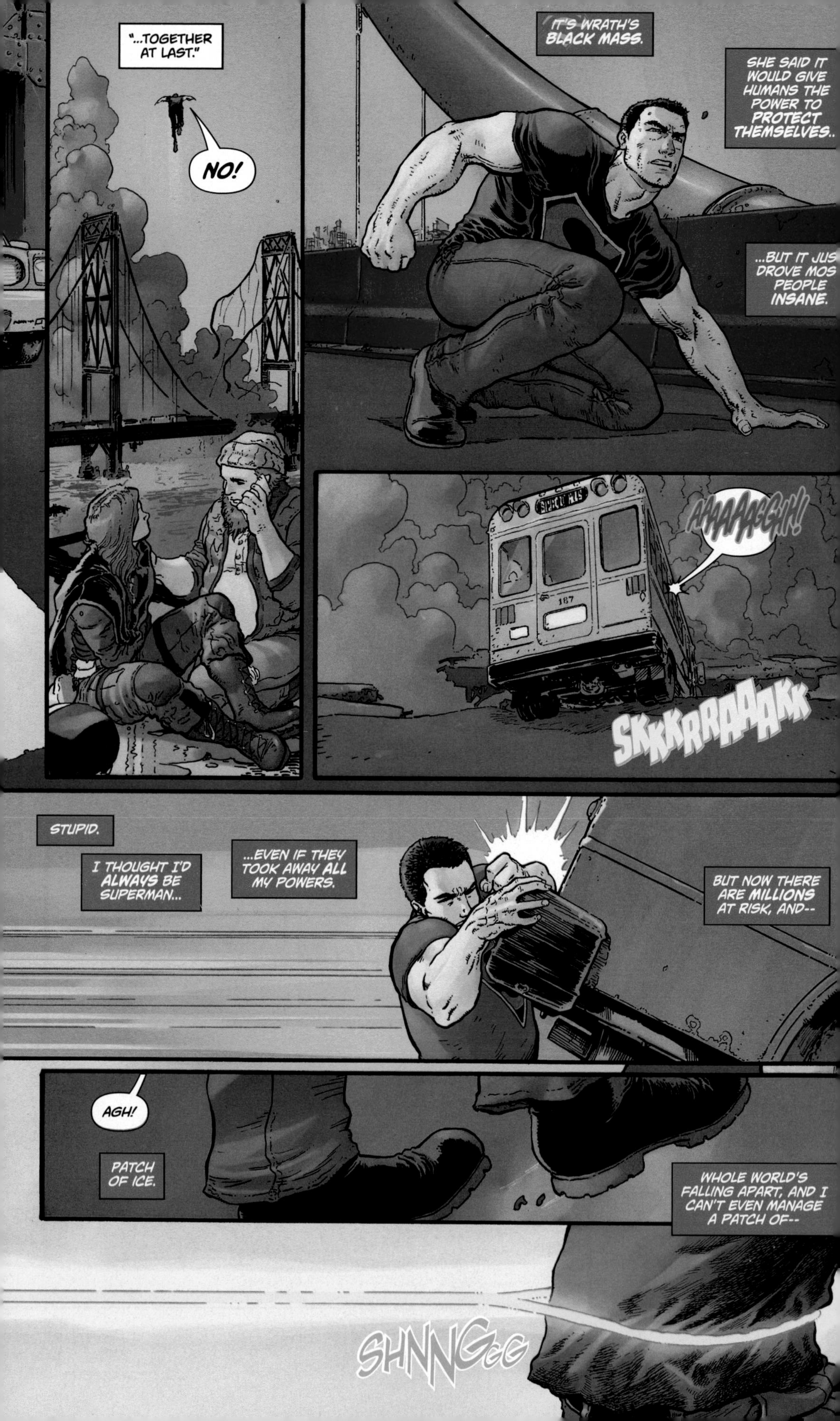
"...TOGETHER AT LAST."
NO!
IT'S WRATH'S BLACK MASS.
SHE SAID IT WOULD GIVE HUMANS THE POWER TO PROTECT THEMSELVES...
...BUT IT JUS DROVE MOS PEOPLE INSANE.
AAAAAAGGHH!
187
SKKRRAAAKK
STUPID.
I THOUGHT I'D ALWAYS BE SUPERMAN...
...EVEN IF THEY TOOK AWAY ALL MY POWERS.
BUT NOW THERE ARE MILLIONS AT RISK, AND--
AGH!
PATCH OF ICE.
WHOLE WORLD'S FALLING APART, AND I CAN'T EVEN MANAGE A PATCH OF--
SHNNGGG

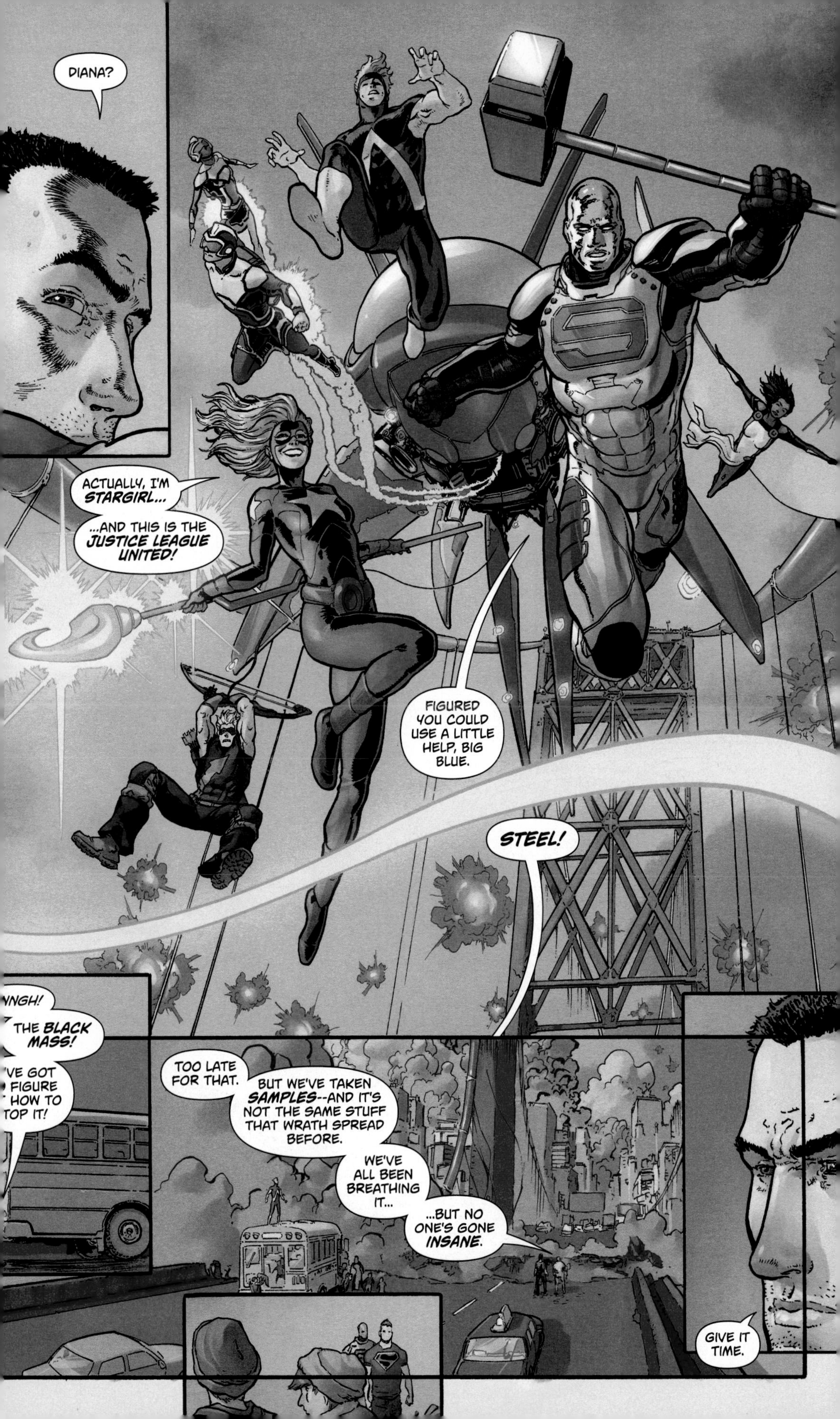

DIANA?
ACTUALLY, I'M STARGIRL...
...AND THIS IS THE JUSTICE LEAGUE UNITED!
FIGURED YOU COULD USE A LITTLE HELP, BIG BLUE.
STEEL!
NGH!
THE BLACK MASS!
'VE GOT FIGURE HOW TO TOP IT!
TOO LATE FOR THAT.
BUT WE'VE TAKEN SAMPLES--AND IT'S NOT THE SAME STUFF THAT WRATH SPREAD BEFORE.
WE'VE ALL BEEN BREATHING IT...
...BUT NO ONE'S GONE INSANE.
GIVE IT TIME.

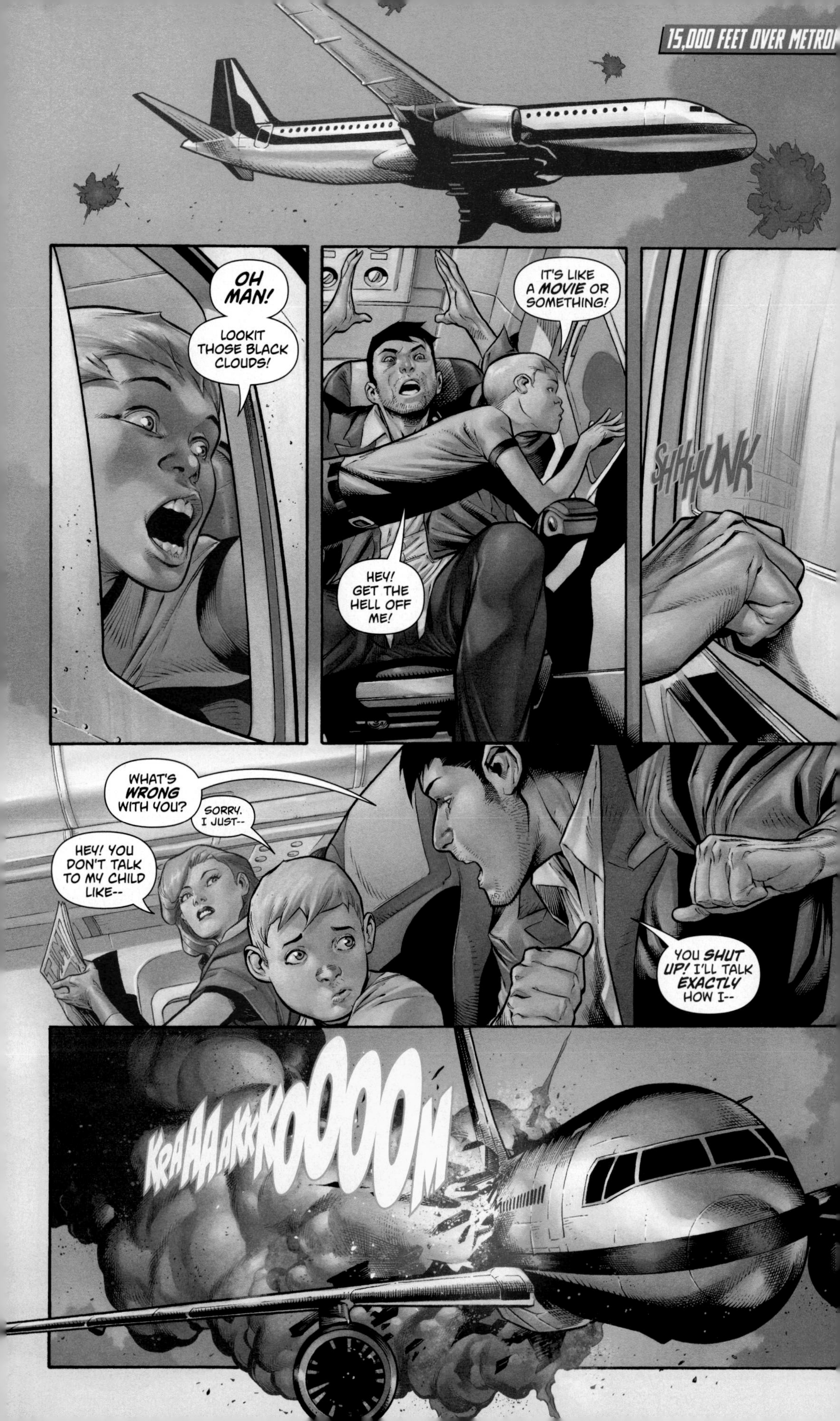
15,000 FEET OVER METRO
OH MAN!
LOOKIT THOSE BLACK CLOUDS!
IT'S LIKE A MOVIE OR SOMETHING!
HEY! GET THE HELL OFF ME!
SHHHUNK
WHAT'S WRONG WITH YOU?
SORRY. I JUST--
HEY! YOU DON'T TALK TO MY CHILD LIKE--
YOU SHUT UP! I'LL TALK EXACTLY HOW I--
KRAAAAKKKOOOOM

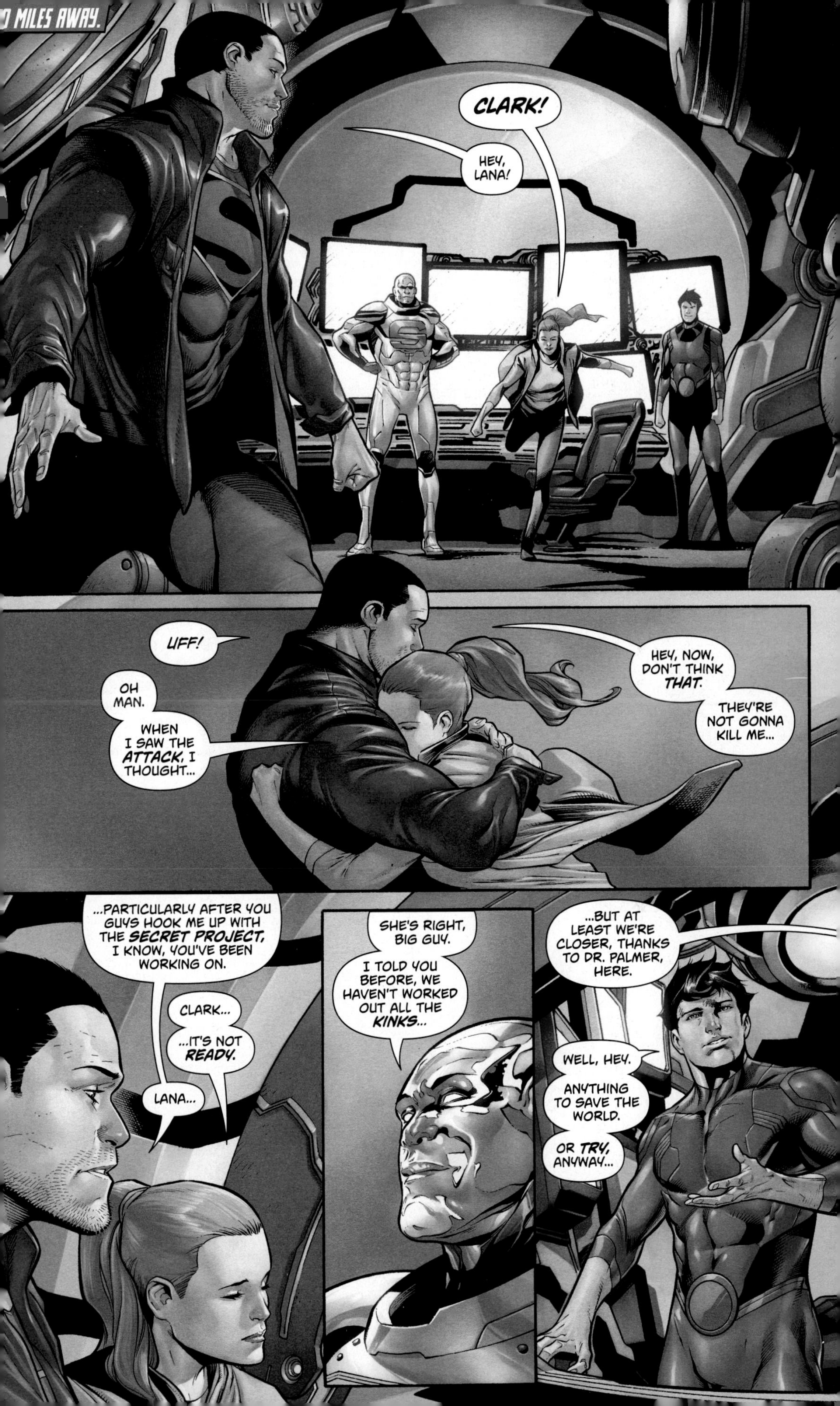

...0 MILES AWAY.
CLARK!
HEY, LANA!
UFF!
OH MAN.
WHEN I SAW THE ATTACK, I THOUGHT...
HEY, NOW, DON'T THINK THAT.
THEY'RE NOT GONNA KILL ME...
...PARTICULARLY AFTER YOU GUYS HOOK ME UP WITH THE SECRET PROJECT, I KNOW, YOU'VE BEEN WORKING ON.
CLARK...
...IT'S NOT READY.
LANA...
SHE'S RIGHT, BIG GUY.
I TOLD YOU BEFORE, WE HAVEN'T WORKED OUT ALL THE KINKS...
...BUT AT LEAST WE'RE CLOSER, THANKS TO DR. PALMER, HERE.
WELL, HEY.
ANYTHING TO SAVE THE WORLD.
OR TRY, ANYWAY...

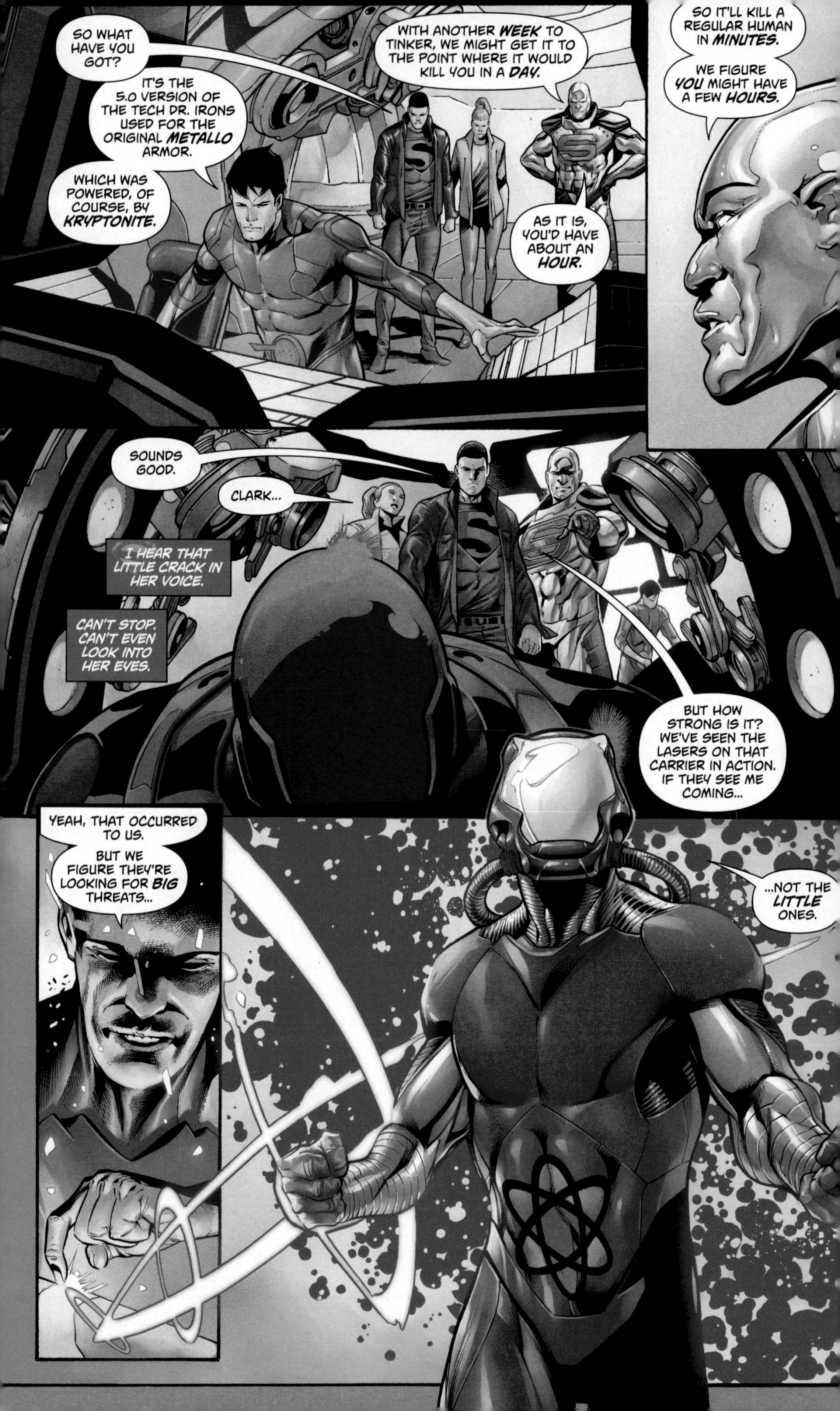
SO WHAT HAVE YOU GOT?
IT'S THE 5.0 VERSION OF THE TECH DR. IRONS USED FOR THE ORIGINAL METALLO ARMOR.
WHICH WAS POWERED, OF COURSE, BY KRYPTONITE.
WITH ANOTHER WEEK TO TINKER, WE MIGHT GET IT TO THE POINT WHERE IT WOULD KILL YOU IN A DAY.
AS IT IS, YOU'D HAVE ABOUT AN HOUR.
SO IT'LL KILL A REGULAR HUMAN IN MINUTES.
WE FIGURE YOU MIGHT HAVE A FEW HOURS.
SOUNDS GOOD.
CLARK...
I HEAR THAT LITTLE CRACK IN HER VOICE.
CAN'T STOP. CAN'T EVEN LOOK INTO HER EYES.
BUT HOW STRONG IS IT? WE'VE SEEN THE LASERS ON THAT CARRIER IN ACTION. IF THEY SEE ME COMING...
YEAH, THAT OCCURRED TO US.
BUT WE FIGURE THEY'RE LOOKING FOR BIG THREATS...
...NOT THE LITTLE ONES.

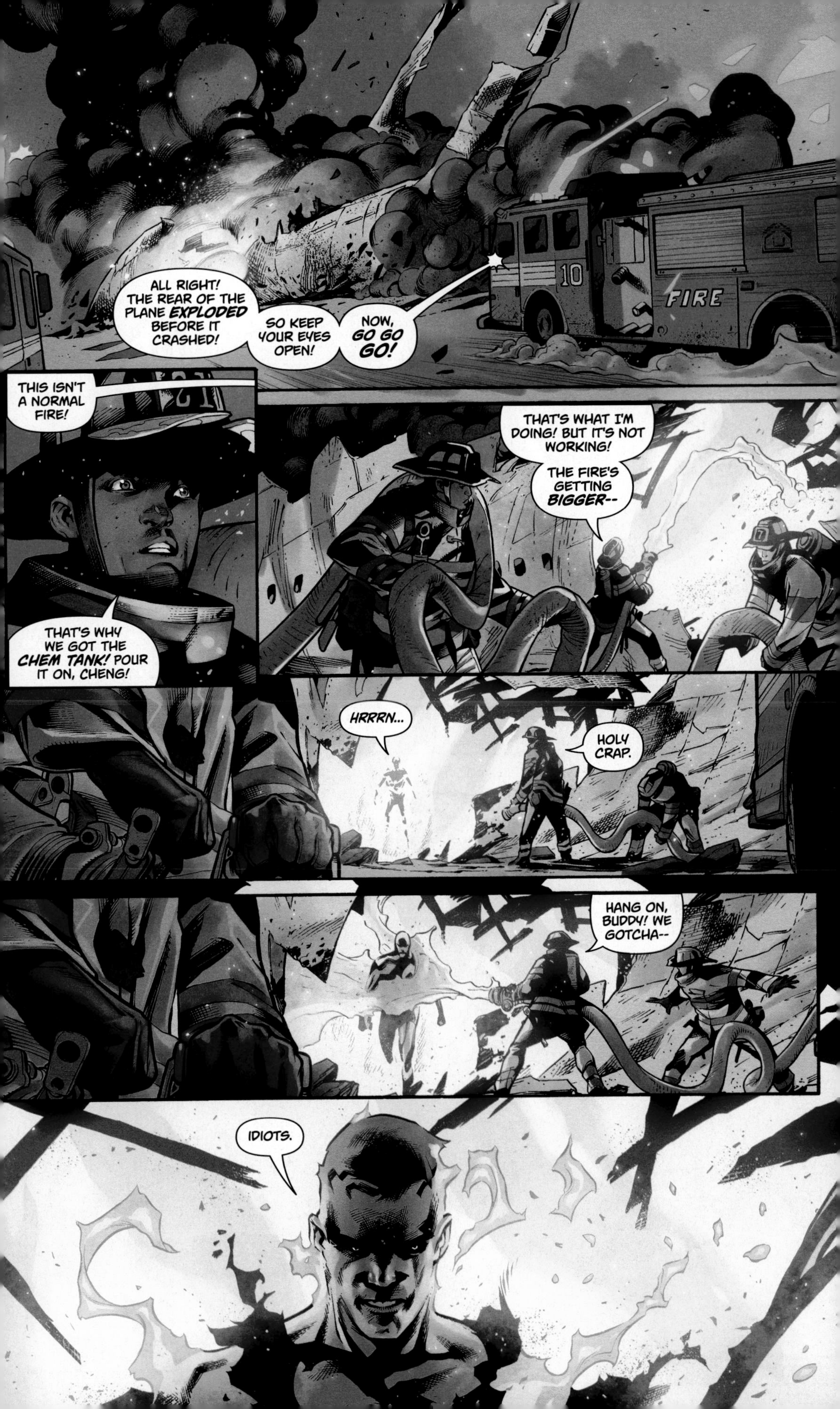
ALL RIGHT! THE REAR OF THE PLANE EXPLODED BEFORE IT CRASHED!
SO KEEP YOUR EYES OPEN!
NOW, GO GO GO!
THIS ISN'T A NORMAL FIRE!
THAT'S WHY WE GOT THE CHEM TANK! POUR IT ON, CHENG!
THAT'S WHAT I'M DOING! BUT IT'S NOT WORKING!
THE FIRE'S GETTING BIGGER--
HRRRN...
HOLY CRAP.
HANG ON, BUDDY! WE GOTCHA--
IDIOTS.

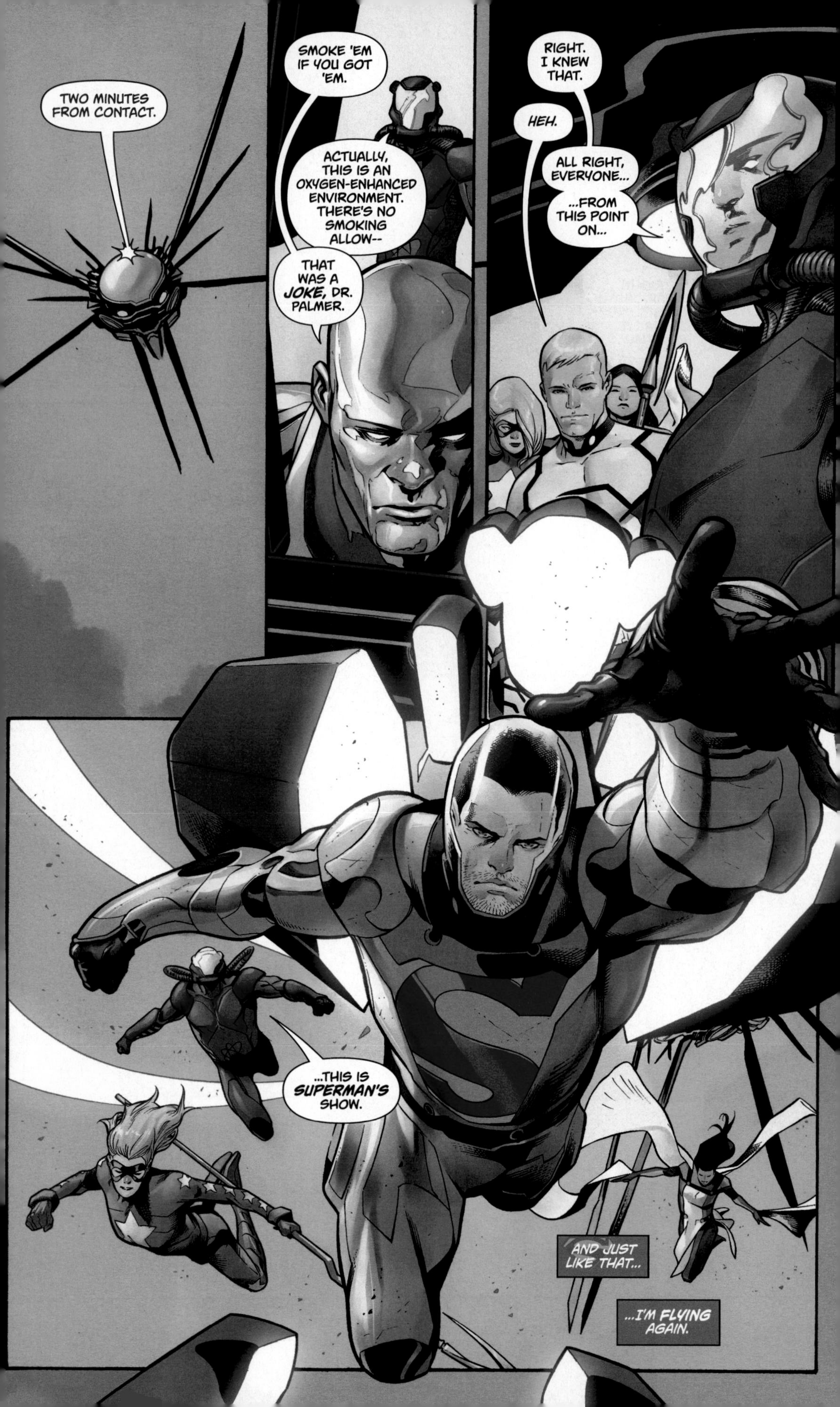
TWO MINUTES FROM CONTACT.
SMOKE 'EM IF YOU GOT 'EM.
ACTUALLY, THIS IS AN OXYGEN-ENHANCED ENVIRONMENT. THERE'S NO SMOKING ALLOW--
THAT WAS A JOKE, DR. PALMER.
RIGHT. I KNEW THAT.
HEH.
ALL RIGHT, EVERYONE...
...FROM THIS POINT ON...
...THIS IS SUPERMAN'S SHOW.
AND JUST LIKE THAT...
...I'M FLYING AGAIN.

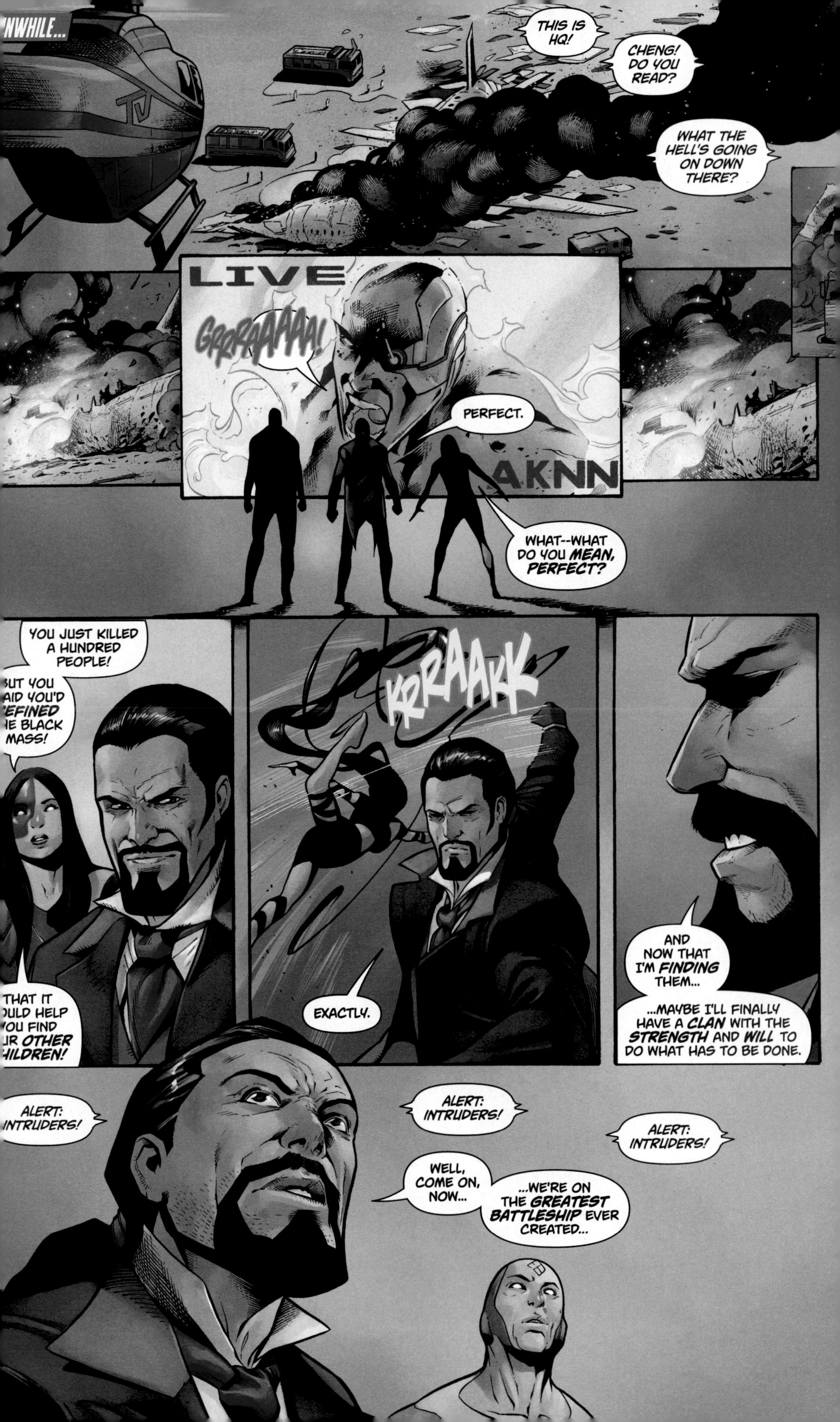
NWHILE...
THIS IS HQ!
CHENG! DO YOU READ?
WHAT THE HELL'S GOING ON DOWN THERE?
LIVE
GRRRAAAAA!
PERFECT.
AKNN
WHAT--WHAT DO YOU MEAN, PERFECT?
YOU JUST KILLED A HUNDRED PEOPLE!
UT YOU AID YOU'D EFINED E BLACK MASS!
THAT IT OULD HELP YOU FIND R OTHER HILDREN!
KRRAAKK
EXACTLY.
AND NOW THAT I'M FINDING THEM...
...MAYBE I'LL FINALLY HAVE A CLAN WITH THE STRENGTH AND WILL TO DO WHAT HAS TO BE DONE.
ALERT: INTRUDERS!
ALERT: INTRUDERS!
ALERT: INTRUDERS!
WELL, COME ON, NOW...
...WE'RE ON THE GREATEST BATTLESHIP EVER CREATED...

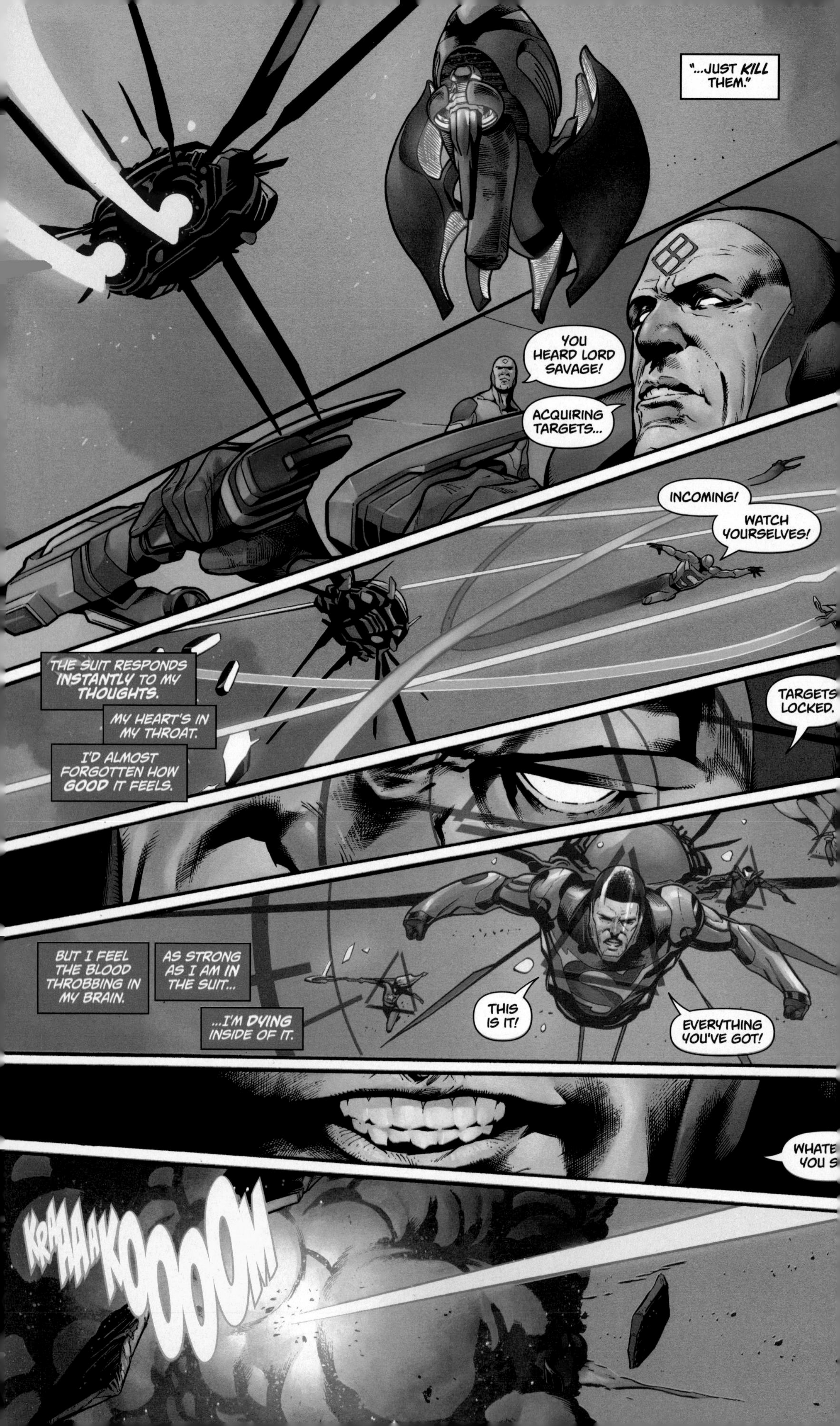
"...JUST KILL THEM."
YOU HEARD LORD SAVAGE!
ACQUIRING TARGETS...
INCOMING!
WATCH YOURSELVES!
THE SUIT RESPONDS INSTANTLY TO MY THOUGHTS.
MY HEART'S IN MY THROAT.
I'D ALMOST FORGOTTEN HOW GOOD IT FEELS.
TARGETS LOCKED.
BUT I FEEL THE BLOOD THROBBING IN MY BRAIN.
AS STRONG AS I AM IN THE SUIT...
...I'M DYING INSIDE OF IT.
THIS IS IT!
EVERYTHING YOU'VE GOT!
KRAAAAKOOOOM

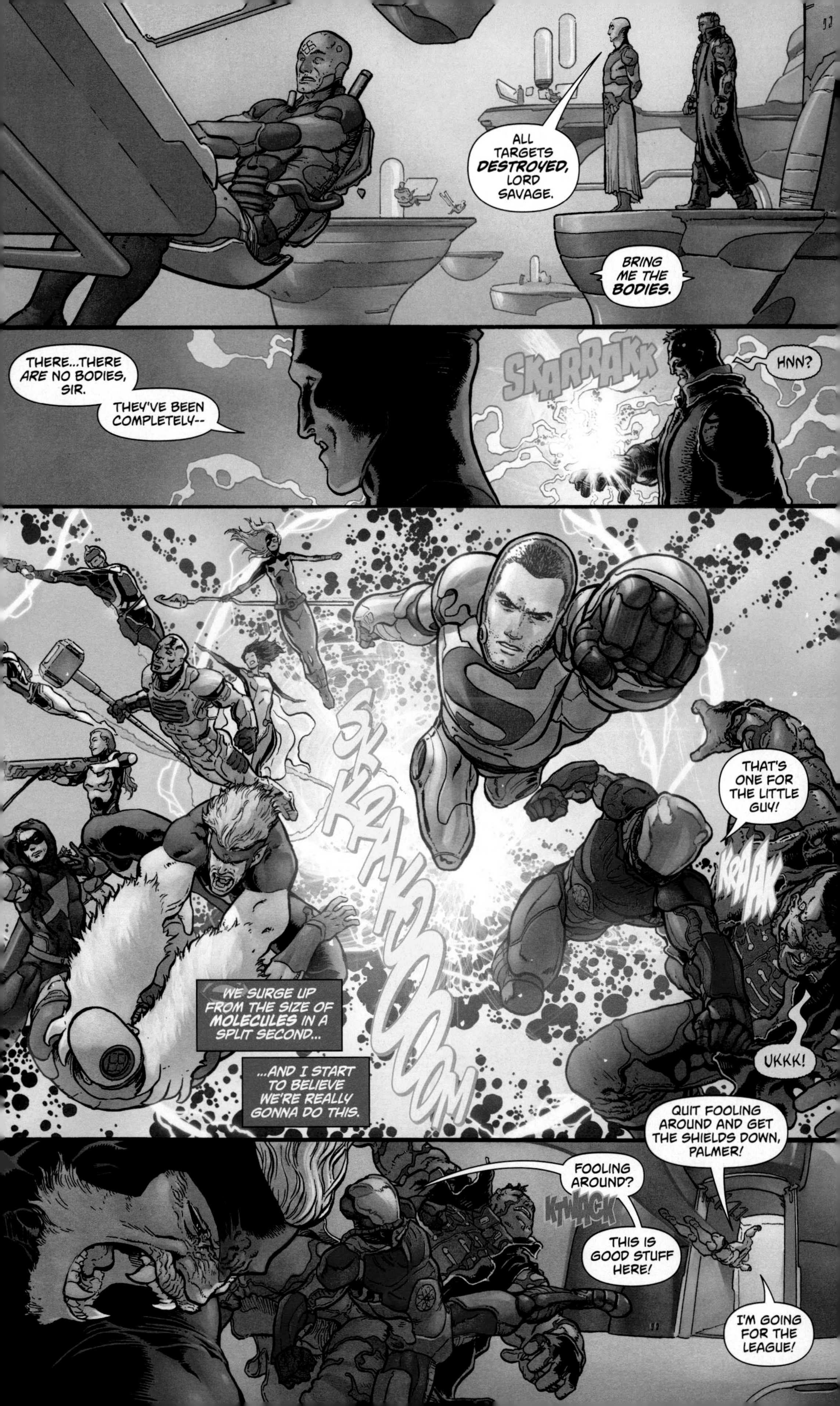

ALL TARGETS DESTROYED, LORD SAVAGE.
BRING ME THE BODIES.
THERE...THERE ARE NO BODIES, SIR.
THEY'VE BEEN COMPLETELY--
SKARRAKK
HNN?
SKKRAKKOOOOM
WE SURGE UP FROM THE SIZE OF MOLECULES IN A SPLIT SECOND...
...AND I START TO BELIEVE WE'RE REALLY GONNA DO THIS.
THAT'S ONE FOR THE LITTLE GUY!
KRAAK
UKKK!
QUIT FOOLING AROUND AND GET THE SHIELDS DOWN, PALMER!
FOOLING AROUND?
KTWACK
THIS IS GOOD STUFF HERE!
I'M GOING FOR THE LEAGUE!

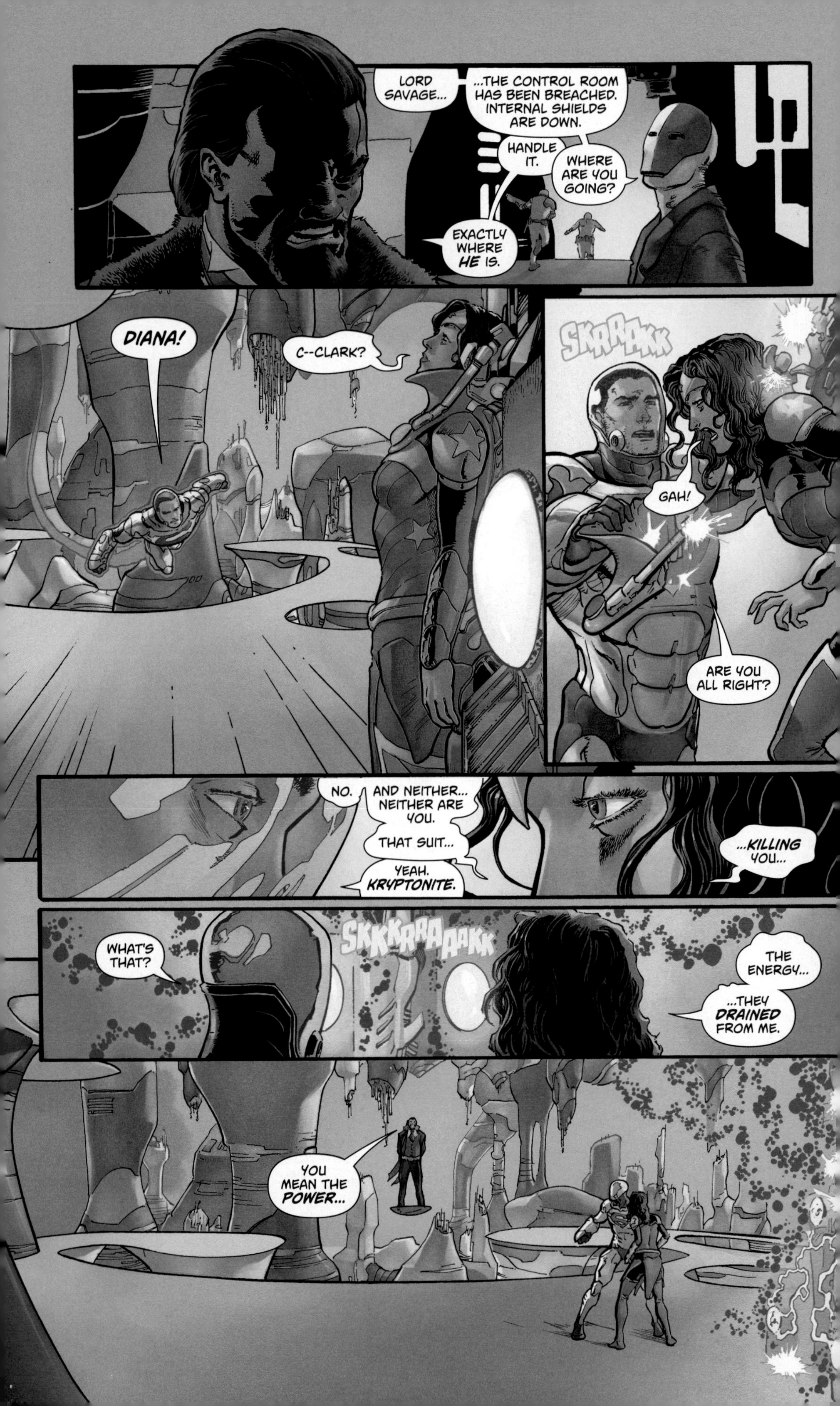
LORD SAVAGE...
...THE CONTROL ROOM HAS BEEN BREACHED. INTERNAL SHIELDS ARE DOWN.
HANDLE IT.
WHERE ARE YOU GOING?
EXACTLY WHERE HE IS.
DIANA!
C--CLARK?
SKRRAAKK
GAH!
ARE YOU ALL RIGHT?
NO.
AND NEITHER... NEITHER ARE YOU.
THAT SUIT...
YEAH. KRYPTONITE.
...KILLING YOU...
WHAT'S THAT?
SKKKRRAAAKK
THE ENERGY...
...THEY DRAINED FROM ME.
YOU MEAN THE POWER...

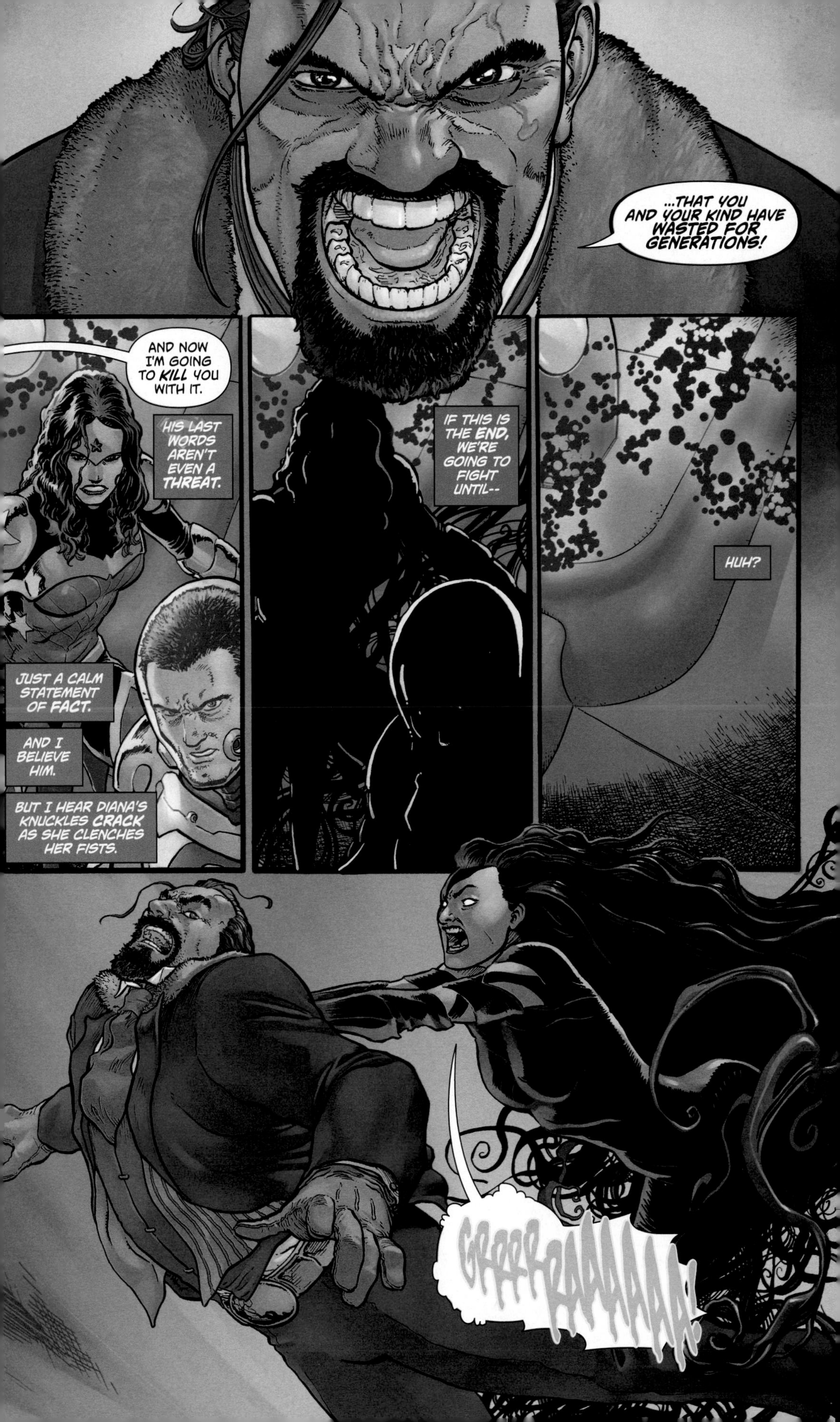
...THAT YOU AND YOUR KIND HAVE WASTED FOR GENERATIONS!
AND NOW I'M GOING TO KILL YOU WITH IT.
HIS LAST WORDS AREN'T EVEN A THREAT.
JUST A CALM STATEMENT OF FACT.
AND I BELIEVE HIM.
BUT I HEAR DIANA'S KNUCKLES CRACK AS SHE CLENCHES HER FISTS.
IF THIS IS THE END, WE'RE GOING TO FIGHT UNTIL--
HUH?
GRRRRAAAAAAA!

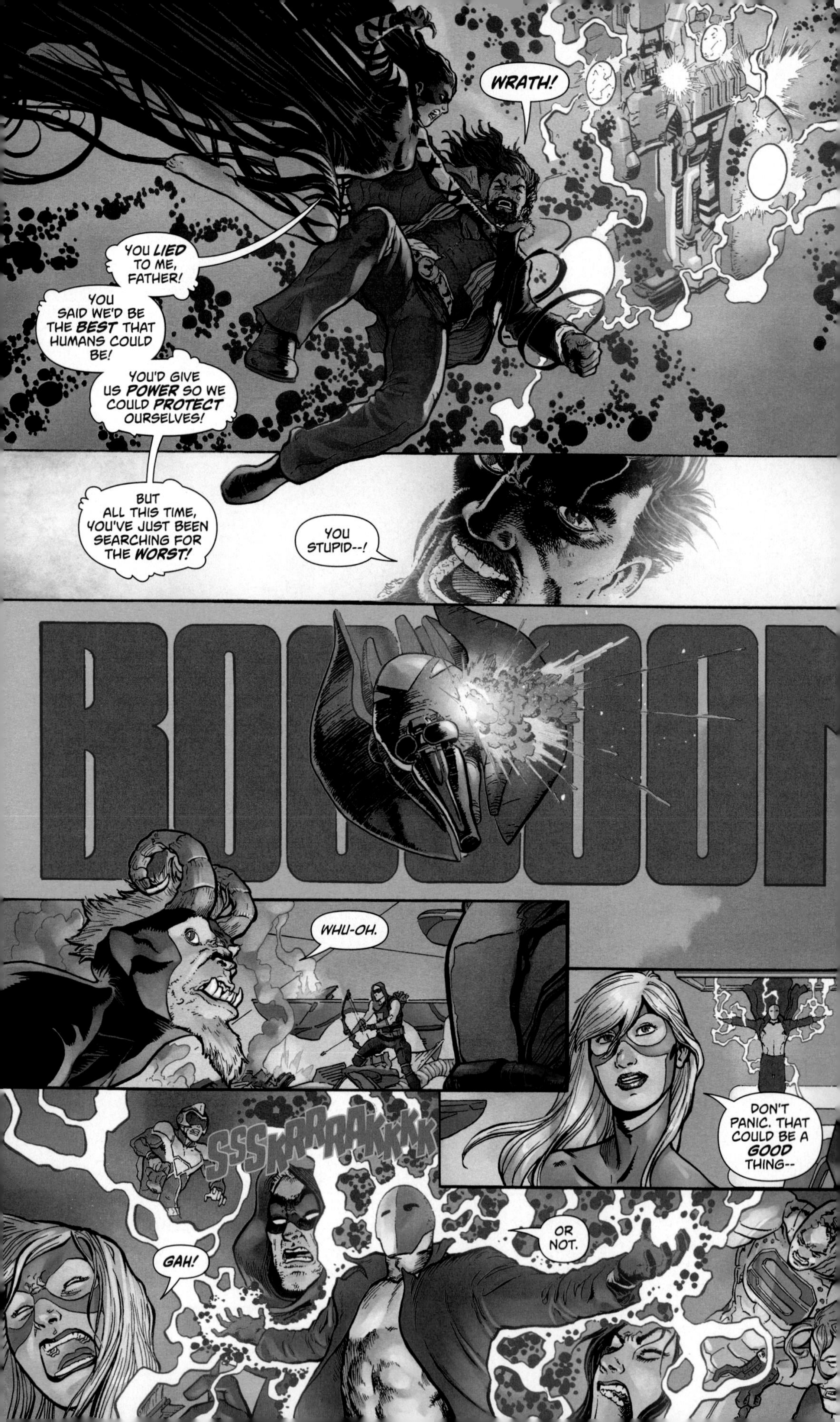
WRATH!
YOU LIED TO ME, FATHER!
YOU SAID WE'D BE THE BEST THAT HUMANS COULD BE!
YOU'D GIVE US POWER SO WE COULD PROTECT OURSELVES!
BUT ALL THIS TIME, YOU'VE JUST BEEN SEARCHING FOR THE WORST!
YOU STUPID--!
BOOOOOM
WHU-OH.
DON'T PANIC. THAT COULD BE A GOOD THING--
SSSKRRRAKKKK
OR NOT.
GAH!

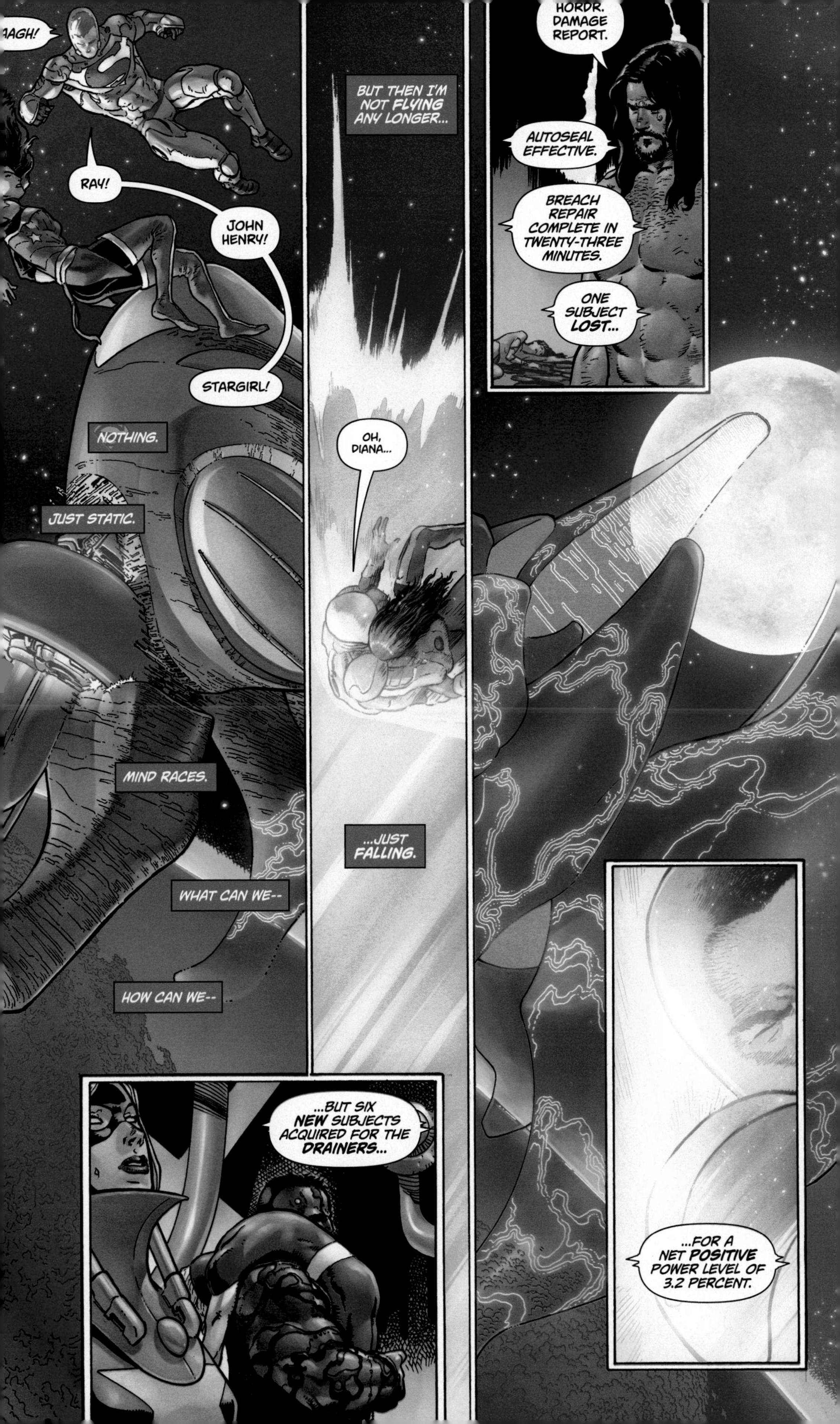
AAGH!
RAY!
JOHN HENRY!
STARGIRL!
NOTHING.
JUST STATIC.
MIND RACES.
WHAT CAN WE--
HOW CAN WE--
BUT THEN I'M NOT FLYING ANY LONGER...
OH, DIANA...
...JUST FALLING.
HORDR. DAMAGE REPORT.
AUTOSEAL EFFECTIVE.
BREACH REPAIR COMPLETE IN TWENTY-THREE MINUTES.
ONE SUBJECT LOST...
...BUT SIX NEW SUBJECTS ACQUIRED FOR THE DRAINERS...
...FOR A NET POSITIVE POWER LEVEL OF 3.2 PERCENT.

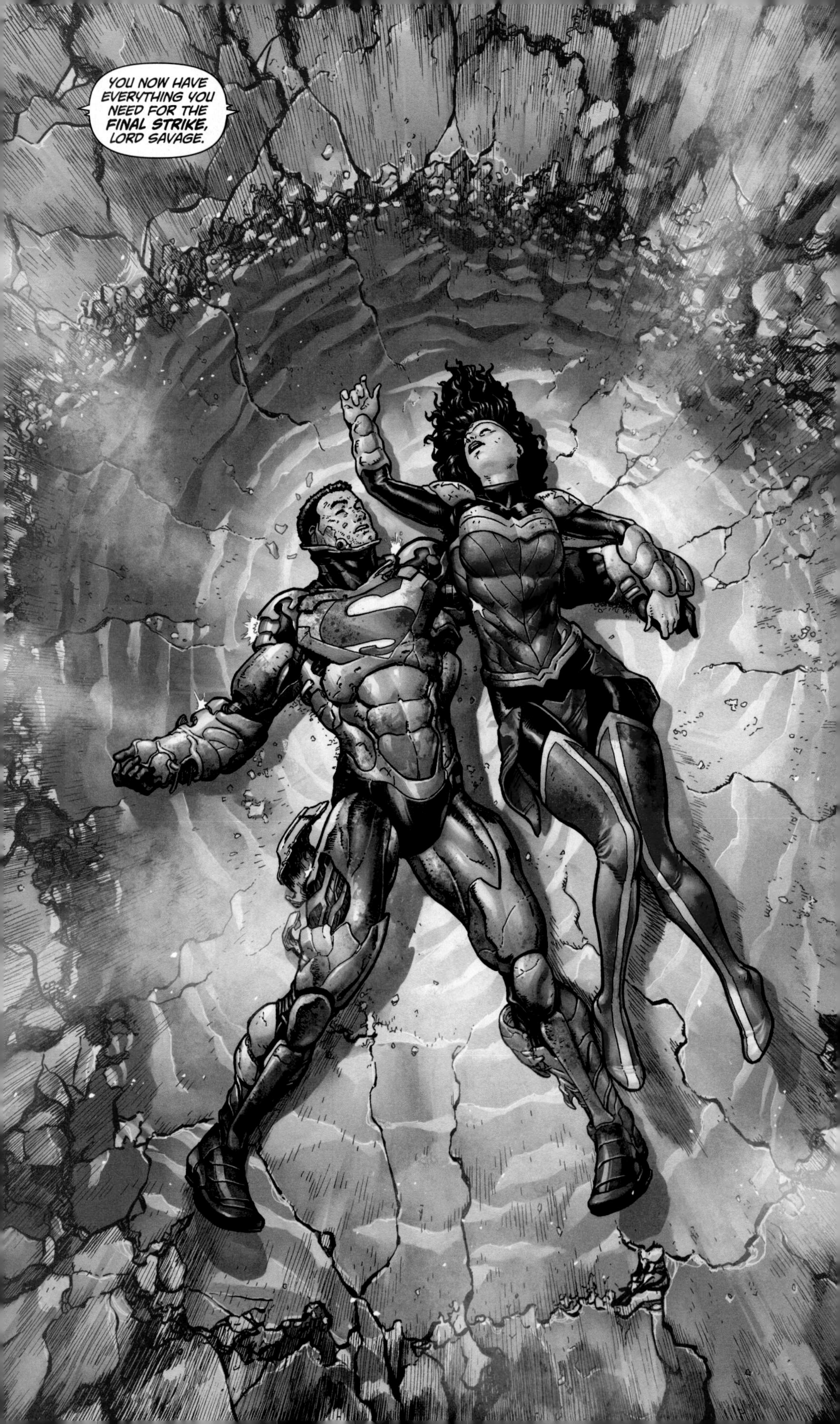
YOU NOW HAVE EVERYTHING YOU NEED FOR THE FINAL STRIKE, LORD SAVAGE.

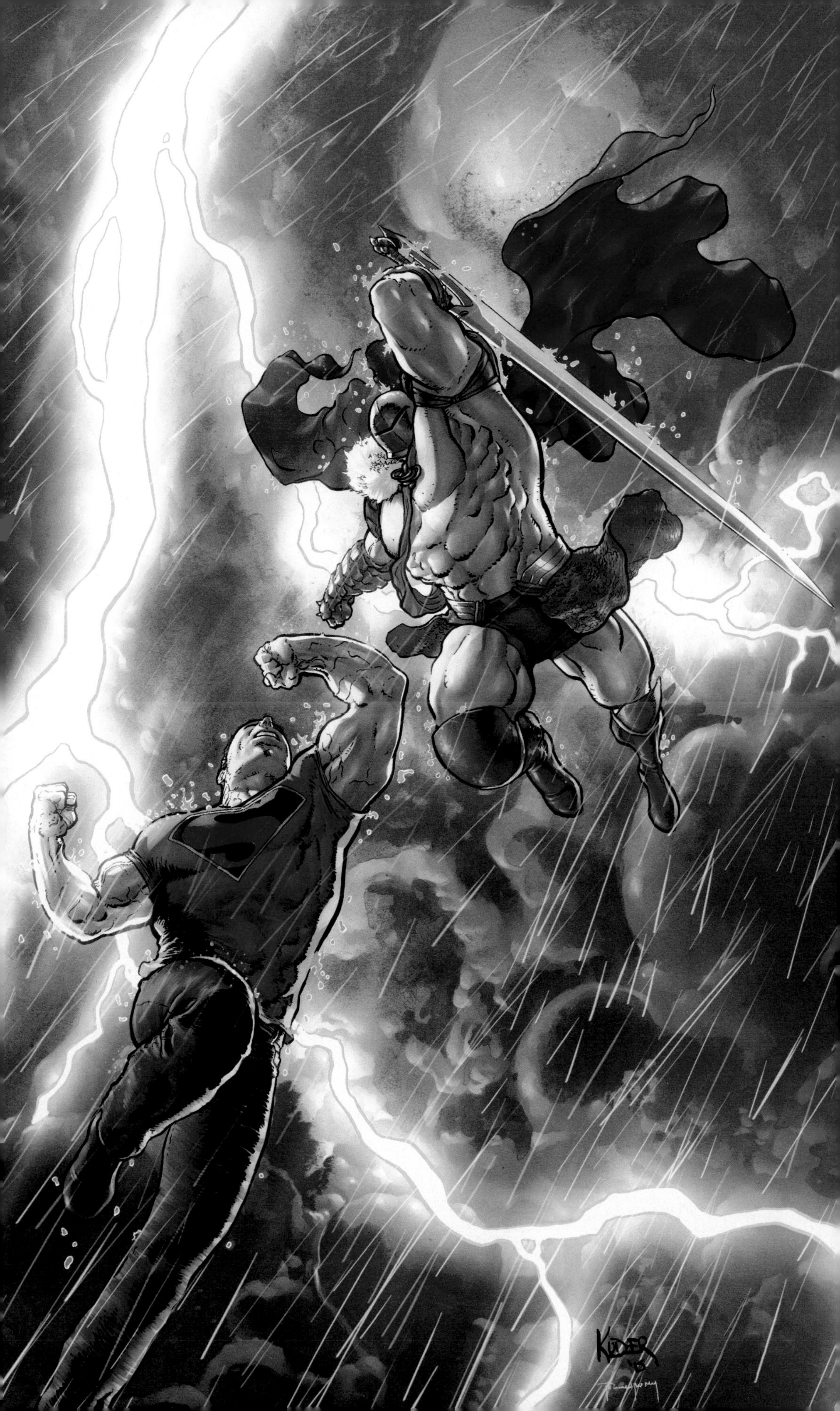

Previously,
in SUPERMAN/WONDER WOMAN #25 and SUPERMAN #48...

With the man she loves so close to death, Wonder Woman brings Superman to Olympus, where the gods put his spiritual form through a grueling "test of valor" before bestowing the Gift of Healing—and rendering him "completely and fully mortal."

Still determined to find a way to regain his powers and stop Vandal Savage, the Man of Steel asks Steve Trevor, Diana's ex and top field agent of A.R.G.U.S. (Advanced Research Group Uniting Super-Humans), to be given access to the compound's massive deposit of Kryptonite. As he theorizes the Kryptonite will burn away the poisoned cells that are preventing him from powering up, the Puzzler, a mechanical menace Savage has ordered to infiltrate the compound, threatens to terminate everyone—and forces Superman to act fast and hurl himself into the chamber housing all of A.R.G.U.S.'s Kryptonite...

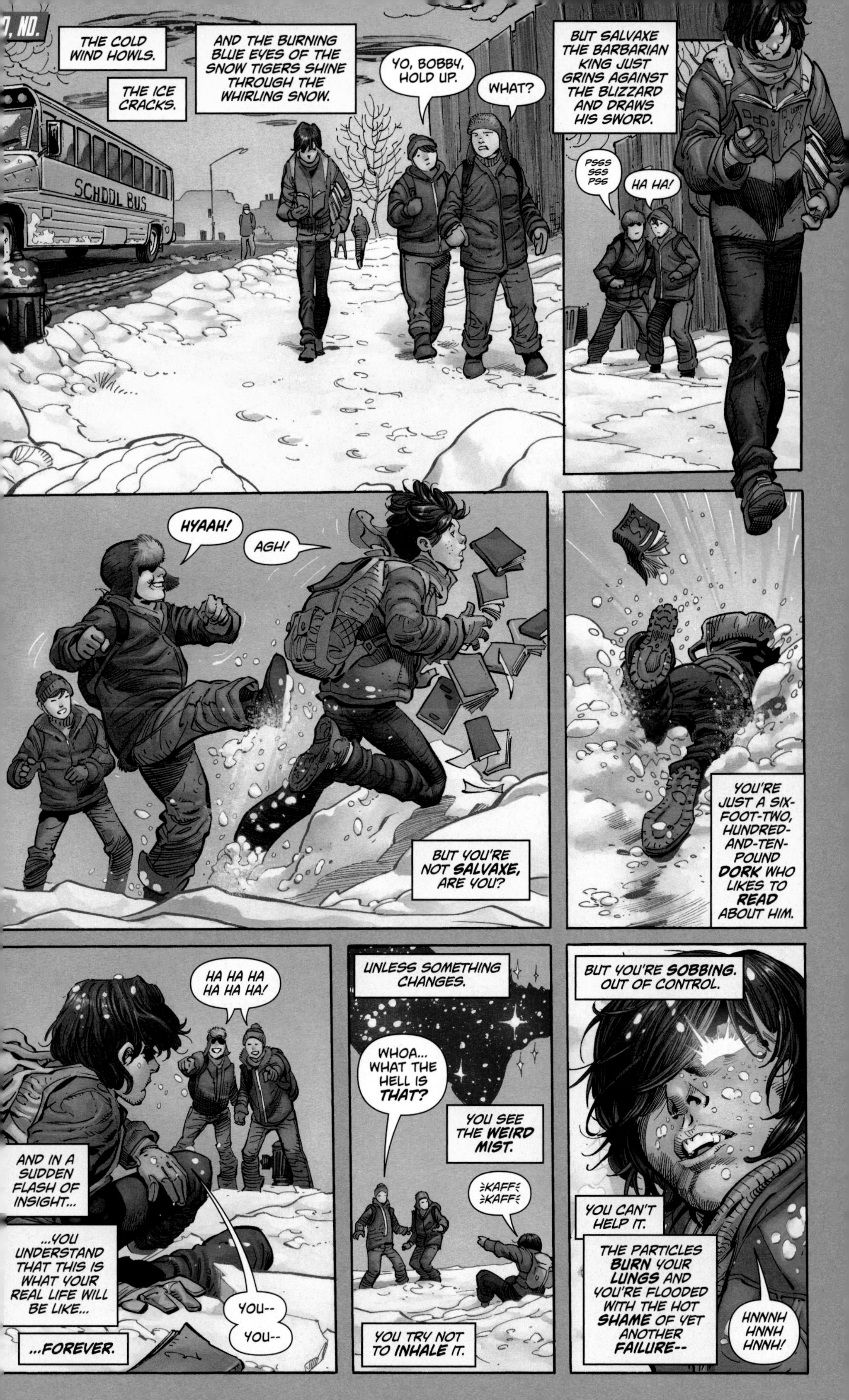

THE COLD WIND HOWLS.
THE ICE CRACKS.
AND THE BURNING BLUE EYES OF THE SNOW TIGERS SHINE THROUGH THE WHIRLING SNOW.
YO, BOBBY, HOLD UP.
WHAT?
SCHOOL BUS
BUT SALVAXE THE BARBARIAN KING JUST GRINS AGAINST THE BLIZZARD AND DRAWS HIS SWORD.
PSSS SSS PSS
HA HA!
HYAAH!
AGH!
BUT YOU'RE NOT SALVAXE, ARE YOU?
YOU'RE JUST A SIX-FOOT-TWO, HUNDRED-AND-TEN-POUND DORK WHO LIKES TO READ ABOUT HIM.
HA HA HA HA HA HA!
AND IN A SUDDEN FLASH OF INSIGHT...
...YOU UNDERSTAND THAT THIS IS WHAT YOUR REAL LIFE WILL BE LIKE...
...FOREVER.
YOU--
YOU--
UNLESS SOMETHING CHANGES.
WHOA... WHAT THE HELL IS THAT?
YOU SEE THE WEIRD MIST.
KAFF KAFF
YOU TRY NOT TO INHALE IT.
BUT YOU'RE SOBBING. OUT OF CONTROL.
YOU CAN'T HELP IT.
THE PARTICLES BURN YOUR LUNGS AND YOU'RE FLOODED WITH THE HOT SHAME OF YET ANOTHER FAILURE--
HNNNH HNNH HNNH!

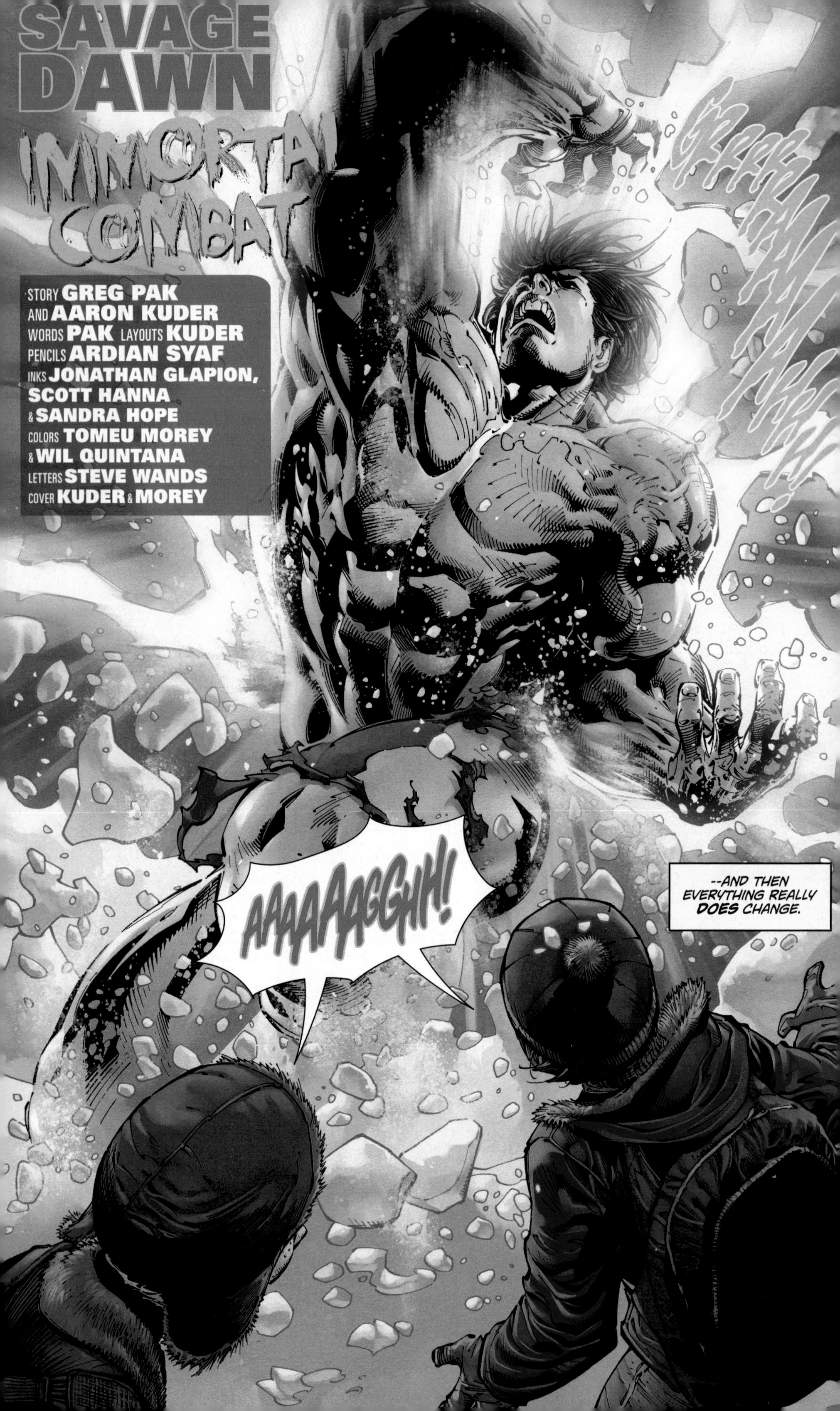
SAVAGE DAWN
IMMORTAL COMBAT
STORY GREG PAK
AND AARON KUDER
WORDS PAK LAYOUTS KUDER
PENCILS ARDIAN SYAF
INKS JONATHAN GLAPION,
SCOTT HANNA
& SANDRA HOPE
COLORS TOMEU MOREY
& WIL QUINTANA
LETTERS STEVE WANDS
COVER KUDER & MOREY
AAAAAAGGHH!
--AND THEN EVERYTHING REALLY DOES CHANGE.

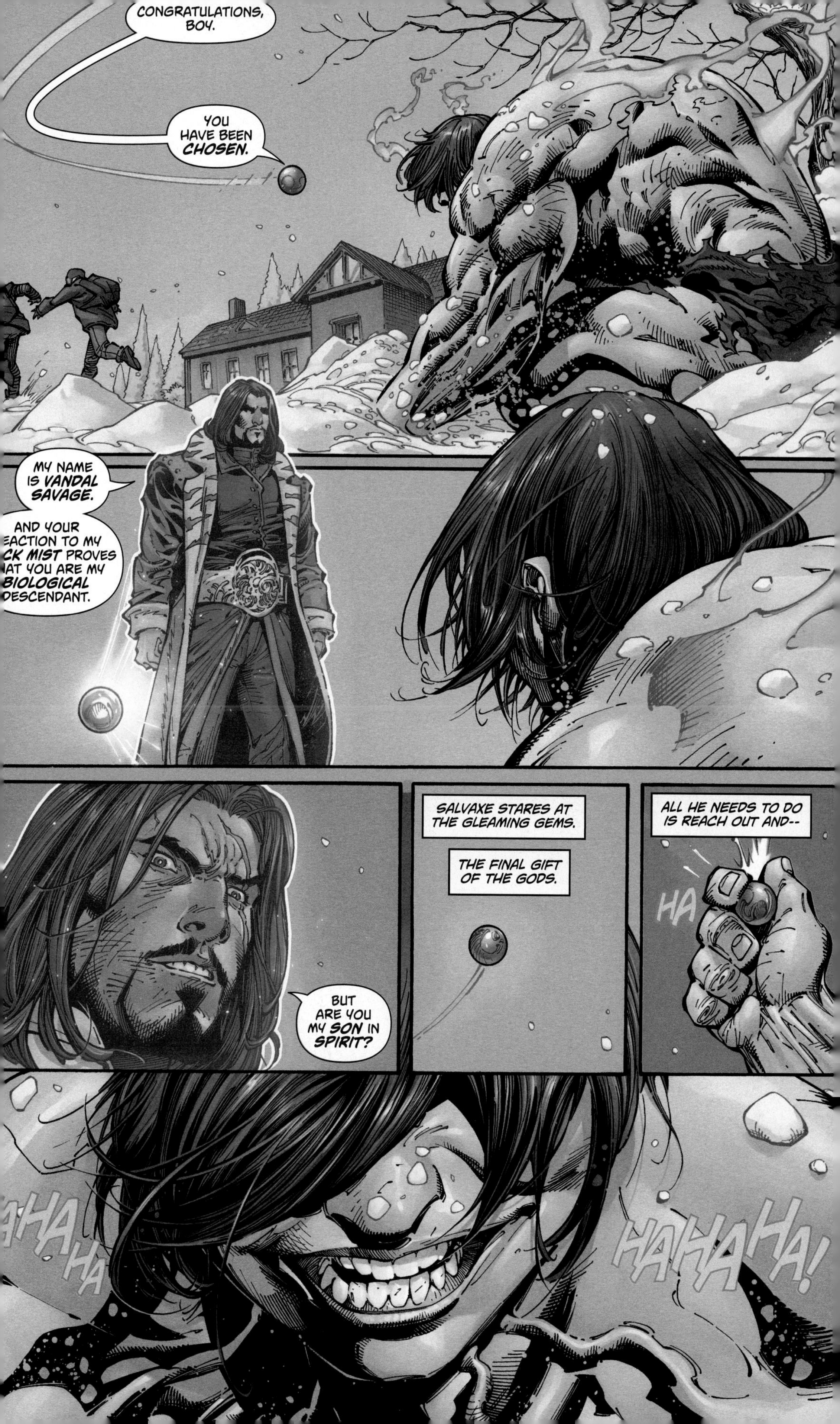
CONGRATULATIONS, BOY.
YOU HAVE BEEN CHOSEN.
MY NAME IS VANDAL SAVAGE.
AND YOUR EACTION TO MY CK MIST PROVES AT YOU ARE MY BIOLOGICAL DESCENDANT.
BUT ARE YOU MY SON IN SPIRIT?
SALVAXE STARES AT THE GLEAMING GEMS.
THE FINAL GIFT OF THE GODS.
ALL HE NEEDS TO DO IS REACH OUT AND--
HA
HAHAHA
HAHAHA!

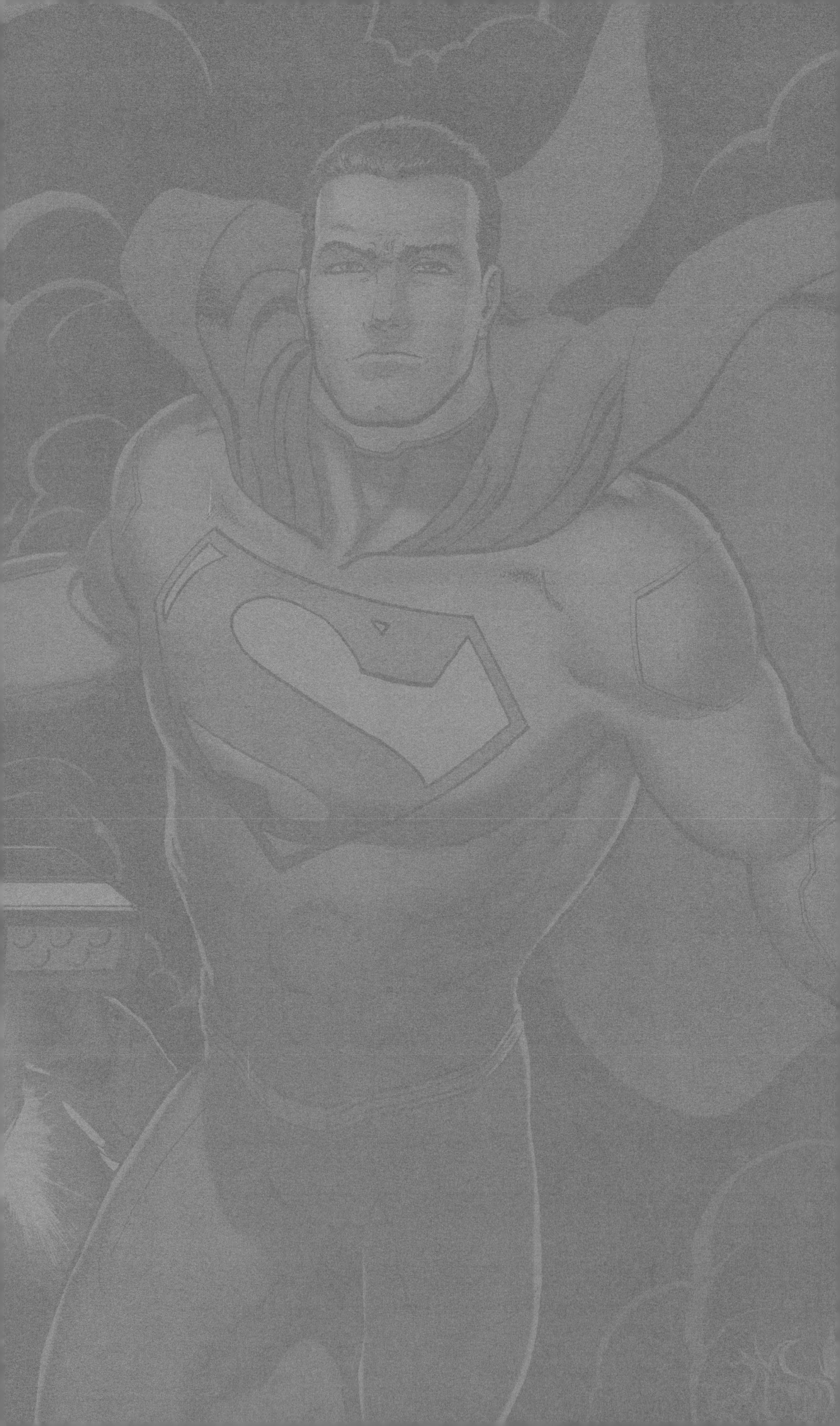

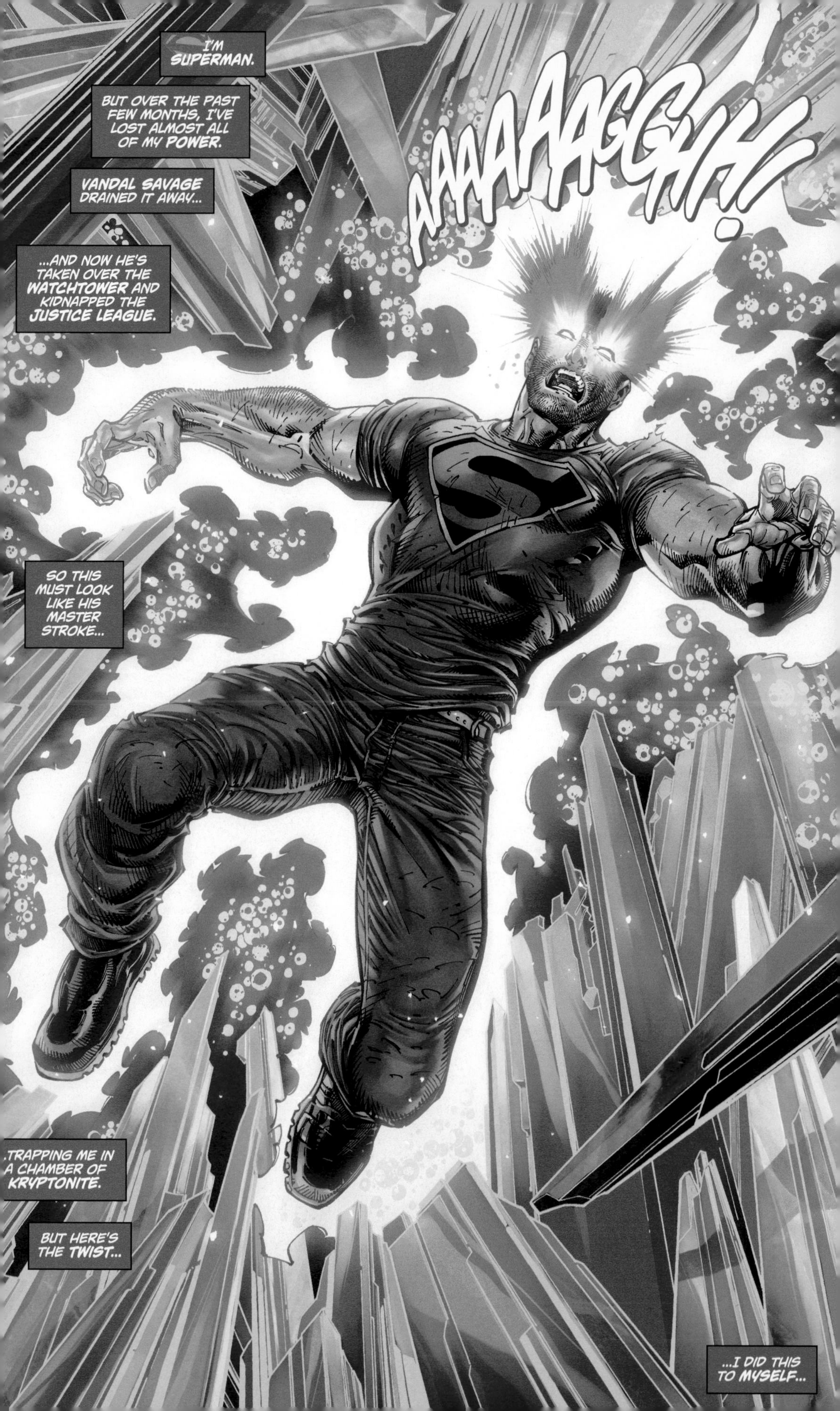
I'M SUPERMAN.
BUT OVER THE PAST FEW MONTHS, I'VE LOST ALMOST ALL OF MY POWER.
VANDAL SAVAGE DRAINED IT AWAY...
...AND NOW HE'S TAKEN OVER THE WATCHTOWER AND KIDNAPPED THE JUSTICE LEAGUE.
AAAAAAGGHH!
SO THIS MUST LOOK LIKE HIS MASTER STROKE...
.TRAPPING ME IN A CHAMBER OF KRYPTONITE.
BUT HERE'S THE TWIST...
...I DID THIS TO MYSELF...

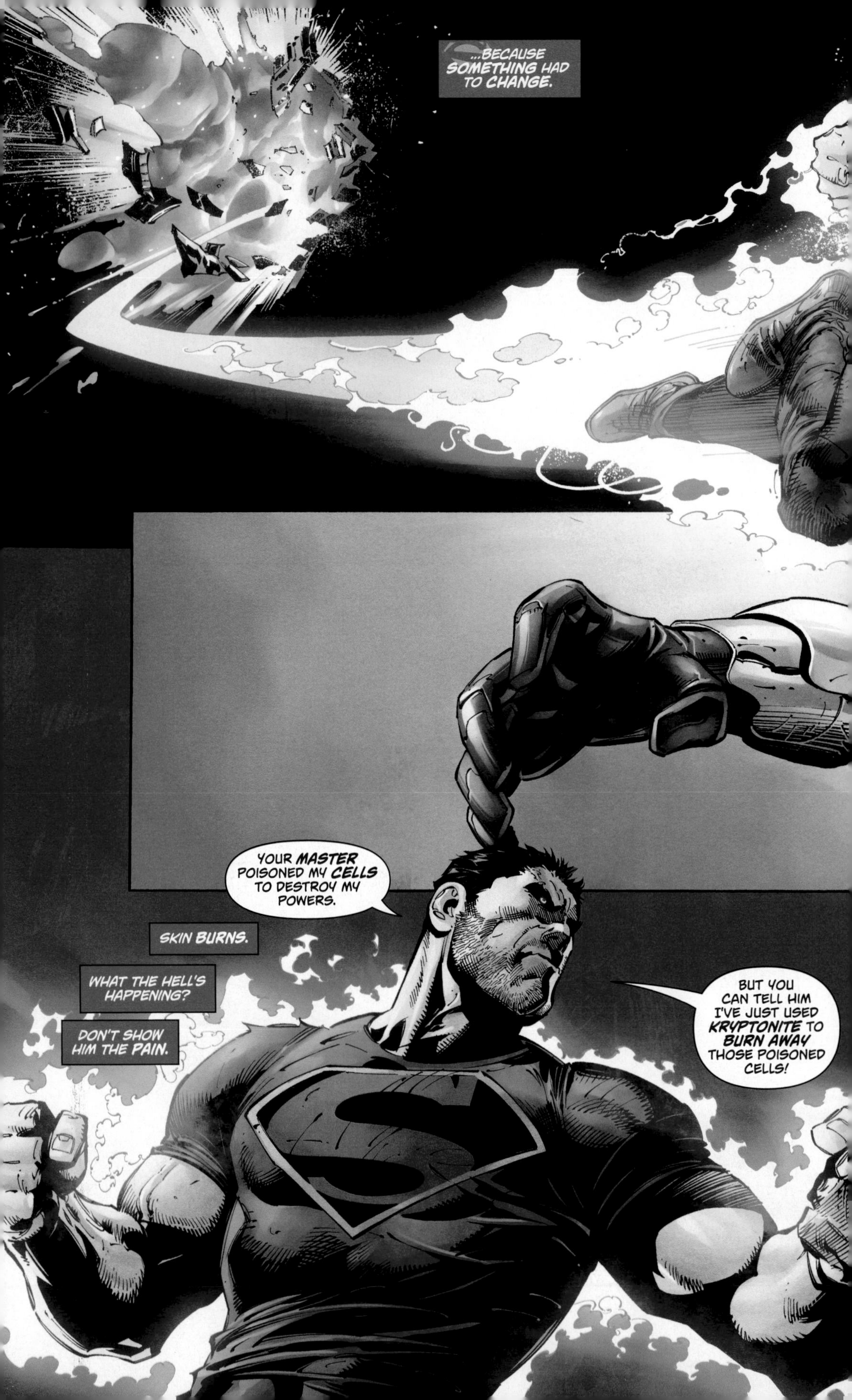
...BECAUSE SOMETHING HAD TO CHANGE.
YOUR MASTER POISONED MY CELLS TO DESTROY MY POWERS.
SKIN BURNS.
WHAT THE HELL'S HAPPENING?
DON'T SHOW HIM THE PAIN.
BUT YOU CAN TELL HIM I'VE JUST USED KRYPTONITE TO BURN AWAY THOSE POISONED CELLS!

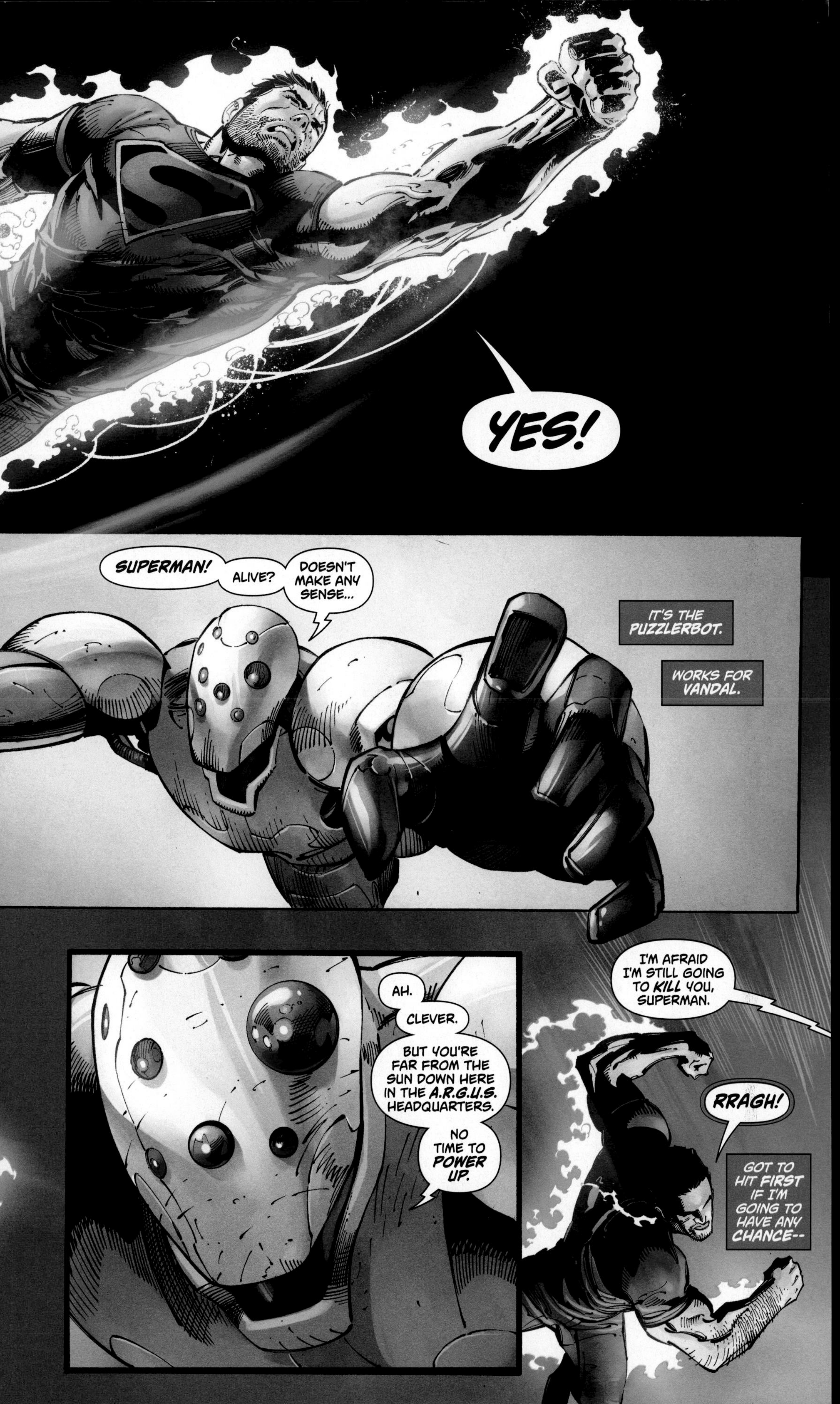

YES!
SUPERMAN!
ALIVE?
DOESN'T MAKE ANY SENSE...
IT'S THE PUZZLERBOT.
WORKS FOR VANDAL.
AH.
CLEVER.
BUT YOU'RE FAR FROM THE SUN DOWN HERE IN THE A.R.G.U.S. HEADQUARTERS.
NO TIME TO POWER UP.
I'M AFRAID I'M STILL GOING TO KILL YOU, SUPERMAN.
RRAGH!
GOT TO HIT FIRST IF I'M GOING TO HAVE ANY CHANCE--

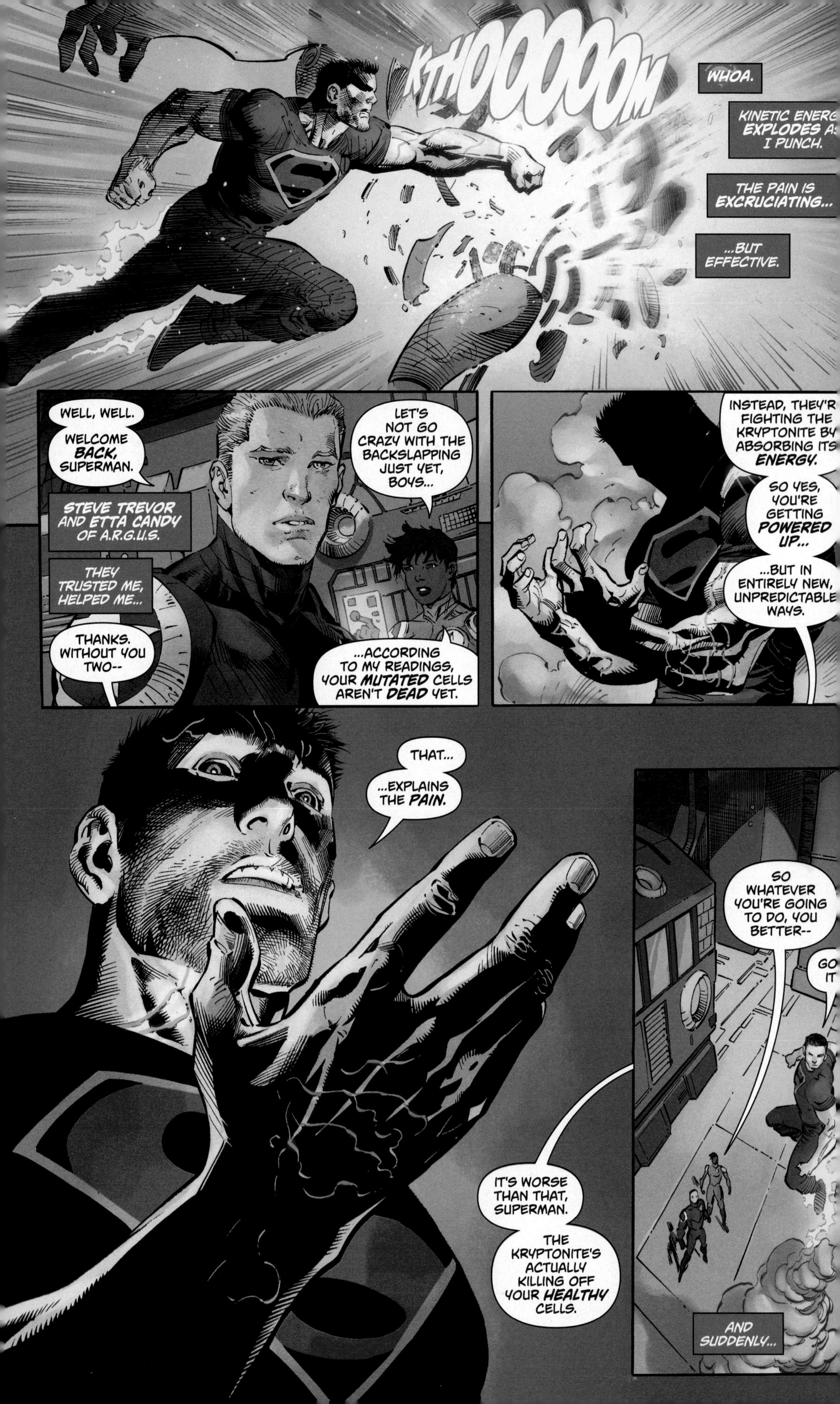
KTHOOOOOM
WHOA.
KINETIC ENERG EXPLODES A I PUNCH.
THE PAIN IS EXCRUCIATING...
...BUT EFFECTIVE.
WELL, WELL.
WELCOME BACK, SUPERMAN.
STEVE TREVOR AND ETTA CANDY OF A.R.G.U.S.
THEY TRUSTED ME, HELPED ME...
THANKS. WITHOUT YOU TWO--
LET'S NOT GO CRAZY WITH THE BACKSLAPPING JUST YET, BOYS...
...ACCORDING TO MY READINGS, YOUR MUTATED CELLS AREN'T DEAD YET.
INSTEAD, THEY'R FIGHTING THE KRYPTONITE BY ABSORBING ITS ENERGY.
SO YES, YOU'RE GETTING POWERED UP...
...BUT IN ENTIRELY NEW, UNPREDICTABLE WAYS.
THAT...
...EXPLAINS THE PAIN.
IT'S WORSE THAN THAT, SUPERMAN.
THE KRYPTONITE'S ACTUALLY KILLING OFF YOUR HEALTHY CELLS.
SO WHATEVER YOU'RE GOING TO DO, YOU BETTER--
GO IT
AND SUDDENLY...

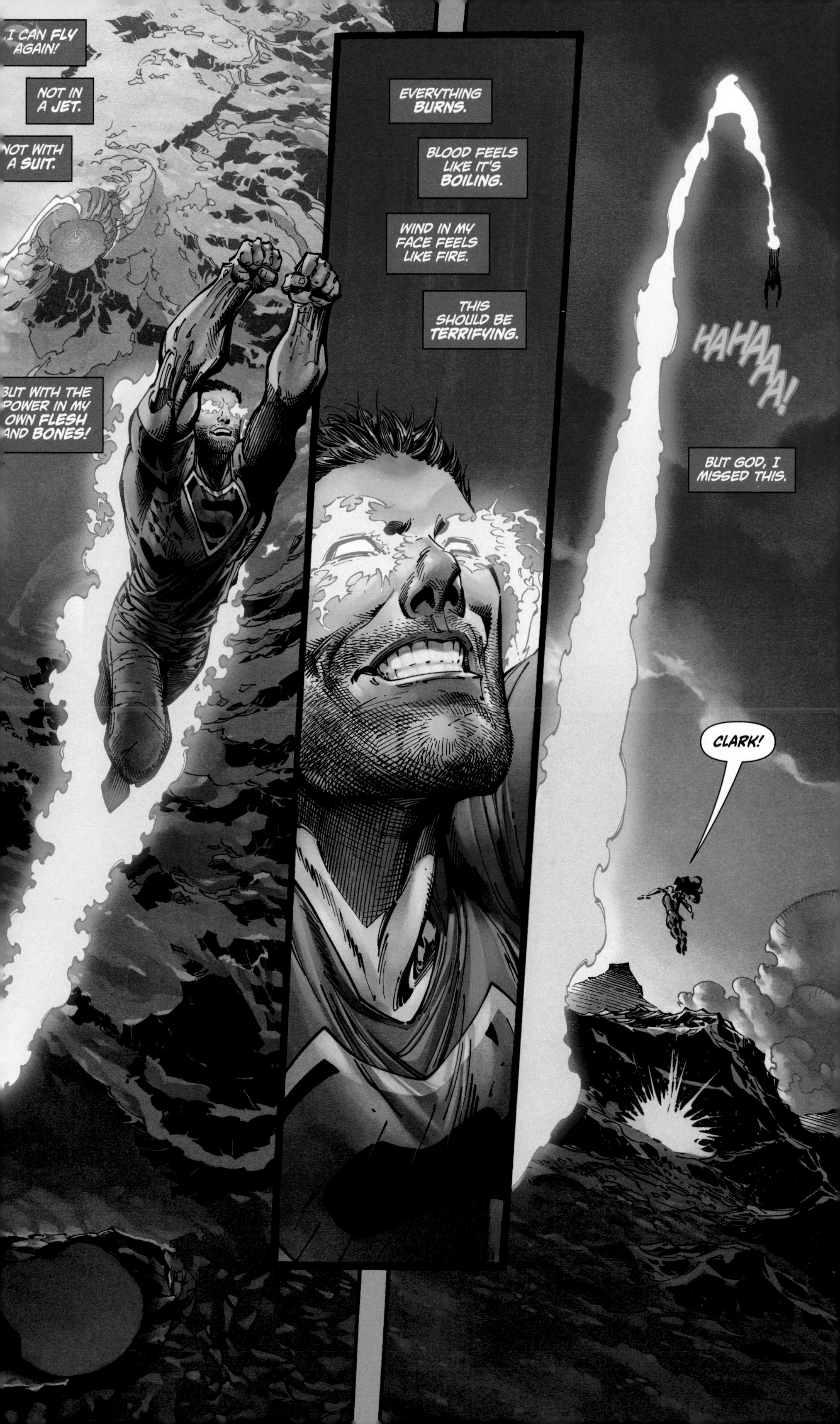

I CAN FLY AGAIN!
NOT IN A JET.
NOT WITH A SUIT.
BUT WITH THE POWER IN MY OWN FLESH AND BONES!
EVERYTHING BURNS.
BLOOD FEELS LIKE IT'S BOILING.
WIND IN MY FACE FEELS LIKE FIRE.
THIS SHOULD BE TERRIFYING.
HAHAAAA!
BUT GOD, I MISSED THIS.
CLARK!

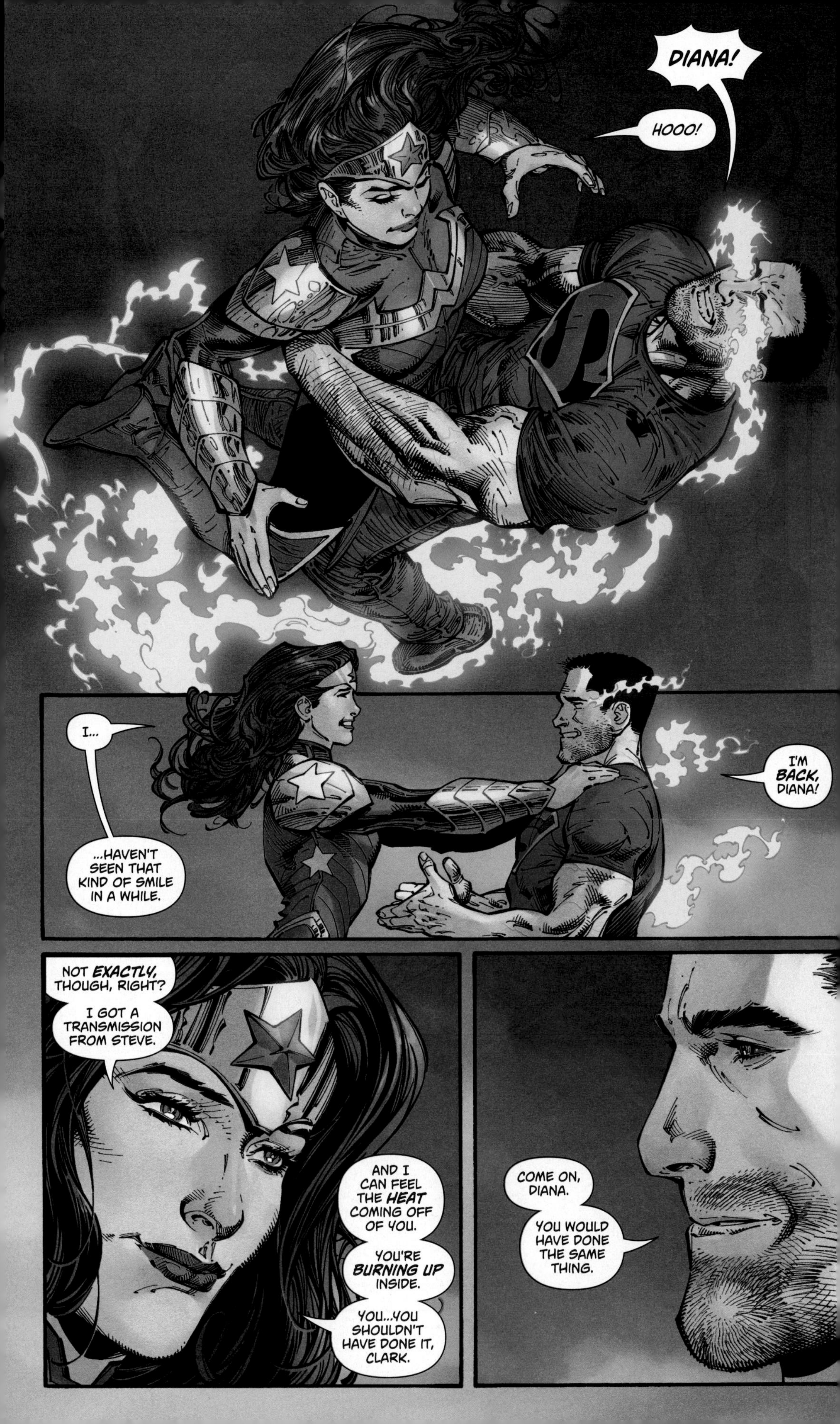
DIANA!
HOOO!
I...
...HAVEN'T SEEN THAT KIND OF SMILE IN A WHILE.
I'M BACK, DIANA!
NOT EXACTLY, THOUGH, RIGHT?
I GOT A TRANSMISSION FROM STEVE.
AND I CAN FEEL THE HEAT COMING OFF OF YOU.
YOU'RE BURNING UP INSIDE.
YOU...YOU SHOULDN'T HAVE DONE IT, CLARK.
COME ON, DIANA.
YOU WOULD HAVE DONE THE SAME THING.

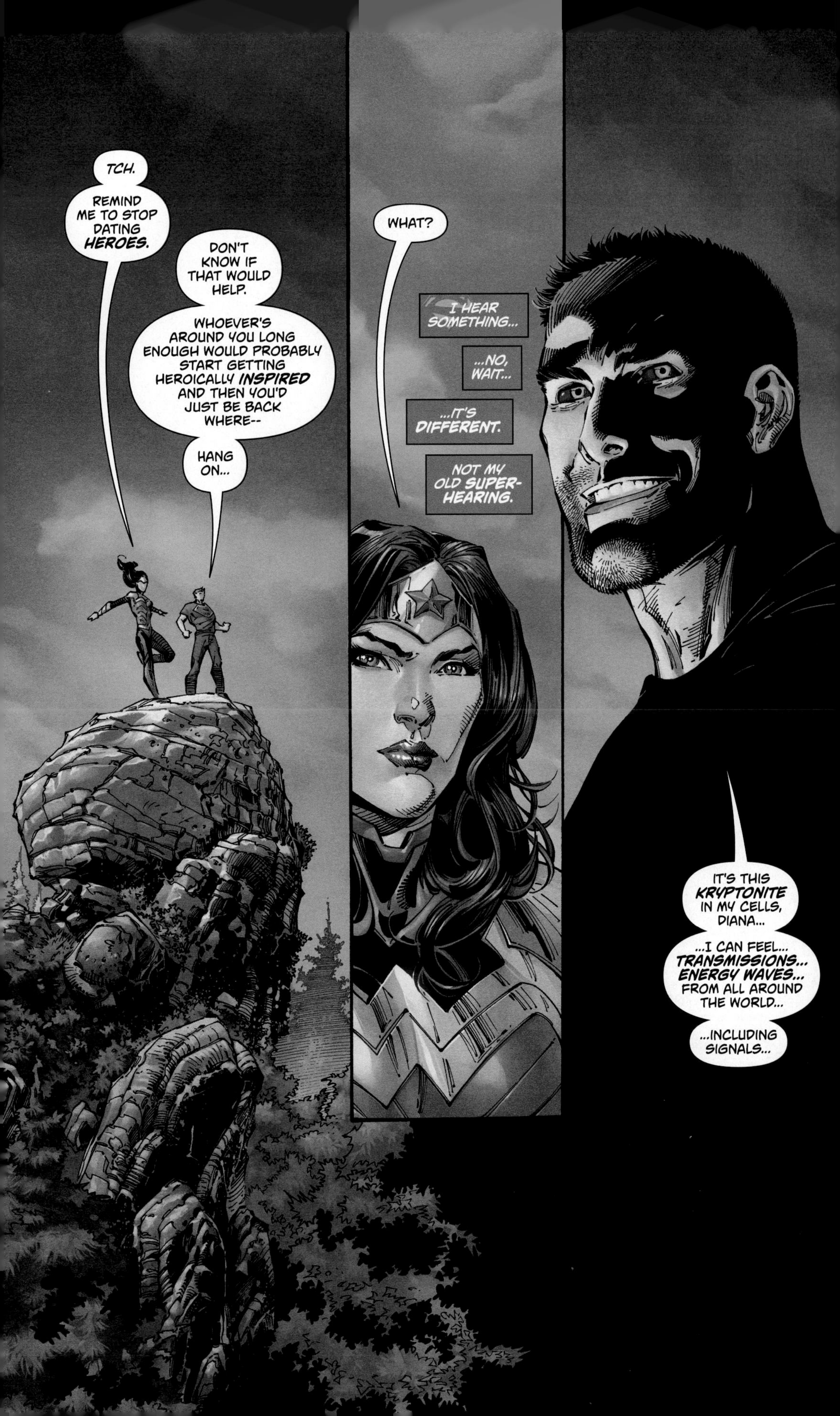

TCH.
REMIND ME TO STOP DATING HEROES.
DON'T KNOW IF THAT WOULD HELP.
WHOEVER'S AROUND YOU LONG ENOUGH WOULD PROBABLY START GETTING HEROICALLY INSPIRED AND THEN YOU'D JUST BE BACK WHERE--
HANG ON...
WHAT?
I HEAR SOMETHING...
...NO, WAIT...
...IT'S DIFFERENT.
NOT MY OLD SUPER-HEARING.
IT'S THIS KRYPTONITE IN MY CELLS, DIANA...
...I CAN FEEL... TRANSMISSIONS... ENERGY WAVES... FROM ALL AROUND THE WORLD...
...INCLUDING SIGNALS...

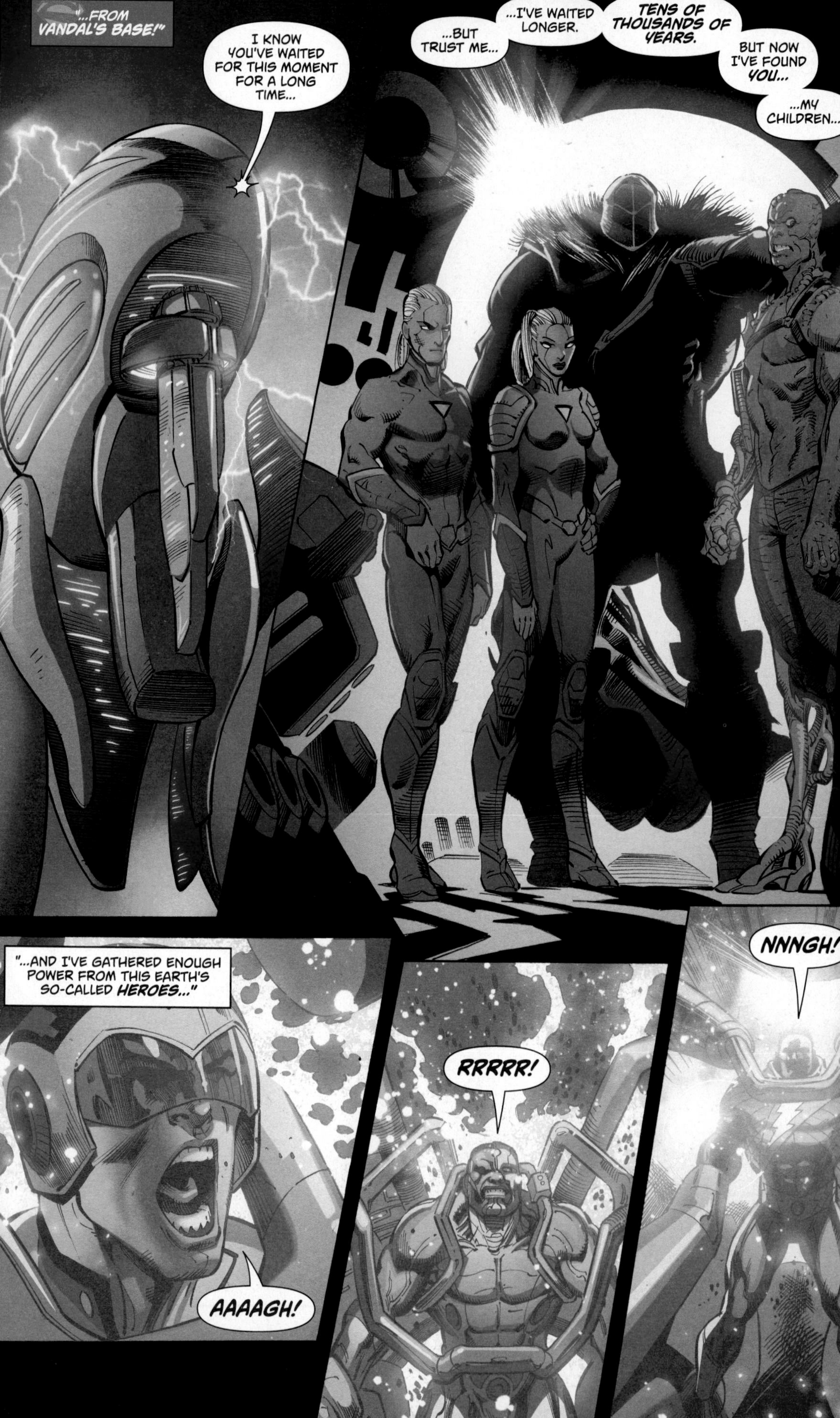
"...FROM VANDAL'S BASE!"
I KNOW YOU'VE WAITED FOR THIS MOMENT FOR A LONG TIME...
...BUT TRUST ME...
...I'VE WAITED LONGER.
TENS OF THOUSANDS OF YEARS.
BUT NOW I'VE FOUND YOU...
...MY CHILDREN...
"...AND I'VE GATHERED ENOUGH POWER FROM THIS EARTH'S SO-CALLED HEROES..."
AAAAGH!
RRRRR!
NNNGH!

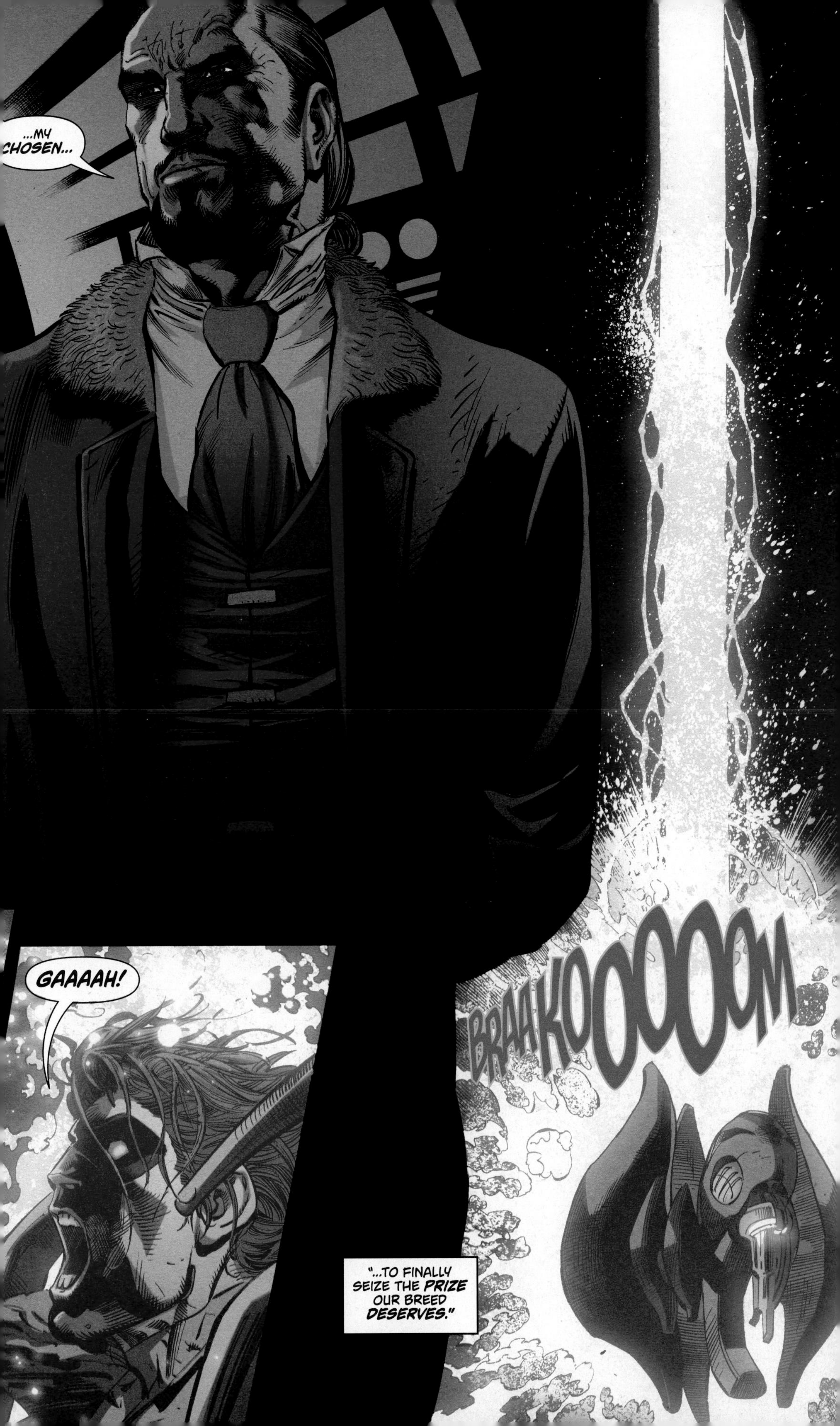

...MY CHOSEN...
GAAAAH!
BRAAKOOOOOM
"...TO FINALLY SEIZE THE *PRIZE* OUR BREED *DESERVES.*"

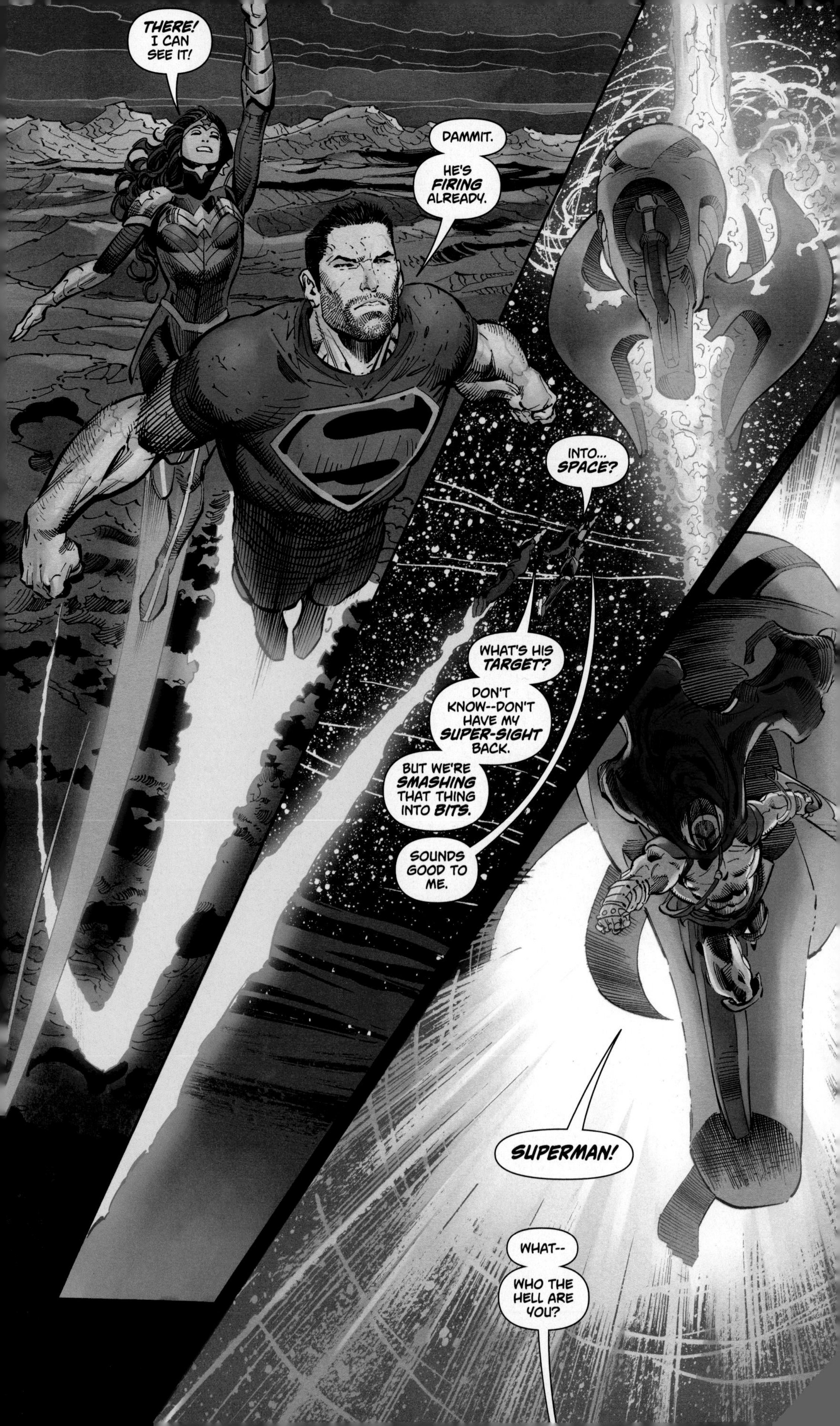
THERE! I CAN SEE IT!
DAMMIT.
HE'S FIRING ALREADY.
INTO... SPACE?
WHAT'S HIS TARGET?
DON'T KNOW--DON'T HAVE MY SUPER-SIGHT BACK.
BUT WE'RE SMASHING THAT THING INTO BITS.
SOUNDS GOOD TO ME.
SUPERMAN!
WHAT--
WHO THE HELL ARE YOU?

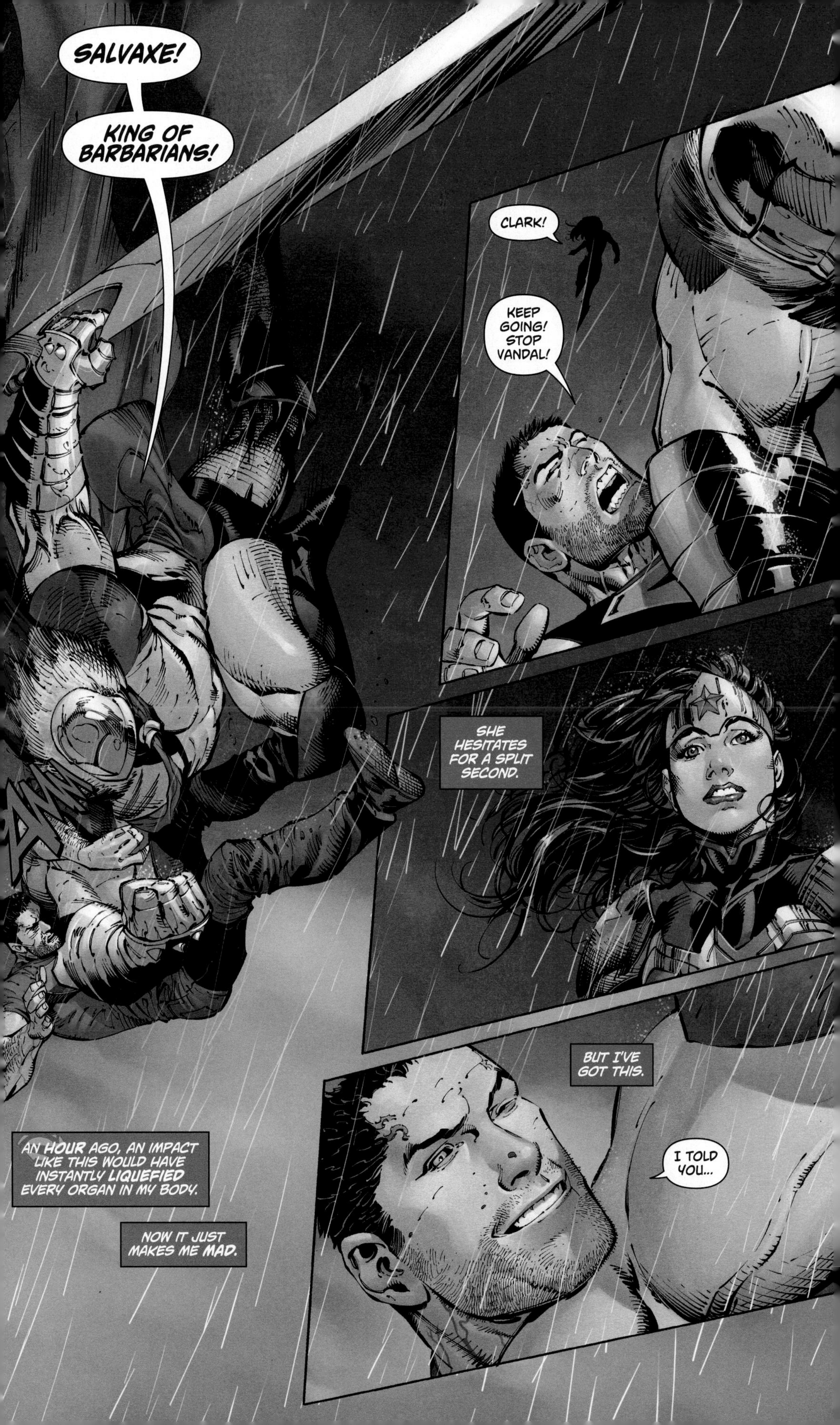
SALVAXE!
KING OF BARBARIANS!
CLARK!
KEEP GOING! STOP VANDAL!
SHE HESITATES FOR A SPLIT SECOND.
BUT I'VE GOT THIS.
AN HOUR AGO, AN IMPACT LIKE THIS WOULD HAVE INSTANTLY LIQUEFIED EVERY ORGAN IN MY BODY.
NOW IT JUST MAKES ME MAD.
I TOLD YOU...

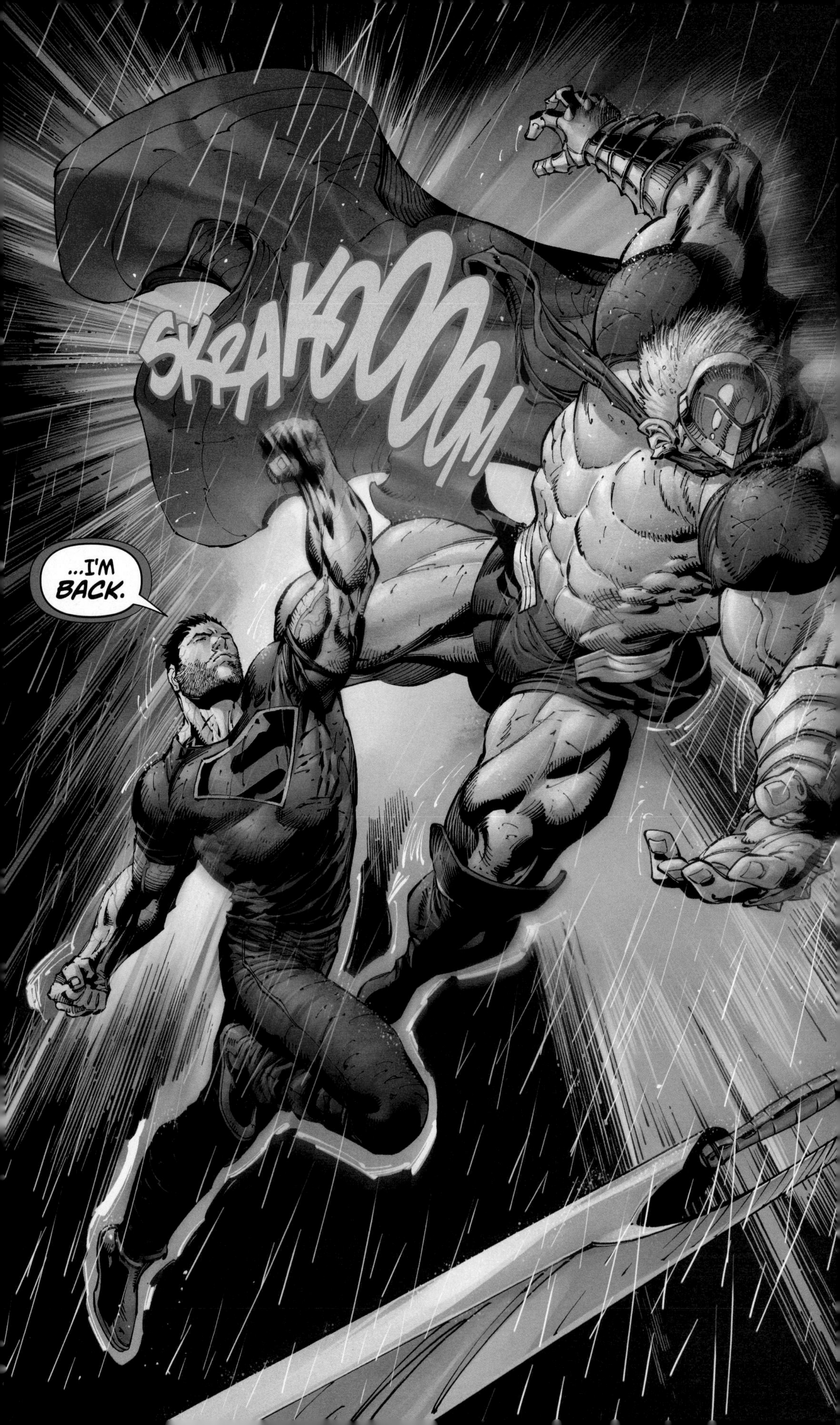
SKRAKOOOOOM
...I'M BACK.

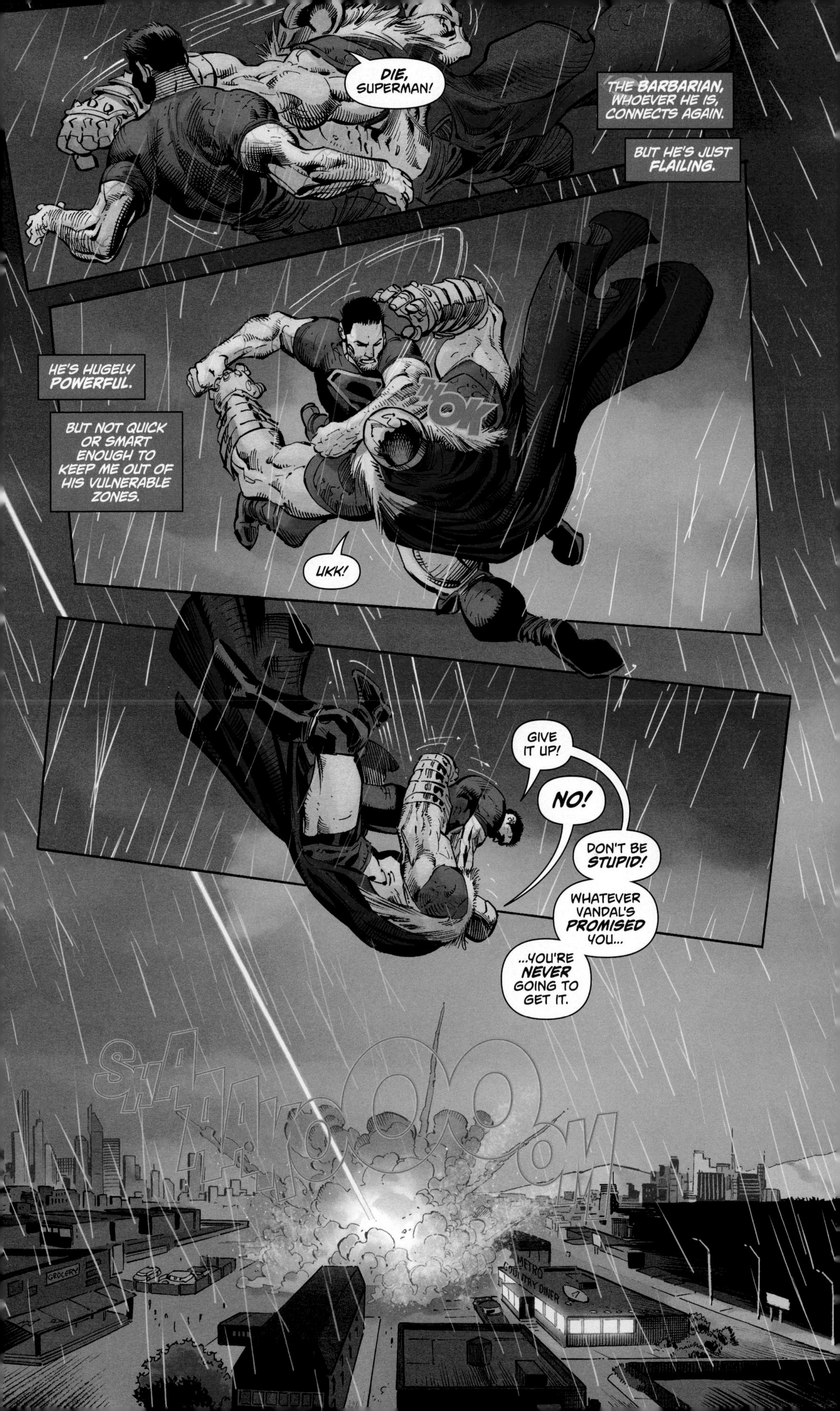

DIE, SUPERMAN!
THE BARBARIAN, WHOEVER HE IS, CONNECTS AGAIN.
BUT HE'S JUST FLAILING.
HE'S HUGELY POWERFUL.
BUT NOT QUICK OR SMART ENOUGH TO KEEP ME OUT OF HIS VULNERABLE ZONES.
THOK
UKK!
GIVE IT UP!
NO!
DON'T BE STUPID!
WHATEVER VANDAL'S PROMISED YOU...
...YOU'RE NEVER GOING TO GET IT.
SHAAKOOOOM
GROCERY
METRO COUNTRY DINER

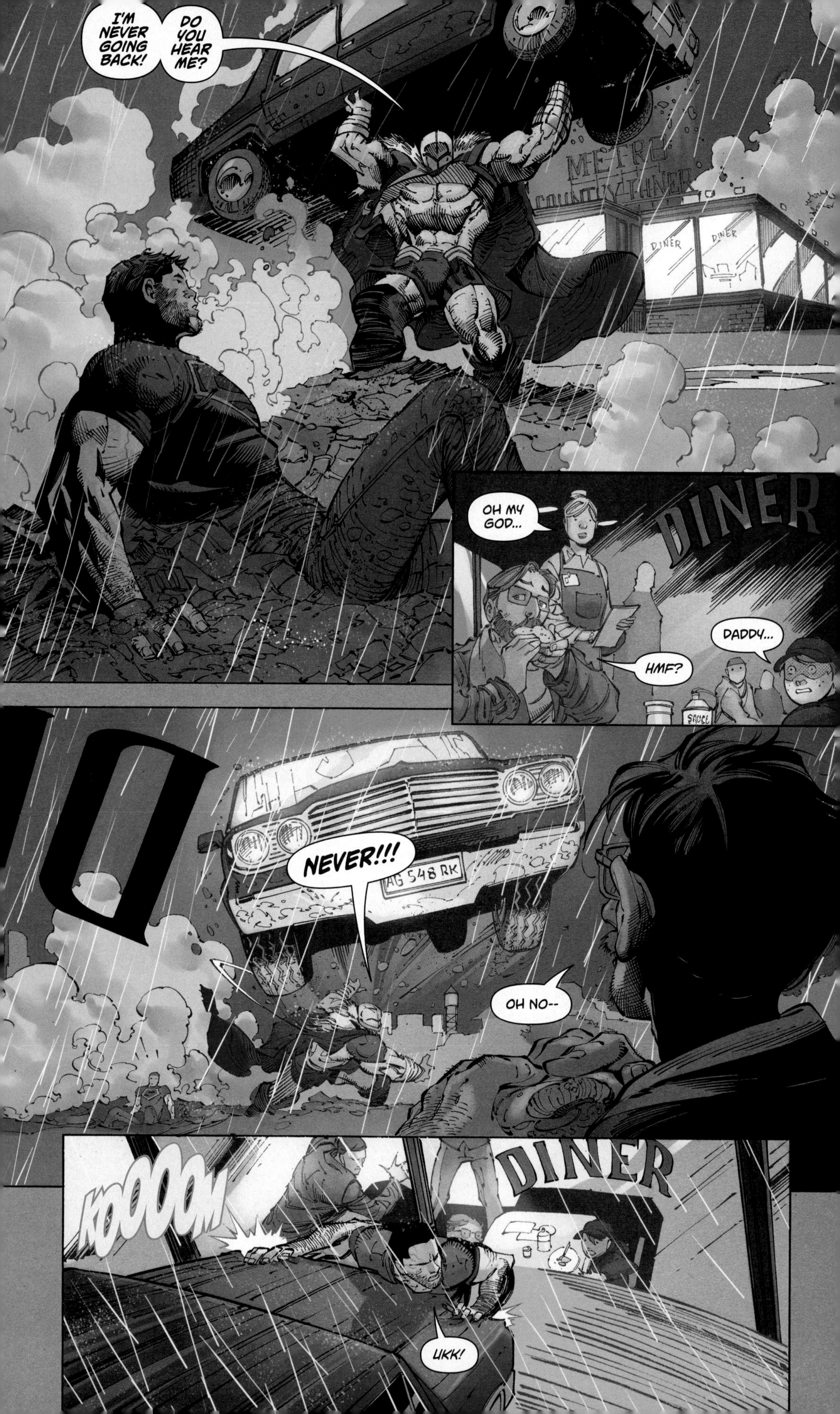
I'M NEVER GOING BACK!
DO YOU HEAR ME?
OH MY GOD...
DADDY...
HMF?
NEVER!!!
OH NO--
KOOOOM
UKK!

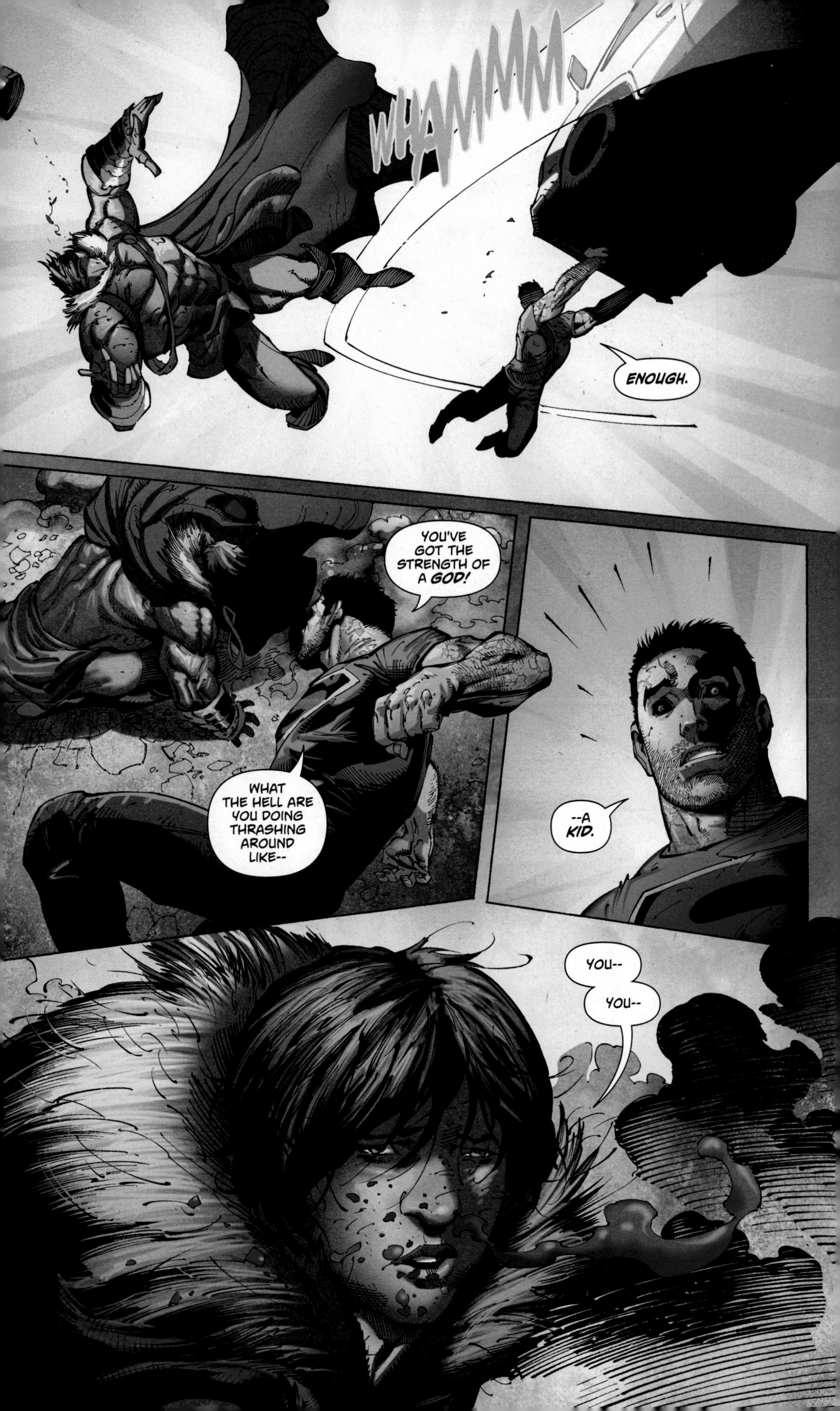
WHAMMMM
ENOUGH.
YOU'VE GOT THE STRENGTH OF A GOD!
WHAT THE HELL ARE YOU DOING THRASHING AROUND LIKE--
--A KID.
YOU--
YOU--

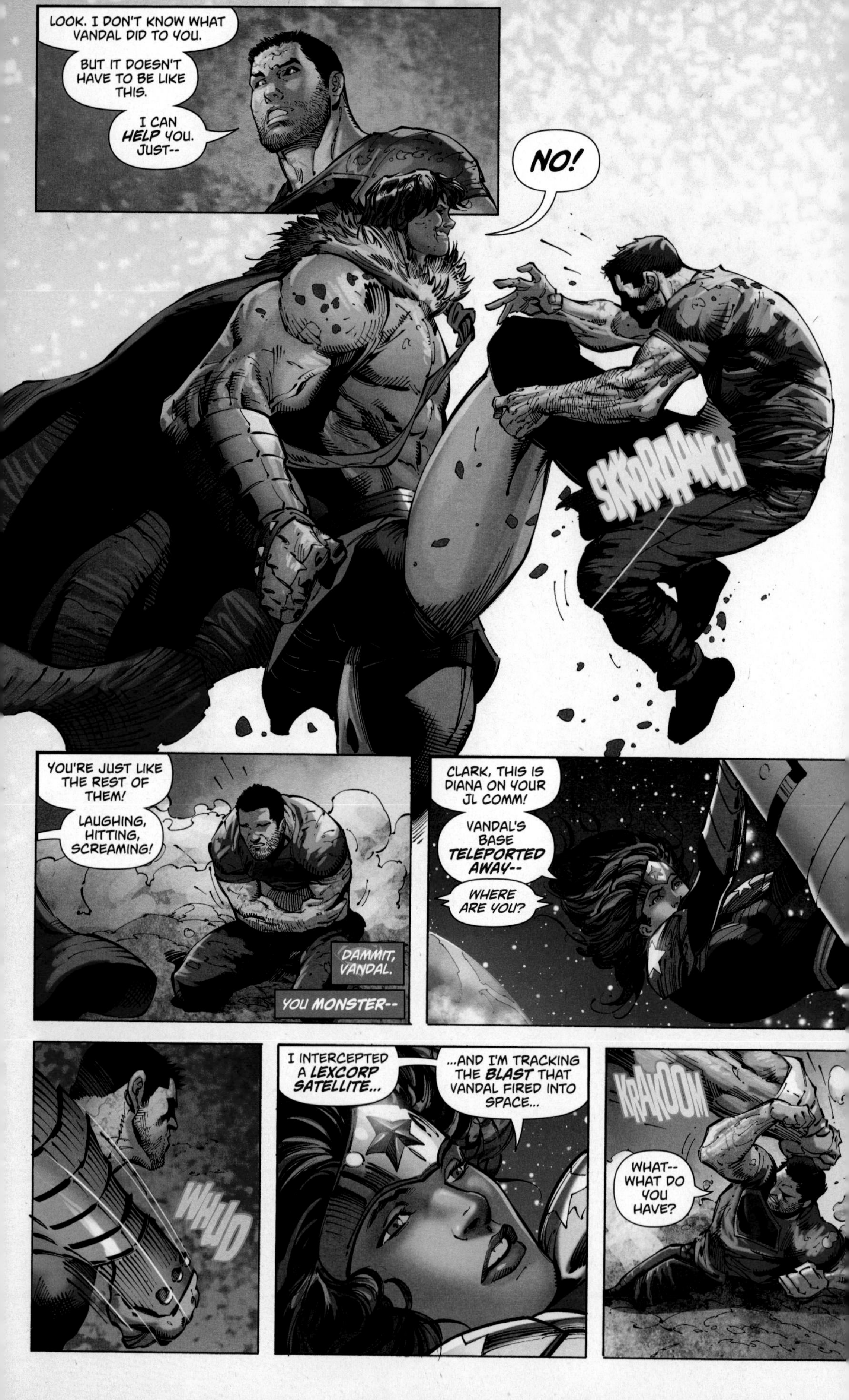

LOOK. I DON'T KNOW WHAT VANDAL DID TO YOU.
BUT IT DOESN'T HAVE TO BE LIKE THIS.
I CAN HELP YOU. JUST--
NO!
SKRRAAANCH
YOU'RE JUST LIKE THE REST OF THEM!
LAUGHING, HITTING, SCREAMING!
DAMMIT, VANDAL.
YOU MONSTER--
CLARK, THIS IS DIANA ON YOUR JL COMM!
VANDAL'S BASE TELEPORTED AWAY--
WHERE ARE YOU?
WHUD
I INTERCEPTED A LEXCORP SATELLITE...
...AND I'M TRACKING THE BLAST THAT VANDAL FIRED INTO SPACE...
KRAKOOM
WHAT-- WHAT DO YOU HAVE?

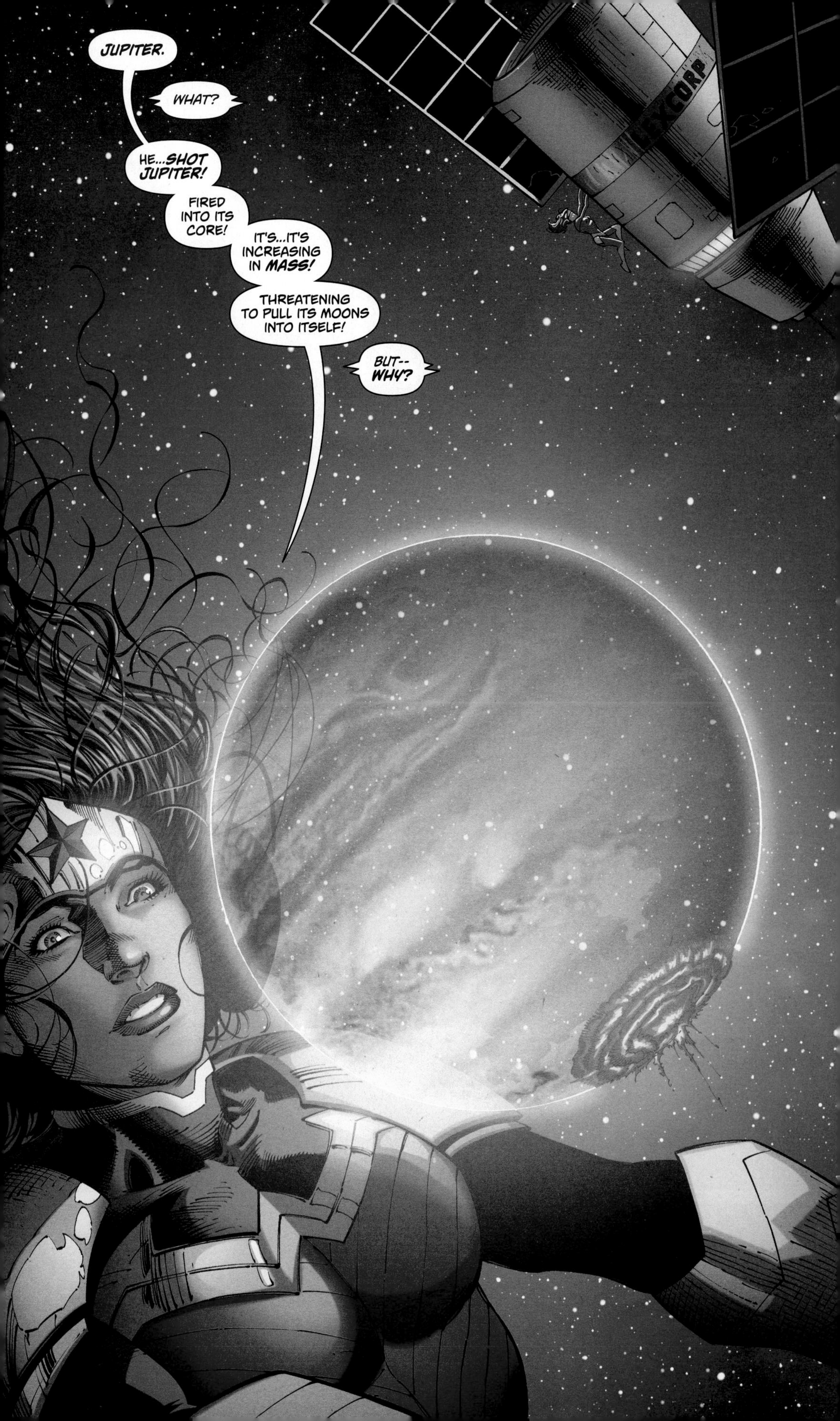
JUPITER.
WHAT?
HE...SHOT JUPITER!
FIRED INTO ITS CORE!
IT'S...IT'S INCREASING IN MASS!
THREATENING TO PULL ITS MOONS INTO ITSELF!
BUT-- WHY?

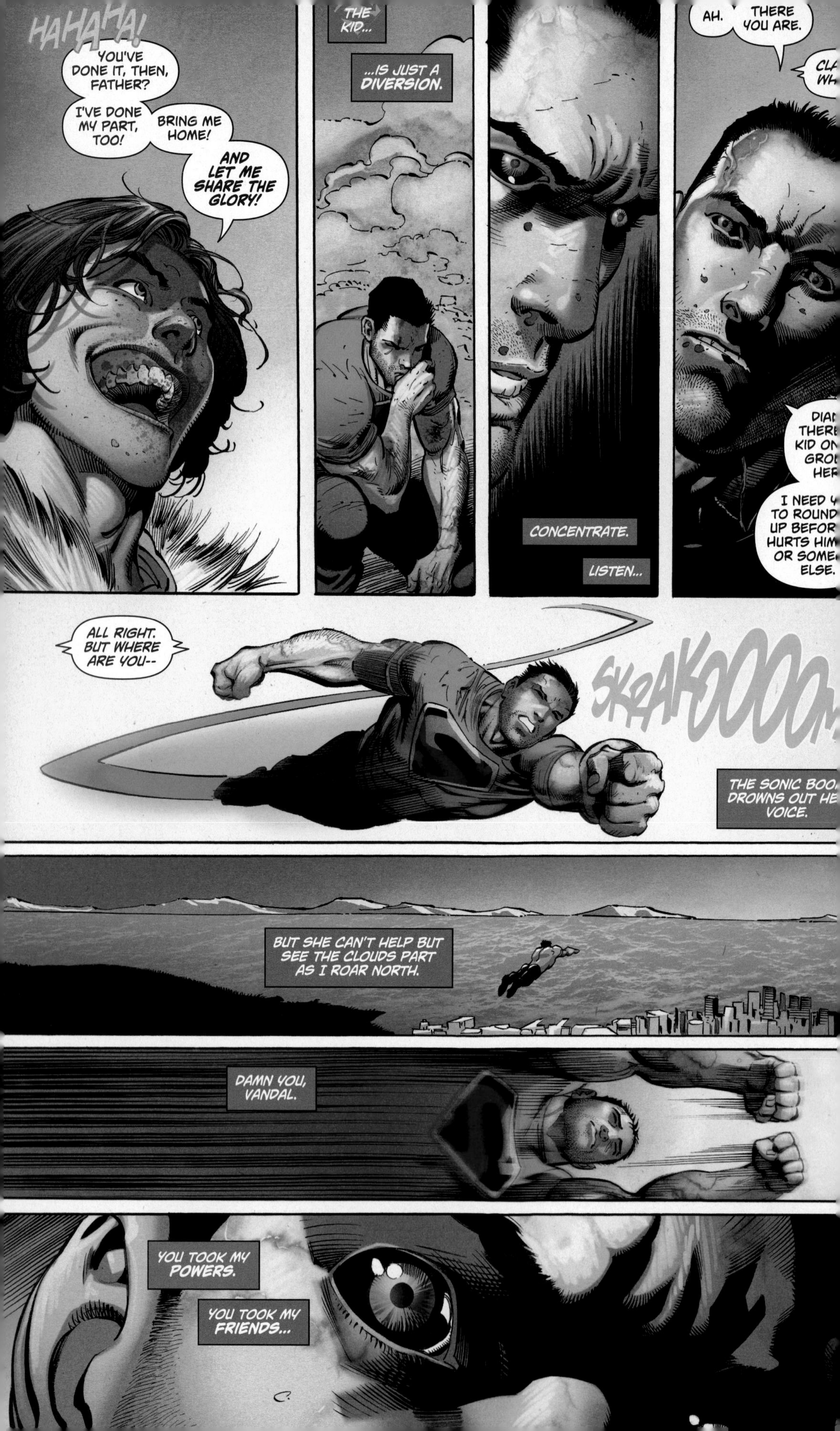
HAHAHA!
YOU'VE DONE IT, THEN, FATHER?
I'VE DONE MY PART, TOO!
BRING ME HOME!
AND LET ME SHARE THE GLORY!
THE KID...
...IS JUST A DIVERSION.
CONCENTRATE.
LISTEN...
AH.
THERE YOU ARE.
ALL RIGHT. BUT WHERE ARE YOU--
SKRAKOOOOM
THE SONIC BOOM DROWNS OUT HER VOICE.
BUT SHE CAN'T HELP BUT SEE THE CLOUDS PART AS I ROAR NORTH.
DAMN YOU, VANDAL.
YOU TOOK MY POWERS.
YOU TOOK MY FRIENDS...

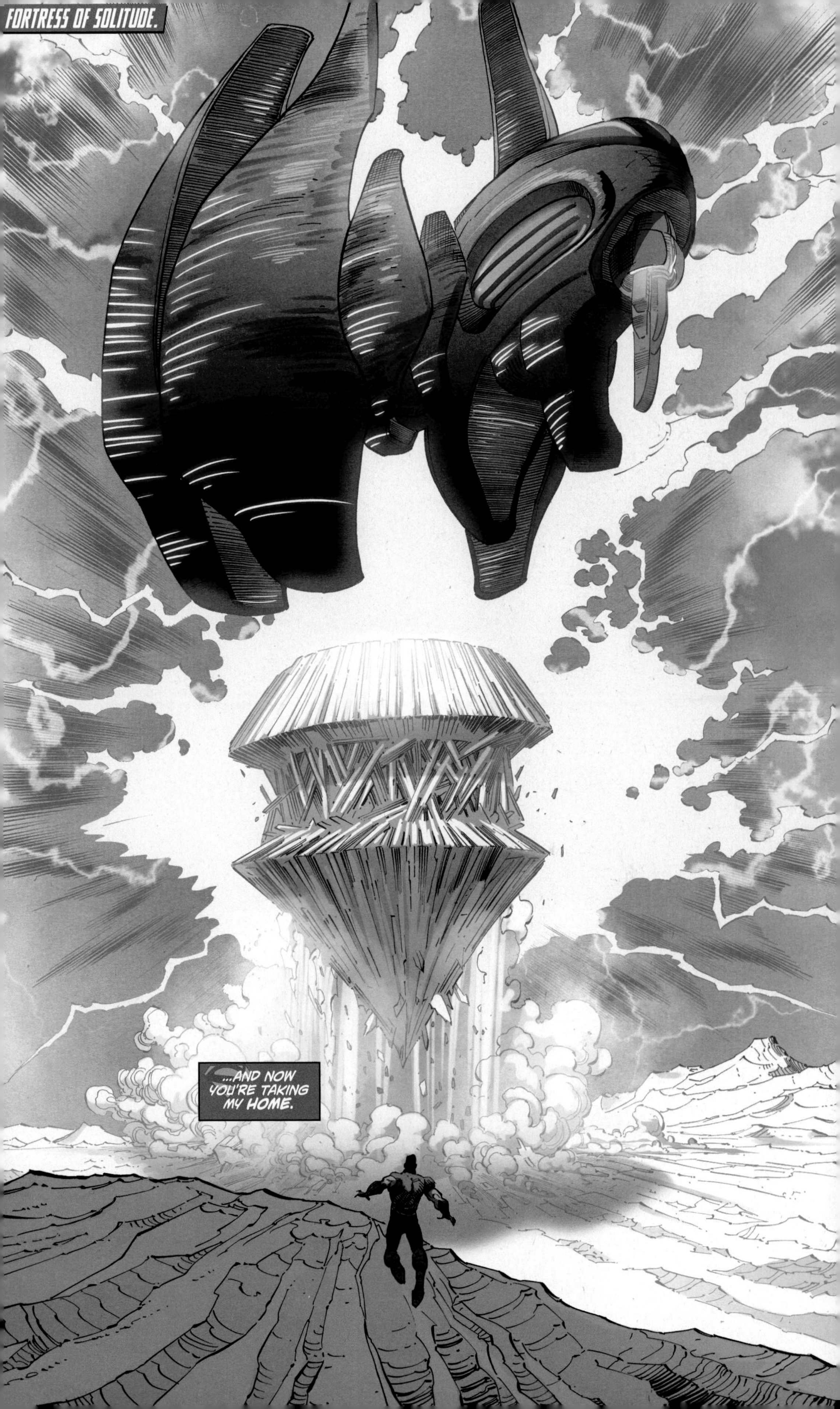
FORTRESS OF SOLITUDE.
...AND NOW YOU'RE TAKING MY HOME.

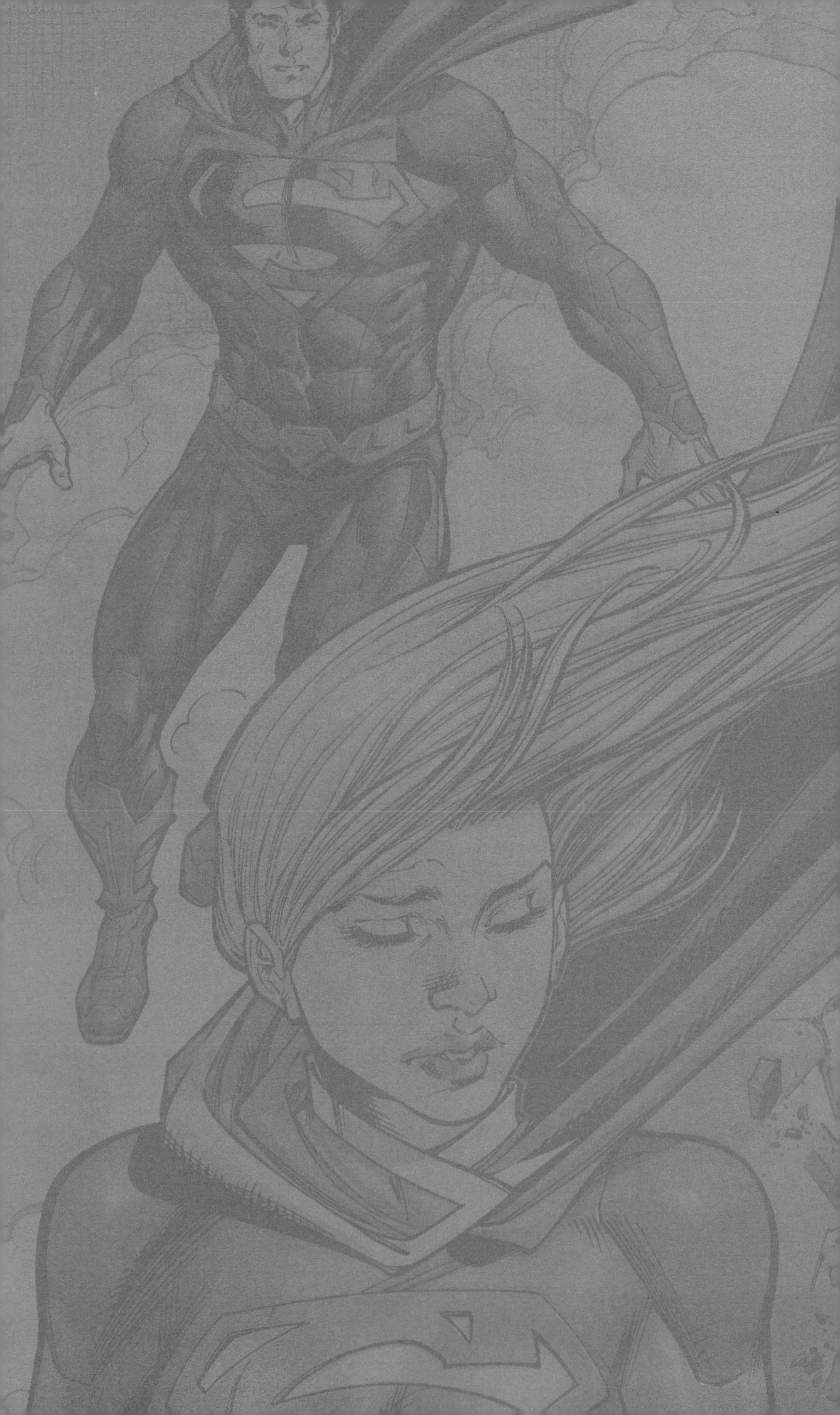

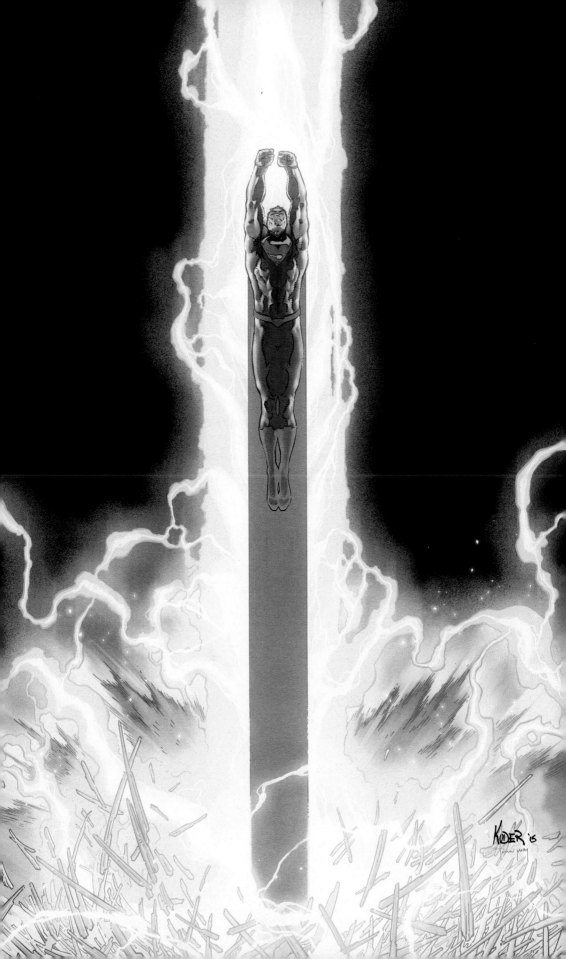

Previously,
in SUPERMAN/WONDER WOMAN #26 and SUPERMAN #49...

With Jupiter's moons realigned and the Fortress of Solitude, Justice League Watchtower and Stormwatch Carrier bonded together, Vandal Savage generates a super-tractor beam strong enough to draw toward Earth the comet that once made him immortal. He has also sent a twin set of his power-mad offspring to destroy Wonder Woman and a Kryptonite-fueled Superman. But when the fused base threatens to crash down in the heart of Metropolis, the Man of Steel foregoes the battle and pushes the structure away from the city—and right on top of him.

As Diana manages to help free Superman, the approaching meteor already gives rise to others who bear Savage's genetic signature. Thankfully, a handful of heroic allies have also entered the fray, while Lois Lane's bodyguard, Metallo, makes the ultimate sacrifice after being fatally wounded: he gives up his Kryptonite heart so the Man of Steel can use it to power up and finish the fight...

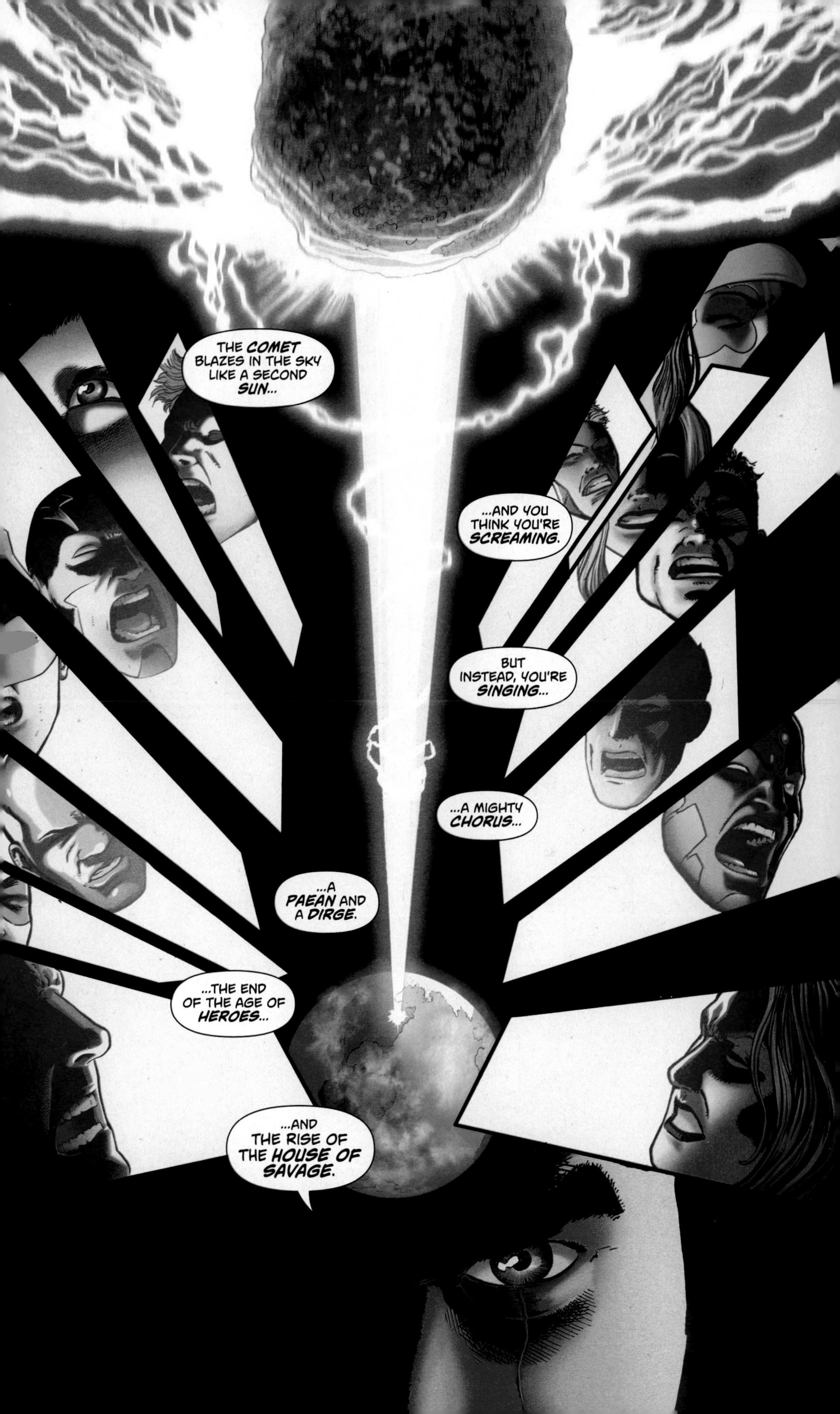
THE COMET BLAZES IN THE SKY LIKE A SECOND SUN...
...AND YOU THINK YOU'RE SCREAMING.
BUT INSTEAD, YOU'RE SINGING...
...A MIGHTY CHORUS...
...A PAEAN AND A DIRGE.
...THE END OF THE AGE OF HEROES...
...AND THE RISE OF THE HOUSE OF SAVAGE.

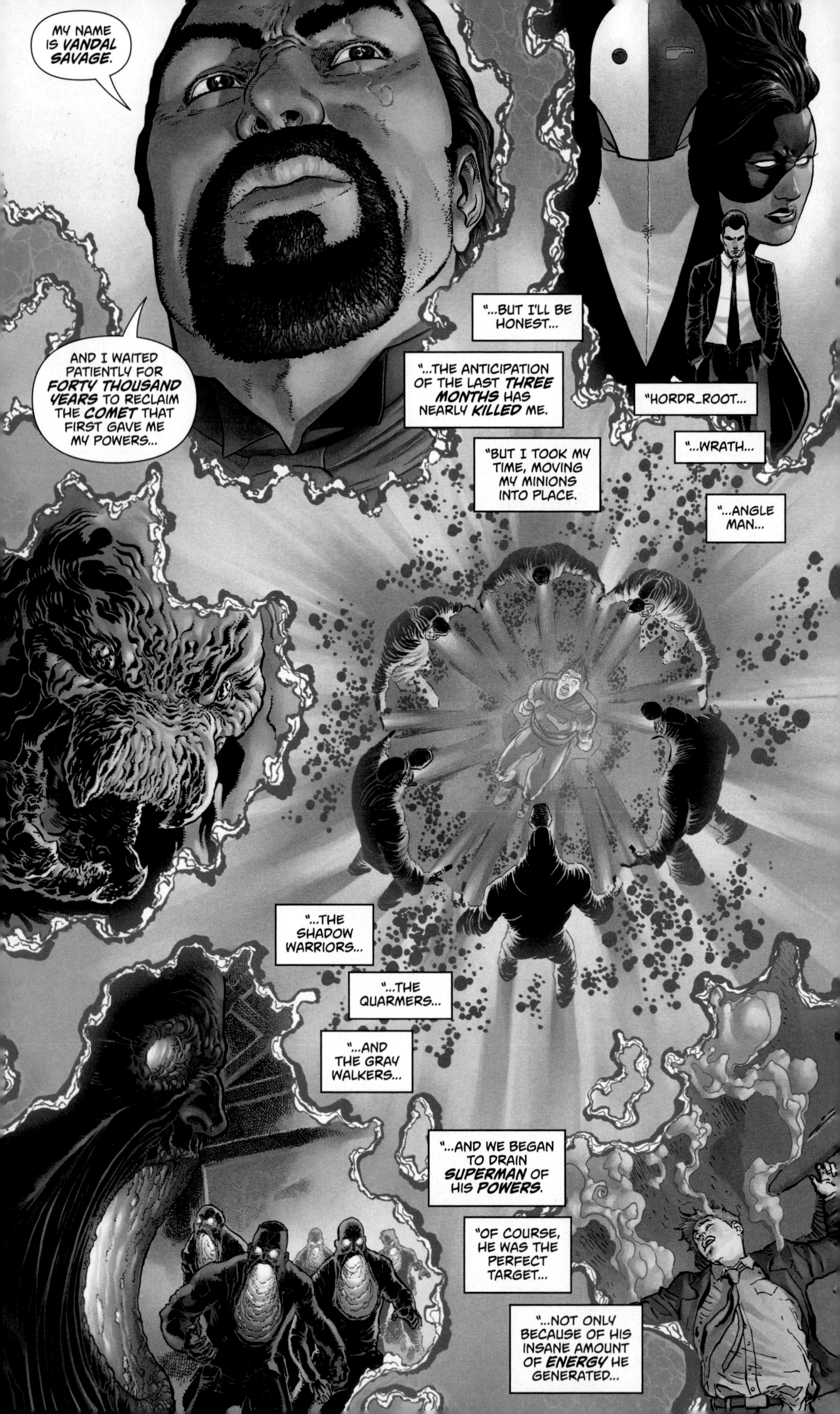
MY NAME IS VANDAL SAVAGE.
AND I WAITED PATIENTLY FOR FORTY THOUSAND YEARS TO RECLAIM THE COMET THAT FIRST GAVE ME MY POWERS...
"...BUT I'LL BE HONEST...
"...THE ANTICIPATION OF THE LAST THREE MONTHS HAS NEARLY KILLED ME.
"BUT I TOOK MY TIME, MOVING MY MINIONS INTO PLACE.
"HORDR_ROOT...
"...WRATH...
"...ANGLE MAN...
"...THE SHADOW WARRIORS...
"...THE QUARMERS...
"...AND THE GRAY WALKERS...
"...AND WE BEGAN TO DRAIN SUPERMAN OF HIS POWERS.
"OF COURSE, HE WAS THE PERFECT TARGET...
"...NOT ONLY BECAUSE OF HIS INSANE AMOUNT OF ENERGY HE GENERATED...

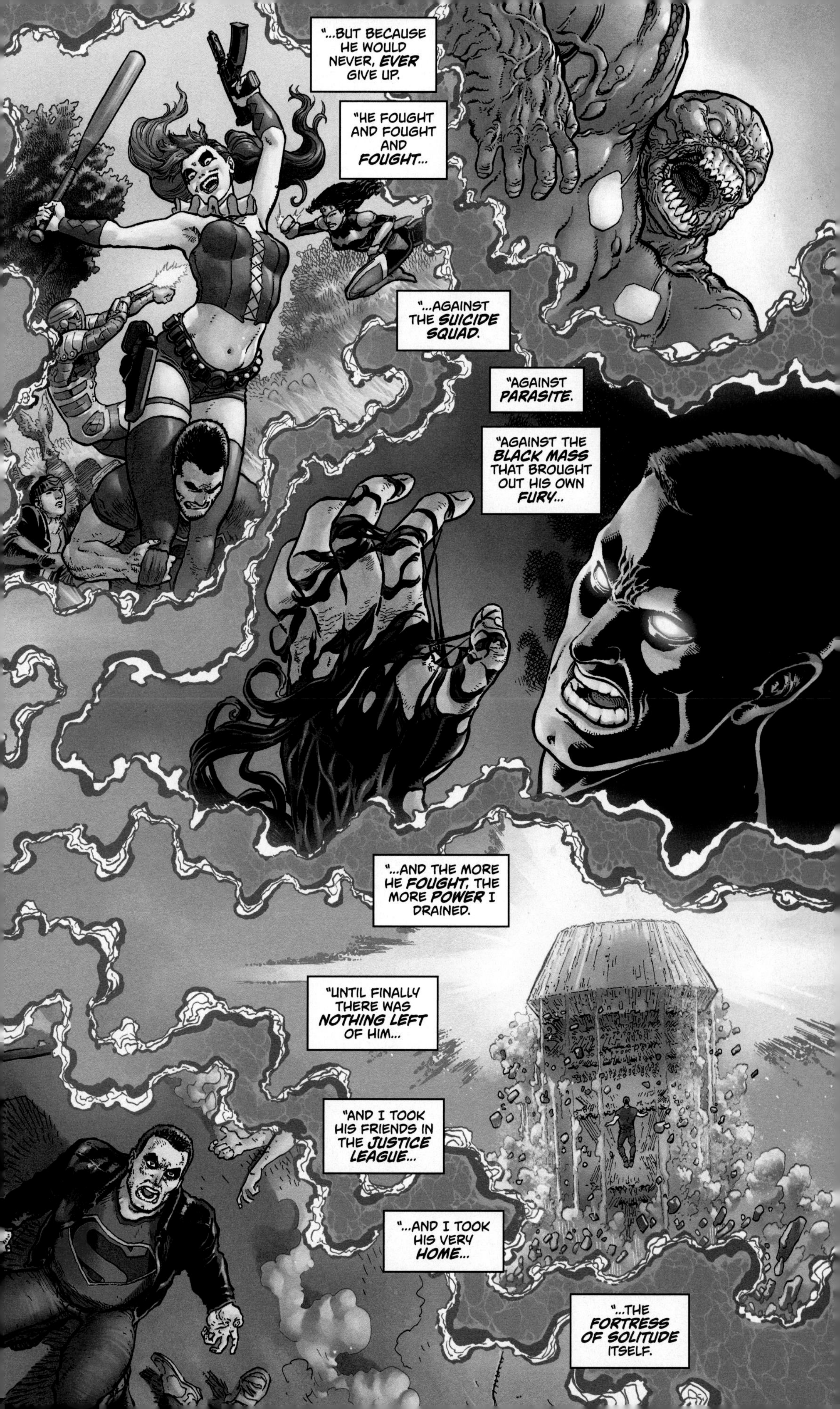
"...BUT BECAUSE HE WOULD NEVER, EVER GIVE UP.
"HE FOUGHT AND FOUGHT AND FOUGHT...
"...AGAINST THE SUICIDE SQUAD.
"AGAINST PARASITE.
"AGAINST THE BLACK MASS THAT BROUGHT OUT HIS OWN FURY...
"...AND THE MORE HE FOUGHT, THE MORE POWER I DRAINED.
"UNTIL FINALLY THERE WAS NOTHING LEFT OF HIM...
"AND I TOOK HIS FRIENDS IN THE JUSTICE LEAGUE...
"...AND I TOOK HIS VERY HOME...
"...THE FORTRESS OF SOLITUDE ITSELF.

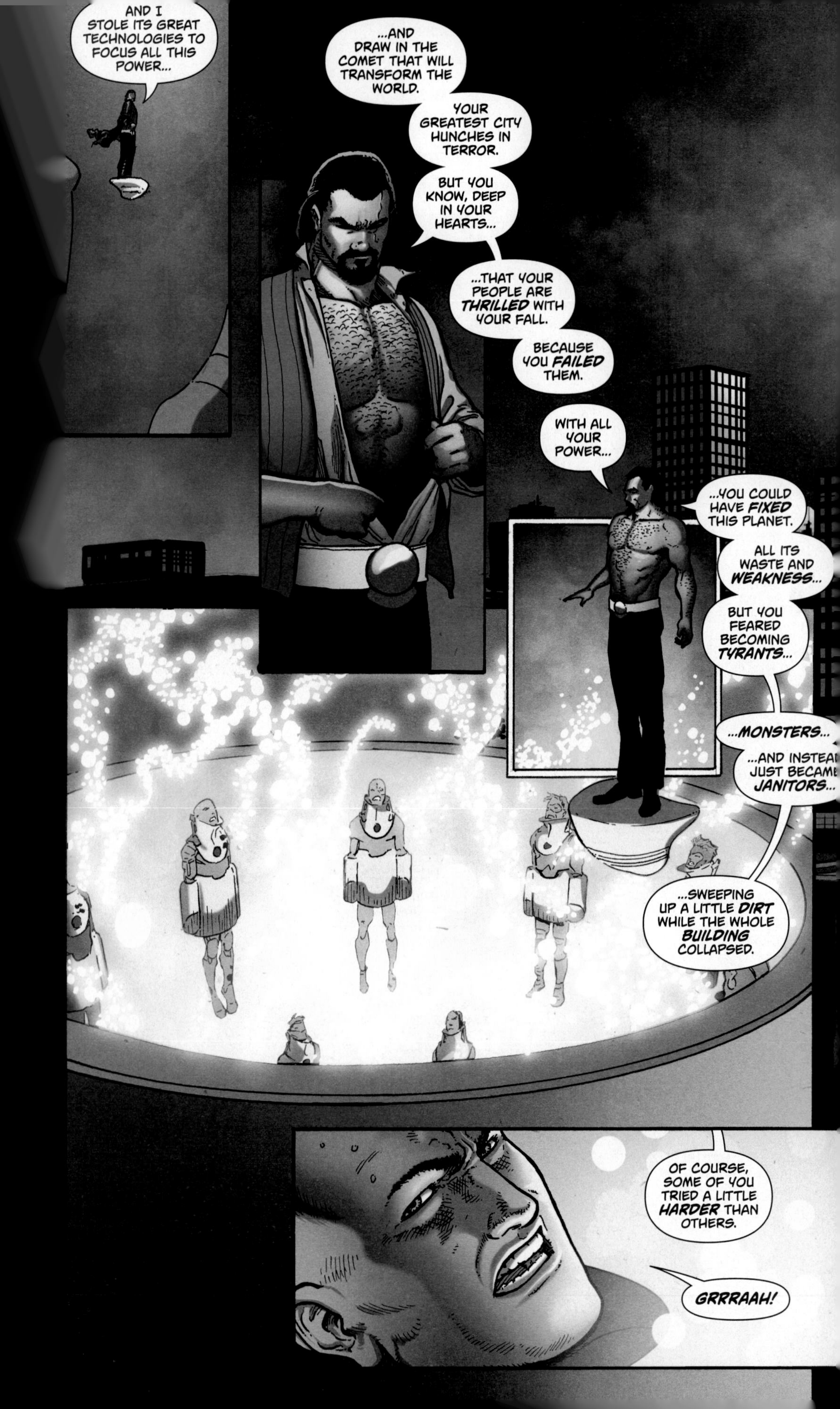
AND I STOLE ITS GREAT TECHNOLOGIES TO FOCUS ALL THIS POWER...
...AND DRAW IN THE COMET THAT WILL TRANSFORM THE WORLD.
YOUR GREATEST CITY HUNCHES IN TERROR.
BUT YOU KNOW, DEEP IN YOUR HEARTS...
...THAT YOUR PEOPLE ARE THRILLED WITH YOUR FALL.
BECAUSE YOU FAILED THEM.
WITH ALL YOUR POWER...
...YOU COULD HAVE FIXED THIS PLANET.
ALL ITS WASTE AND WEAKNESS...
BUT YOU FEARED BECOMING TYRANTS...
...MONSTERS...
...AND INSTEA JUST BECAME JANITORS...
...SWEEPING UP A LITTLE DIRT WHILE THE WHOLE BUILDING COLLAPSED.
OF COURSE, SOME OF YOU TRIED A LITTLE HARDER THAN OTHERS.
GRRRAAH!

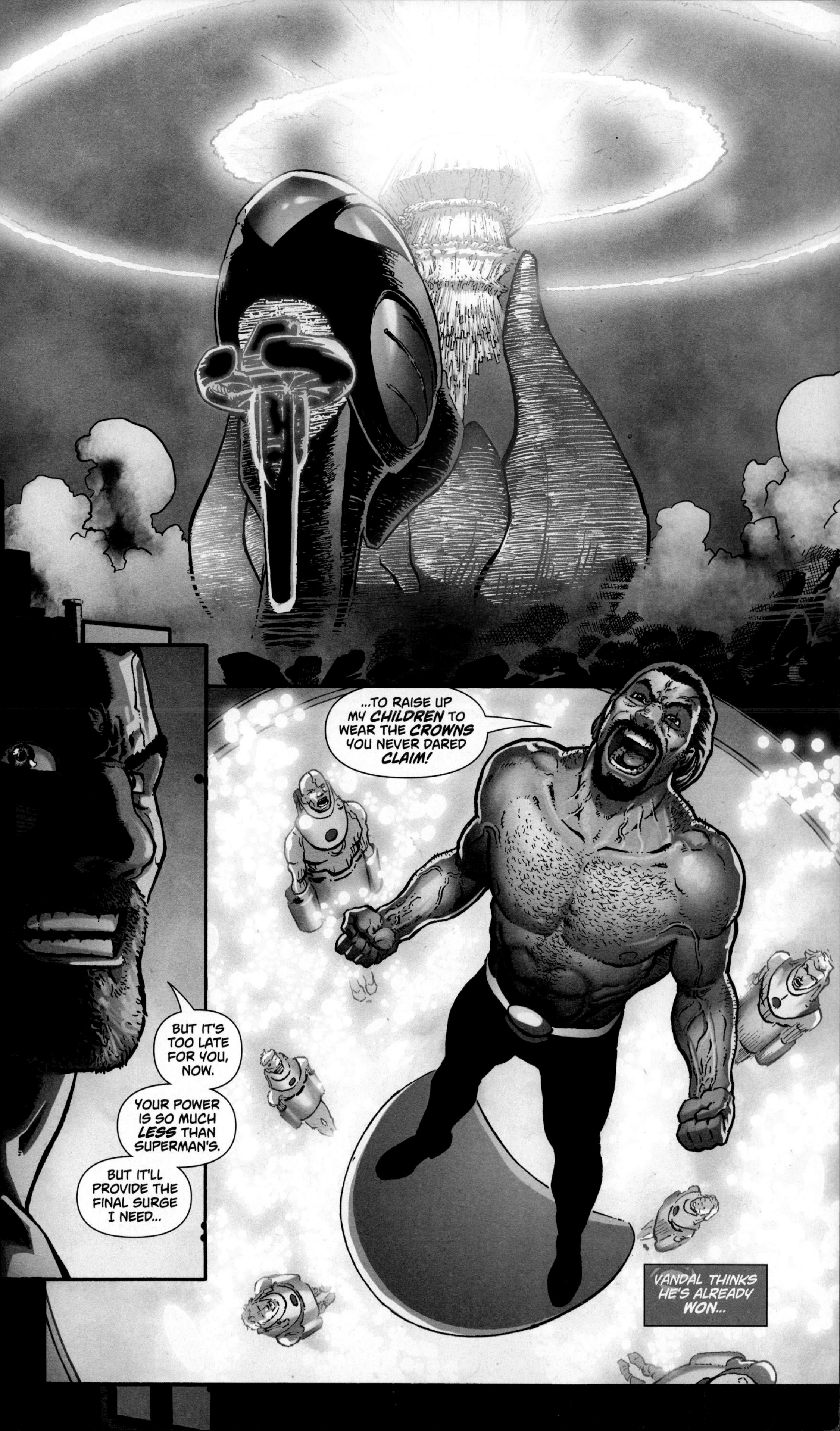
...TO RAISE UP MY CHILDREN TO WEAR THE CROWNS YOU NEVER DARED CLAIM!
BUT IT'S TOO LATE FOR YOU, NOW.
YOUR POWER IS SO MUCH LESS THAN SUPERMAN'S.
BUT IT'LL PROVIDE THE FINAL SURGE I NEED...
VANDAL THINKS HE'S ALREADY WON...

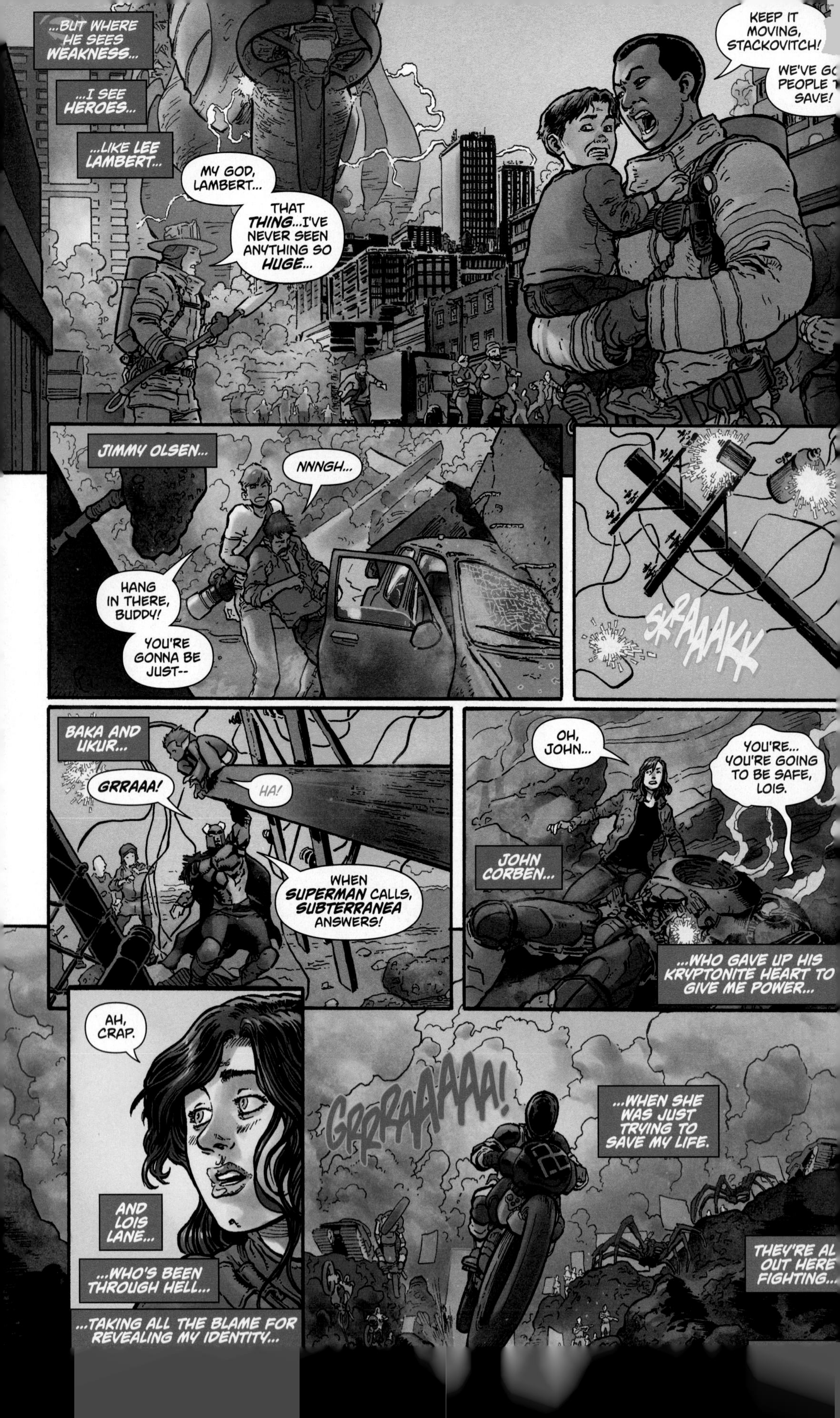
...BUT WHERE HE SEES WEAKNESS...
...I SEE HEROES...
...LIKE LEE LAMBERT...
MY GOD, LAMBERT...
THAT THING...I'VE NEVER SEEN ANYTHING SO HUGE...
KEEP IT MOVING, STACKOVITCH!
WE'VE GO PEOPLE T SAVE!
JIMMY OLSEN...
NNNGH...
HANG IN THERE, BUDDY!
YOU'RE GONNA BE JUST--
SKRAAAKK
BAKA AND UKUR...
GRRAAA!
HA!
WHEN SUPERMAN CALLS, SUBTERRANEA ANSWERS!
OH, JOHN...
YOU'RE... YOU'RE GOING TO BE SAFE, LOIS.
JOHN CORBEN...
...WHO GAVE UP HIS KRYPTONITE HEART TO GIVE ME POWER...
AH, CRAP.
AND LOIS LANE...
...WHO'S BEEN THROUGH HELL...
...TAKING ALL THE BLAME FOR REVEALING MY IDENTITY...
GRRRAAAAAA!
...WHEN SHE WAS JUST TRYING TO SAVE MY LIFE.
THEY'RE AL OUT HERE FIGHTING...

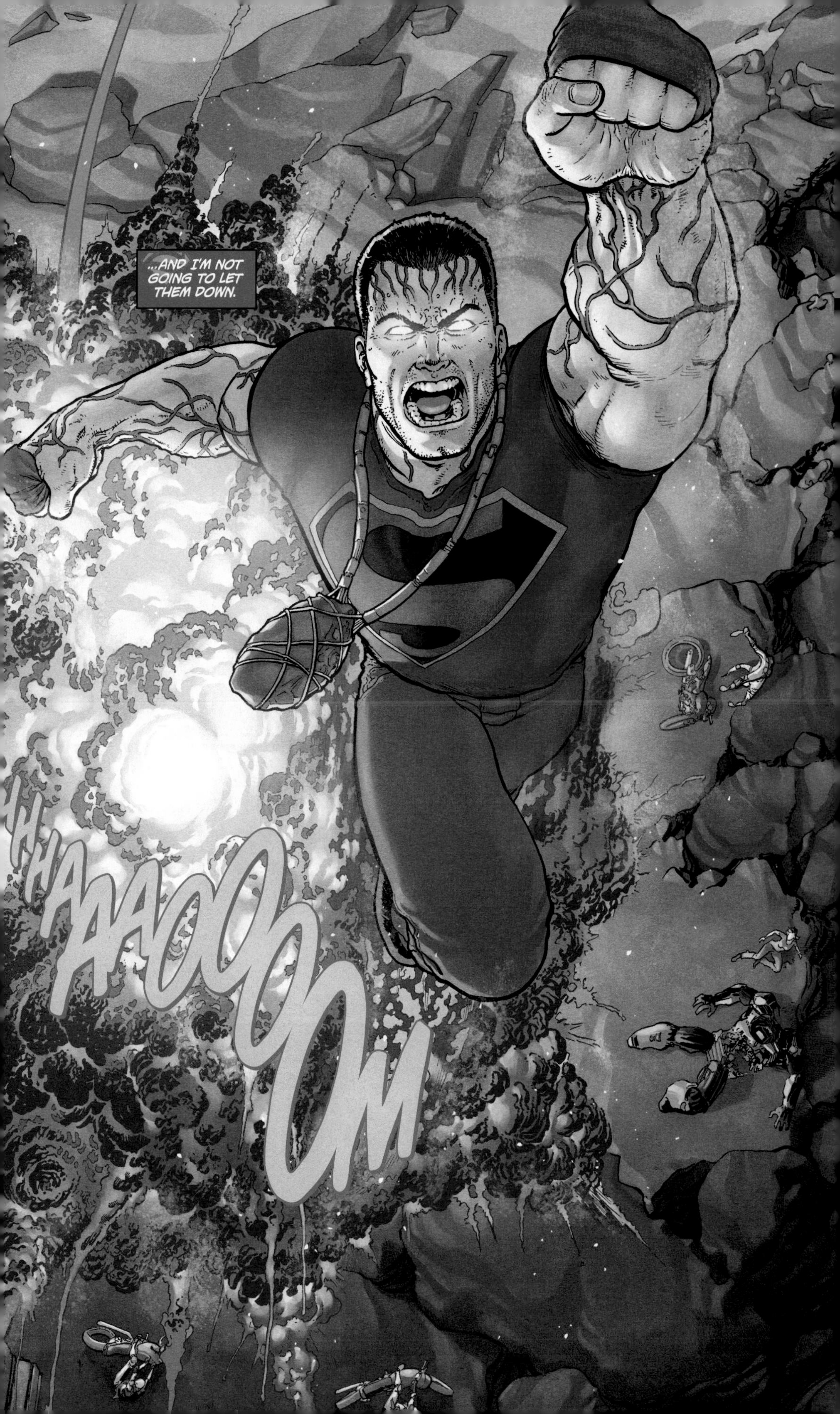
...AND I'M NOT GOING TO LET THEM DOWN.
HHAAAOOOM

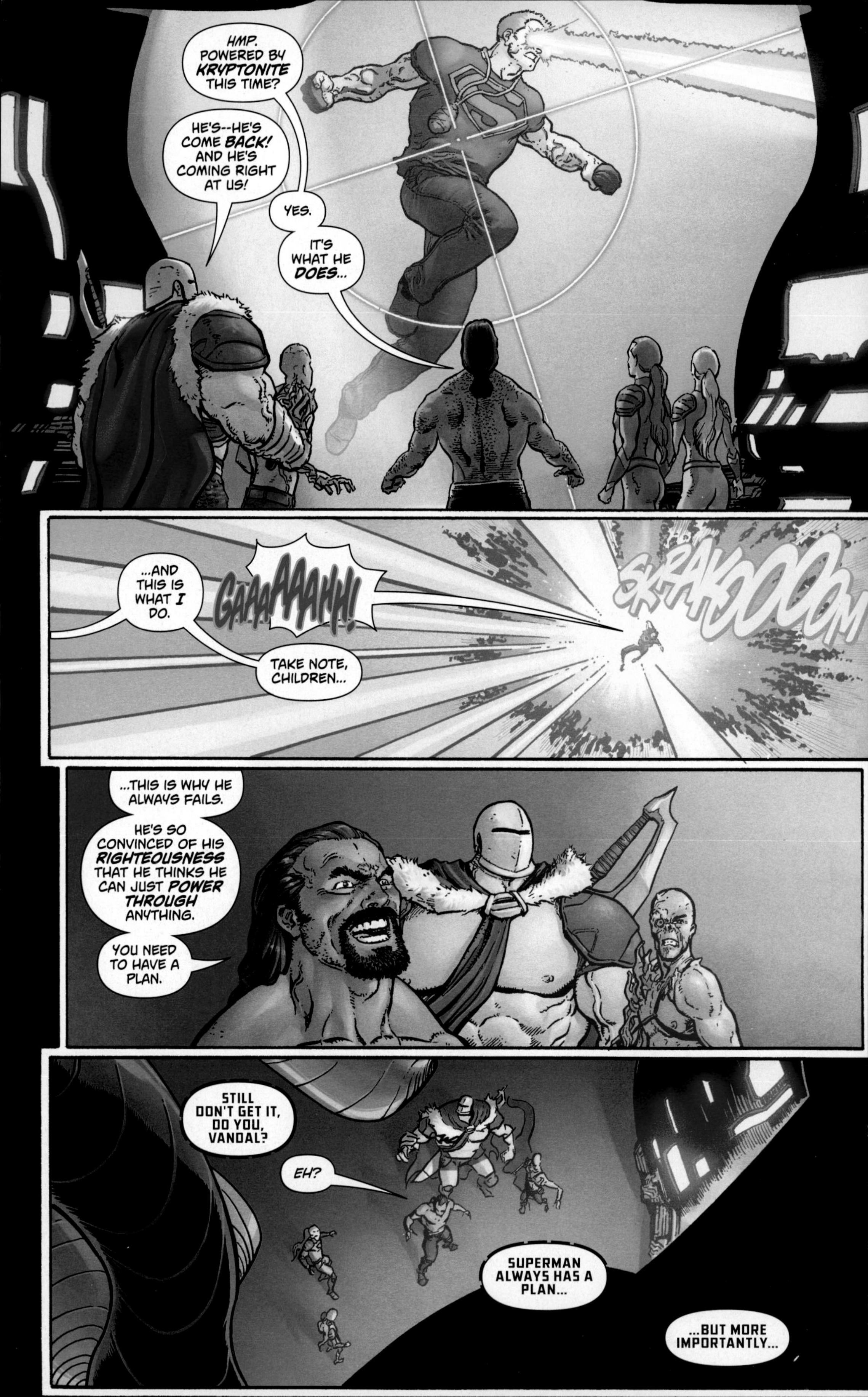
HMP. POWERED BY KRYPTONITE THIS TIME?
HE'S--HE'S COME BACK! AND HE'S COMING RIGHT AT US!
YES.
IT'S WHAT HE DOES...
...AND THIS IS WHAT I DO.
GAAAAAAHH!
SKRAKOOOOM
TAKE NOTE, CHILDREN...
...THIS IS WHY HE ALWAYS FAILS.
HE'S SO CONVINCED OF HIS RIGHTEOUSNESS THAT HE THINKS HE CAN JUST POWER THROUGH ANYTHING.
YOU NEED TO HAVE A PLAN.
STILL DON'T GET IT, DO YOU, VANDAL?
EH?
SUPERMAN ALWAYS HAS A PLAN...
...BUT MORE IMPORTANTLY...

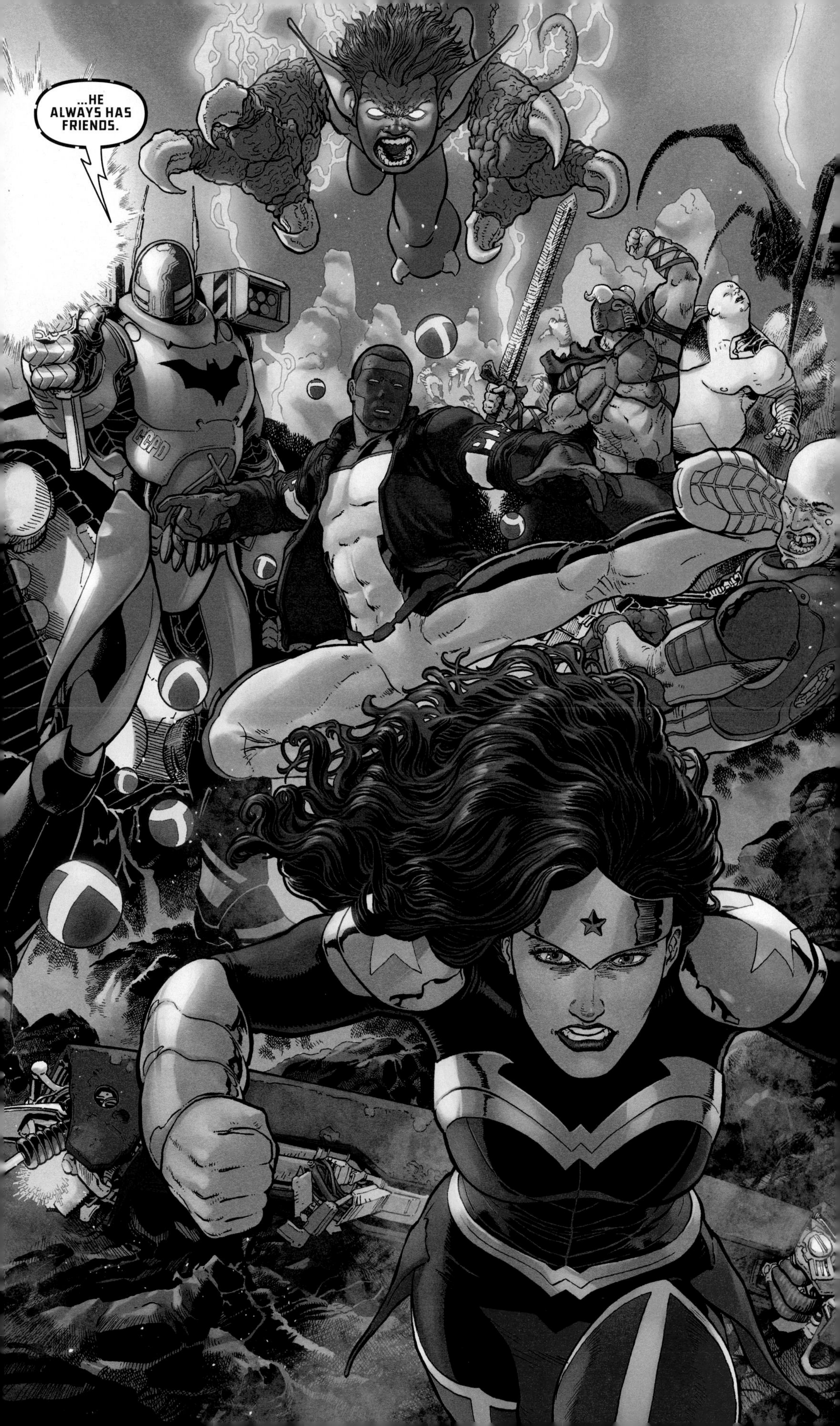
...HE ALWAYS HAS FRIENDS.

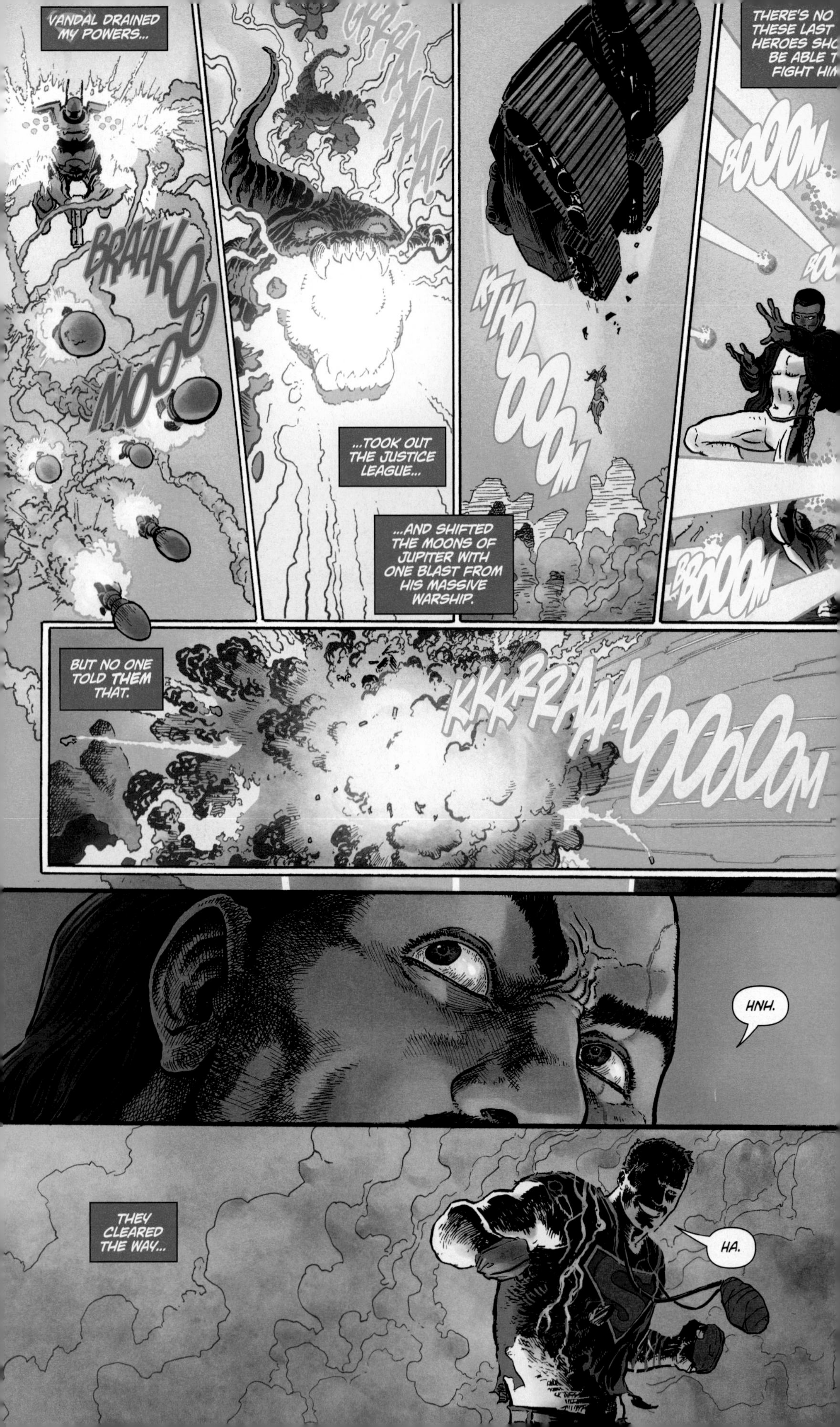
VANDAL DRAINED MY POWERS...
BRAAKOOOMOOO
GKRRAAAAAA!
...TOOK OUT THE JUSTICE LEAGUE...
KTHOOOOOOM
...AND SHIFTED THE MOONS OF JUPITER WITH ONE BLAST FROM HIS MASSIVE WARSHIP.
THERE'S NO
THESE LAST
HEROES SHO
BE ABLE T
FIGHT HIM
BOOOM
BBOOOM
BUT NO ONE TOLD THEM THAT.
KKKRRAAAOOOOOM
HNH.
THEY CLEARED THE WAY...
HA.

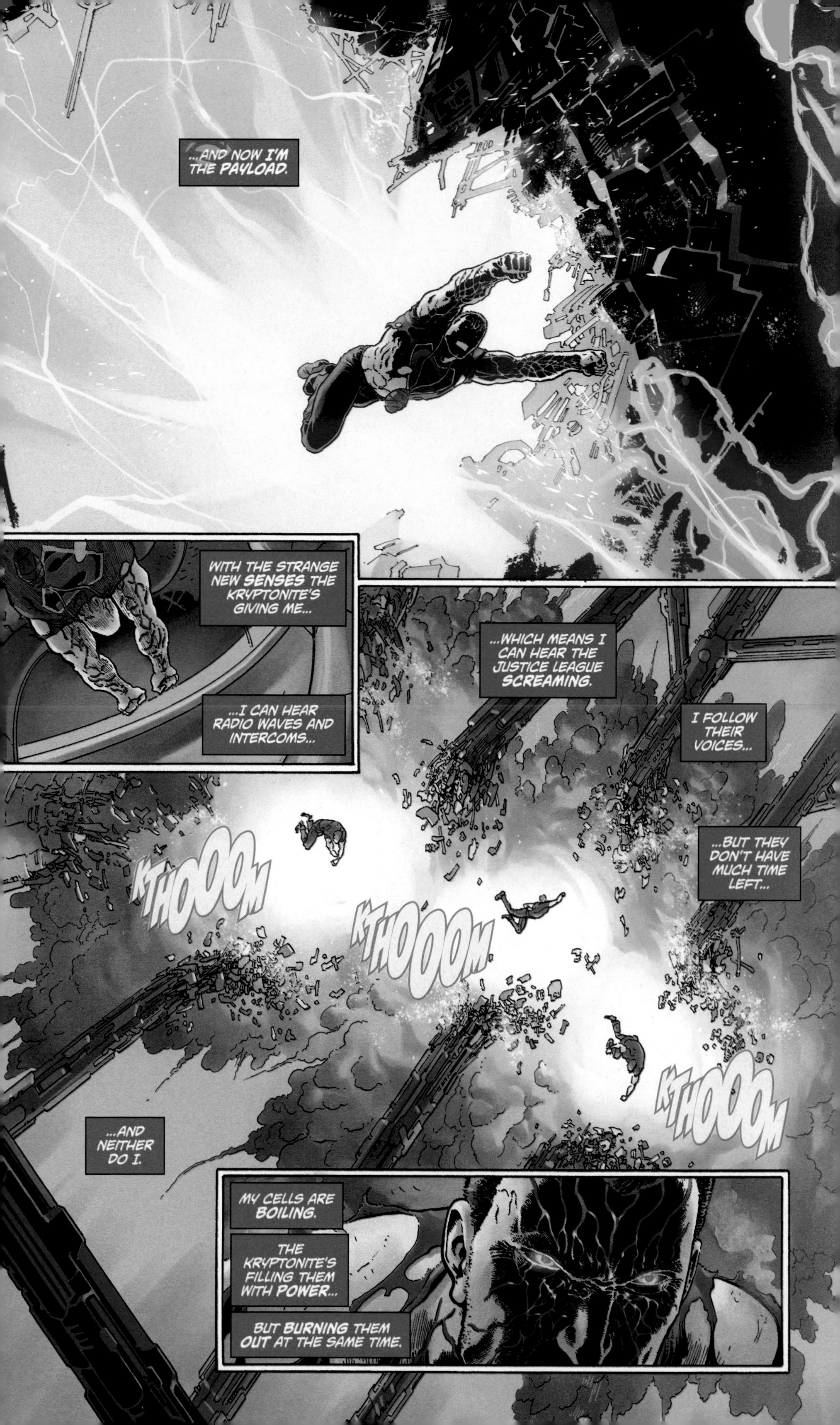
...AND NOW I'M THE PAYLOAD.
WITH THE STRANGE NEW SENSES THE KRYPTONITE'S GIVING ME...
...I CAN HEAR RADIO WAVES AND INTERCOMS...
...WHICH MEANS I CAN HEAR THE JUSTICE LEAGUE SCREAMING.
I FOLLOW THEIR VOICES...
...BUT THEY DON'T HAVE MUCH TIME LEFT...
KTHOOOM
KTHOOOM
KTHOOOM
...AND NEITHER DO I.
MY CELLS ARE BOILING.
THE KRYPTONITE'S FILLING THEM WITH POWER...
BUT BURNING THEM OUT AT THE SAME TIME.

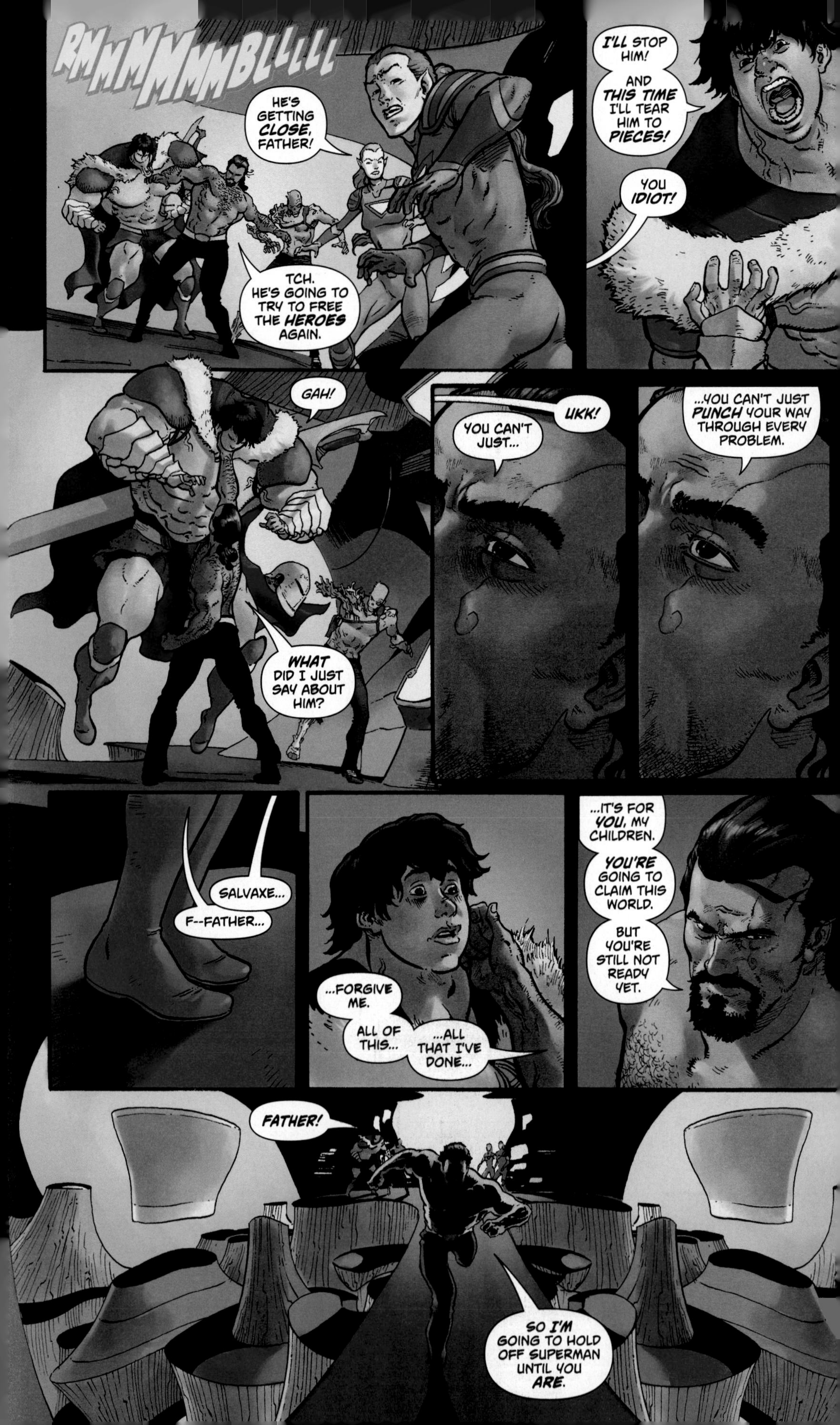
RMMMMMMBLLLLL
HE'S GETTING CLOSE, FATHER!
TCH. HE'S GOING TO TRY TO FREE THE HEROES AGAIN.
I'LL STOP HIM!
AND THIS TIME I'LL TEAR HIM TO PIECES!
YOU IDIOT!
GAH!
WHAT DID I JUST SAY ABOUT HIM?
UKK!
YOU CAN'T JUST...
...YOU CAN'T JUST PUNCH YOUR WAY THROUGH EVERY PROBLEM.
SALVAXE...
F--FATHER...
...FORGIVE ME.
ALL OF THIS...
...ALL THAT I'VE DONE...
...IT'S FOR YOU, MY CHILDREN.
YOU'RE GOING TO CLAIM THIS WORLD.
BUT YOU'RE STILL NOT READY YET.
FATHER!
SO I'M GOING TO HOLD OFF SUPERMAN UNTIL YOU ARE.

ALL RIGHT, SUPES!

I'VE ACCESSED THE CARRIER'S COMPUTER SYSTEM!

TRANSMITTING THE LOCATION OF THE JUSTICE LEAGUE...

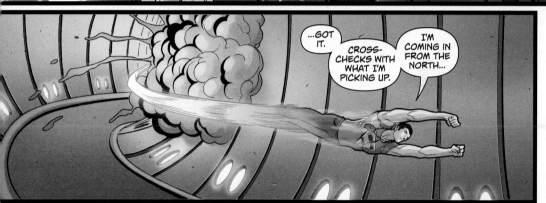

...GOT IT.

CROSS-CHECKS WITH WHAT I'M PICKING UP.

I'M COMING IN FROM THE NORTH...

...AND WE'RE COMING UP FROM THE EAST!

SHOULD BE A CLEAR PATHWAY.

I'M DISARMING THE AUTOMATED CANNONS.

DAMMIT.

THIS IS BAD.

WHAT? WHY?

VANDAL'S TOO SMART TO MAKE IT THIS EASY.

WHERE THE HELL IS HE?

MR. TERRIFIC?

MY NANO-PROBES HAVE JUST PICKED UP TRACES OF HIS DNA...

...OH NO...

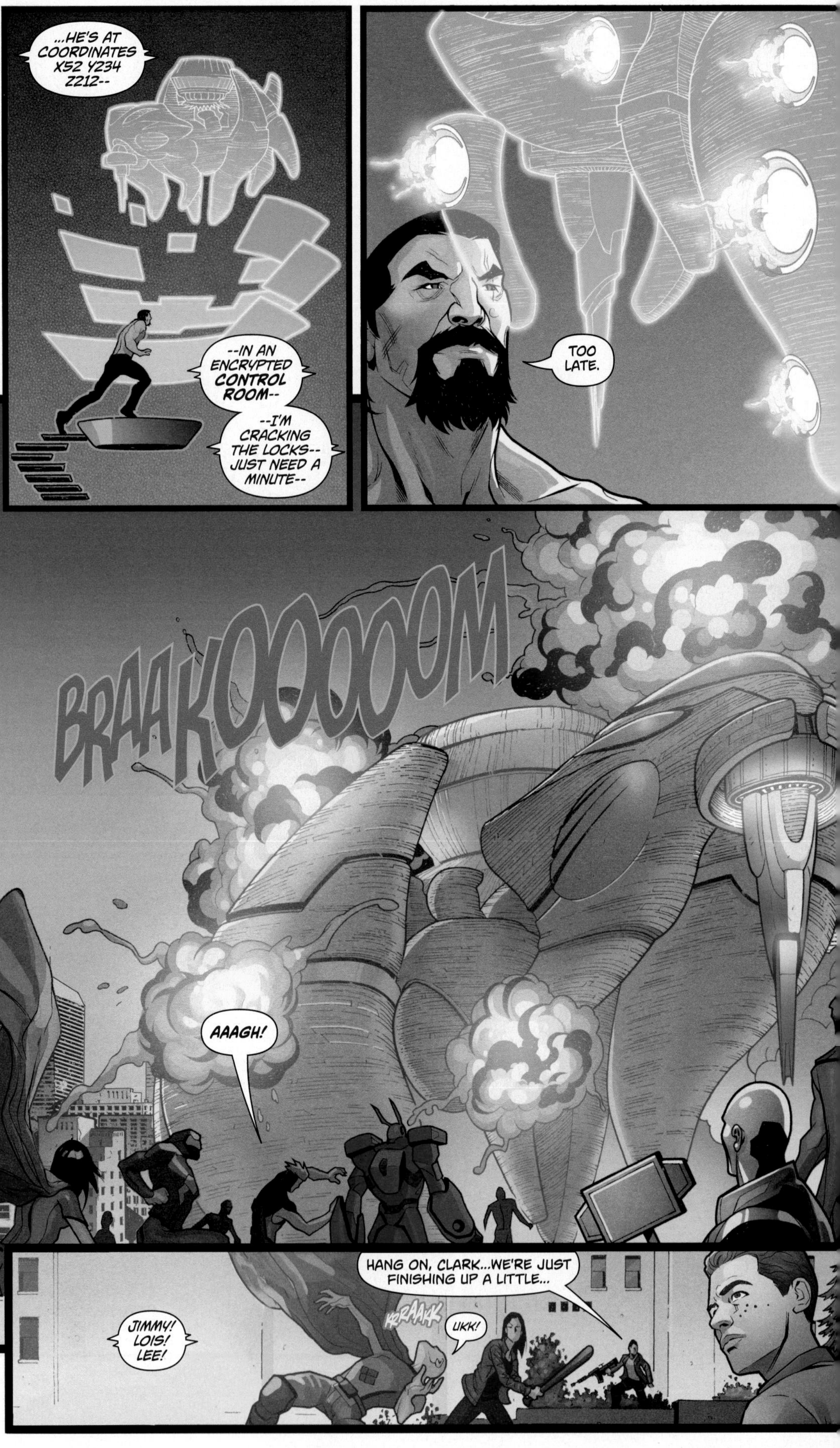
...HE'S AT COORDINATES X52 Y234 Z212--
--IN AN ENCRYPTED CONTROL ROOM--
--I'M CRACKING THE LOCKS-- JUST NEED A MINUTE--
TOO LATE.
BRAAKOOOOOM
AAAGH!
HANG ON, CLARK...WE'RE JUST FINISHING UP A LITTLE...
JIMMY! LOIS! LEE!
KRRAAKK
UKK!

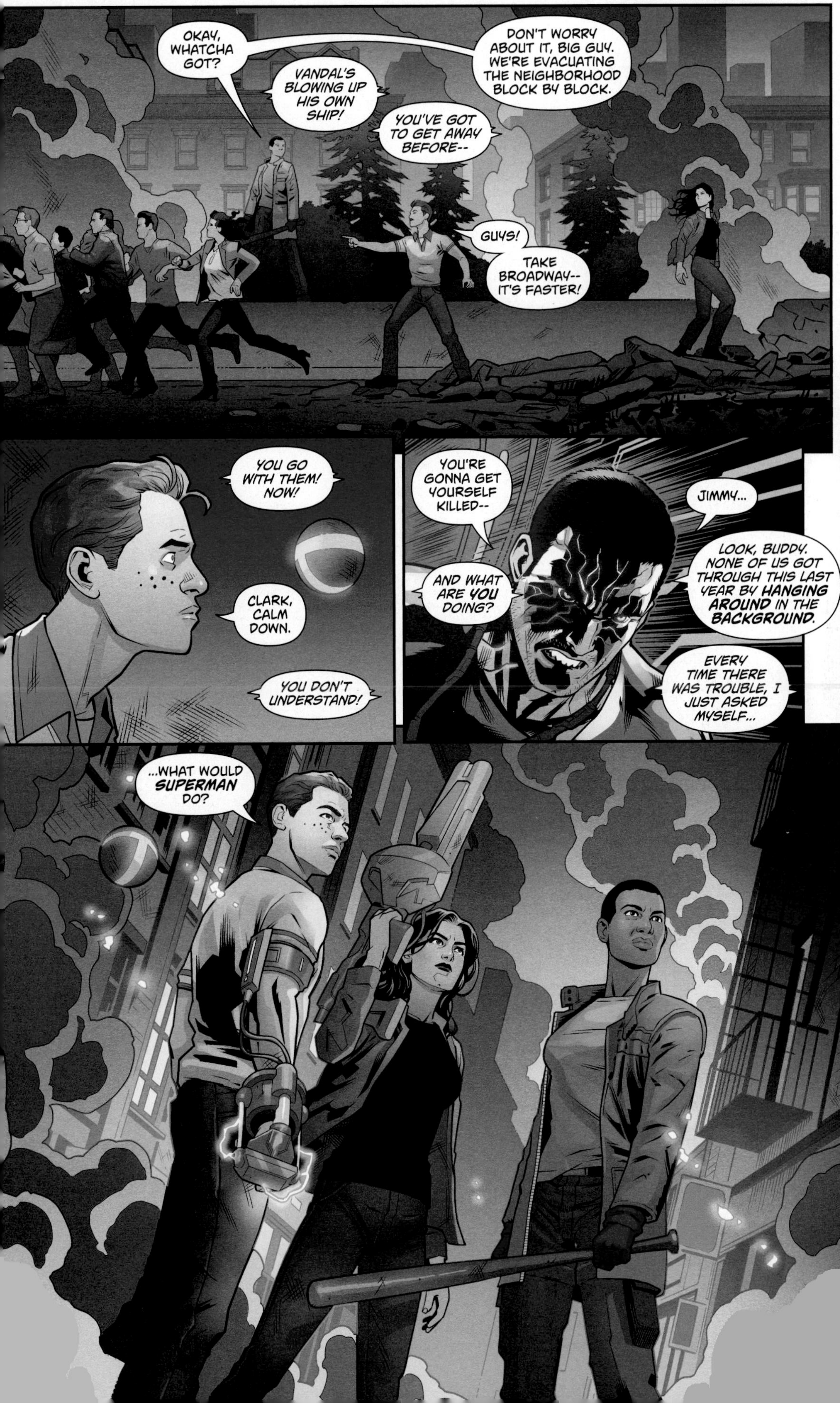

OKAY, WHATCHA GOT?
DON'T WORRY ABOUT IT, BIG GUY. WE'RE EVACUATING THE NEIGHBORHOOD BLOCK BY BLOCK.
VANDAL'S BLOWING UP HIS OWN SHIP!
YOU'VE GOT TO GET AWAY BEFORE--
GUYS!
TAKE BROADWAY-- IT'S FASTER!
YOU GO WITH THEM! NOW!
CLARK, CALM DOWN.
YOU DON'T UNDERSTAND!
YOU'RE GONNA GET YOURSELF KILLED--
AND WHAT ARE YOU DOING?
JIMMY...
LOOK, BUDDY. NONE OF US GOT THROUGH THIS LAST YEAR BY HANGING AROUND IN THE BACKGROUND.
EVERY TIME THERE WAS TROUBLE, I JUST ASKED MYSELF...
...WHAT WOULD SUPERMAN DO?

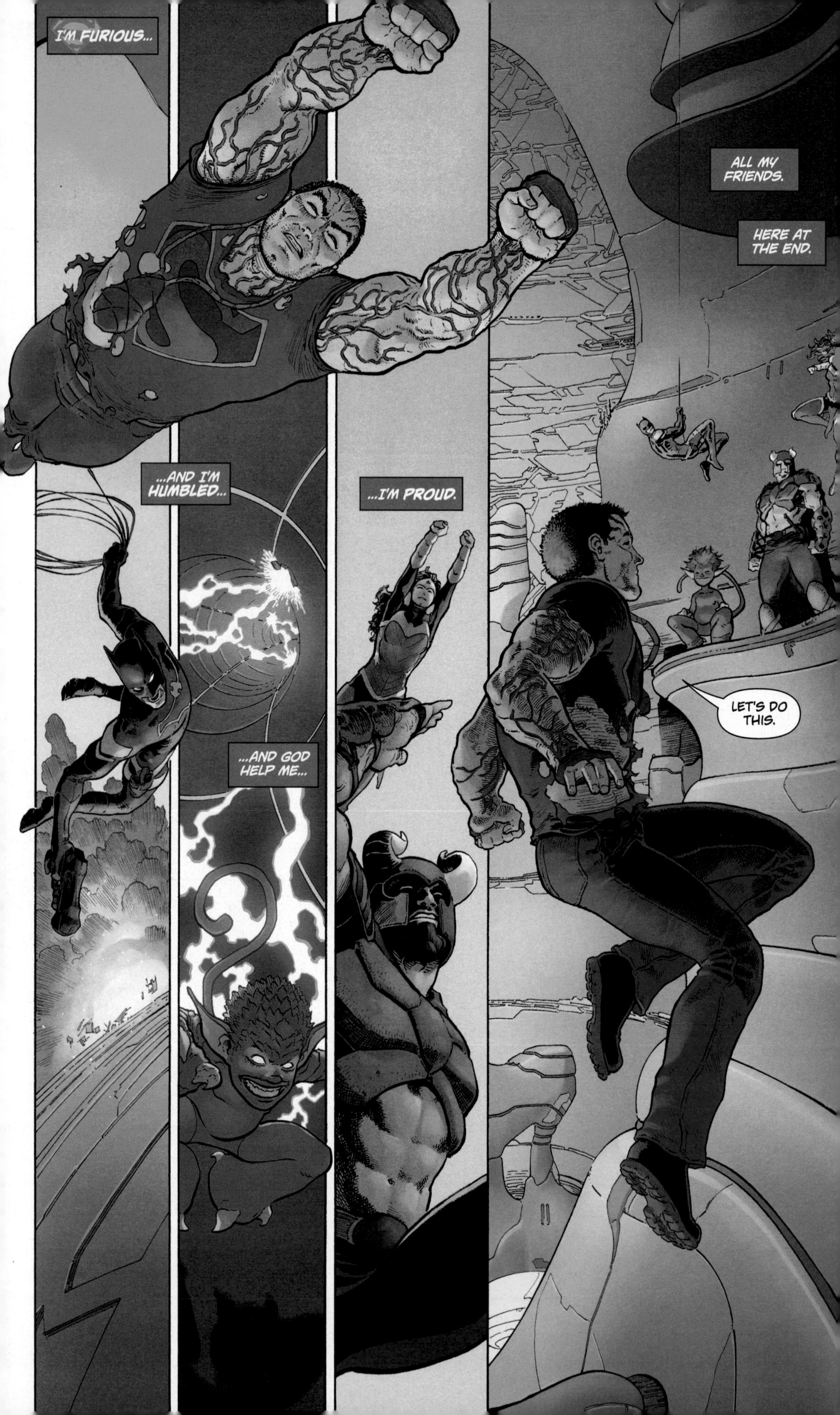
I'M FURIOUS...
...AND I'M HUMBLED...
...AND GOD HELP ME...
...I'M PROUD.
ALL MY FRIENDS.
HERE AT THE END.
LET'S DO THIS.

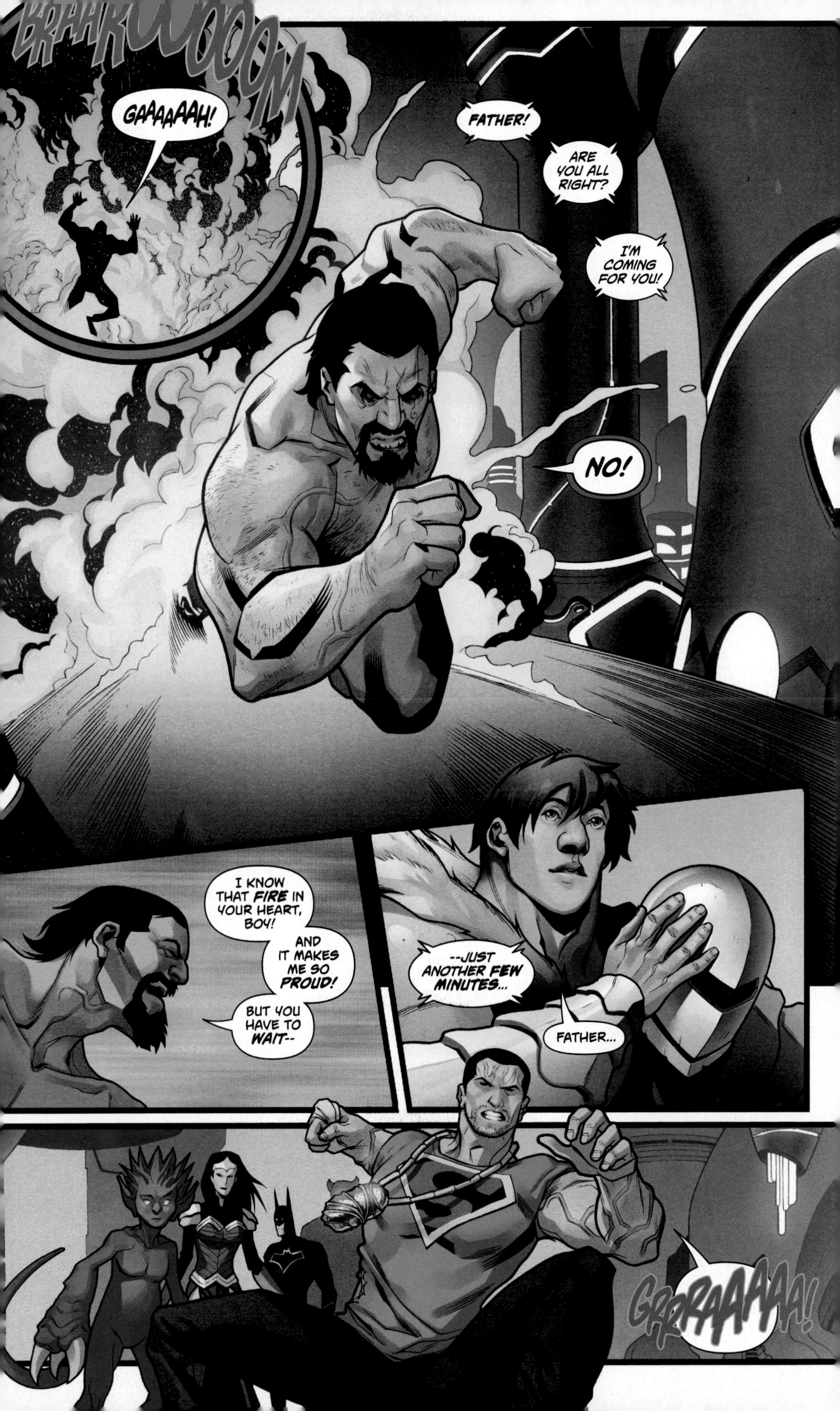
BRAAKOOOOM
GAAAAAAH!
FATHER!
ARE YOU ALL RIGHT?
I'M COMING FOR YOU!
NO!
I KNOW THAT FIRE IN YOUR HEART, BOY!
AND IT MAKES ME SO PROUD!
BUT YOU HAVE TO WAIT--
--JUST ANOTHER FEW MINUTES...
FATHER...
GRRRAAAAAA!

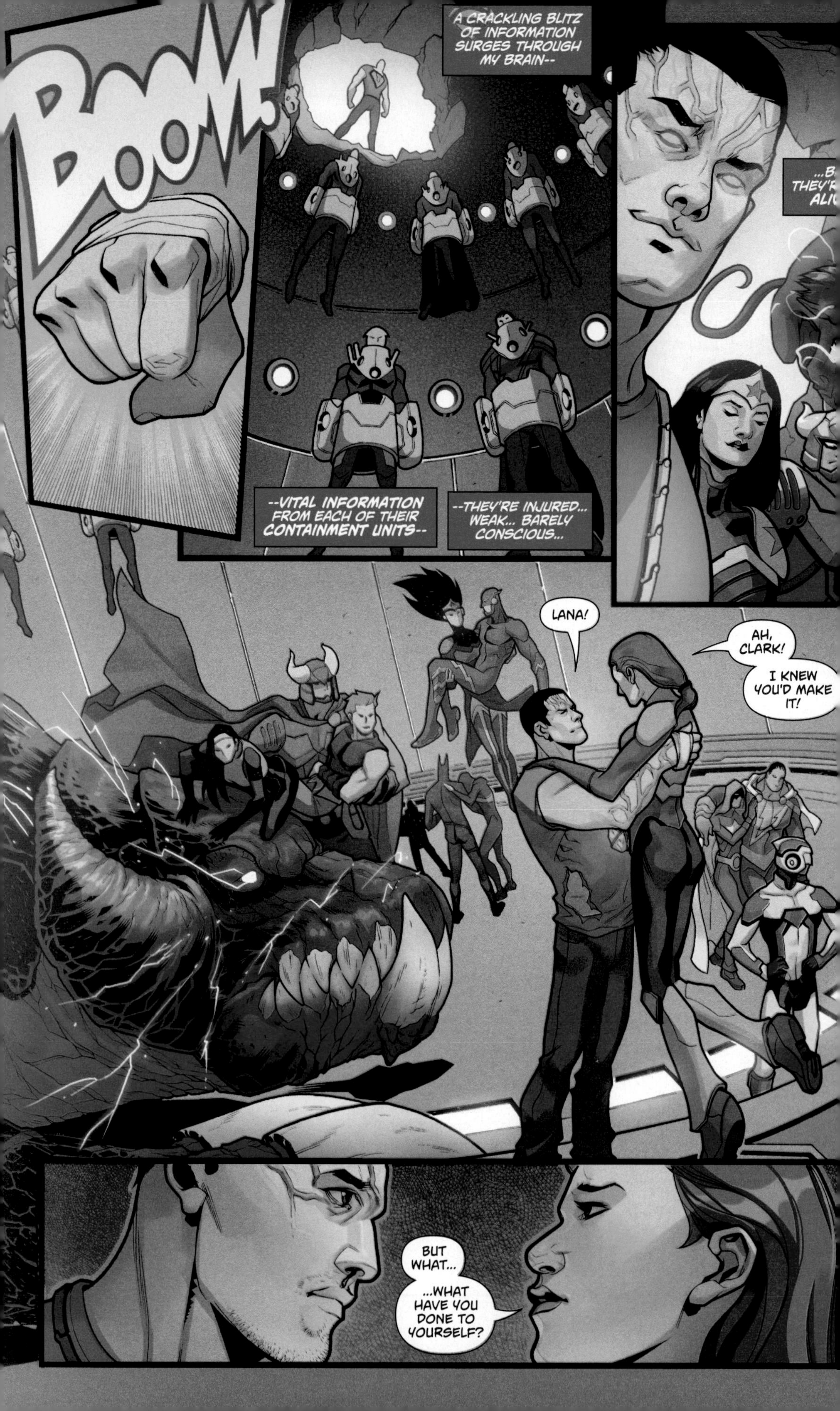
BOOM!
A CRACKLING BLITZ OF INFORMATION SURGES THROUGH MY BRAIN--
--VITAL INFORMATION FROM EACH OF THEIR CONTAINMENT UNITS--
--THEY'RE INJURED... WEAK... BARELY CONSCIOUS...
LANA!
AH, CLARK!
I KNEW YOU'D MAKE IT!
BUT WHAT...
...WHAT HAVE YOU DONE TO YOURSELF?

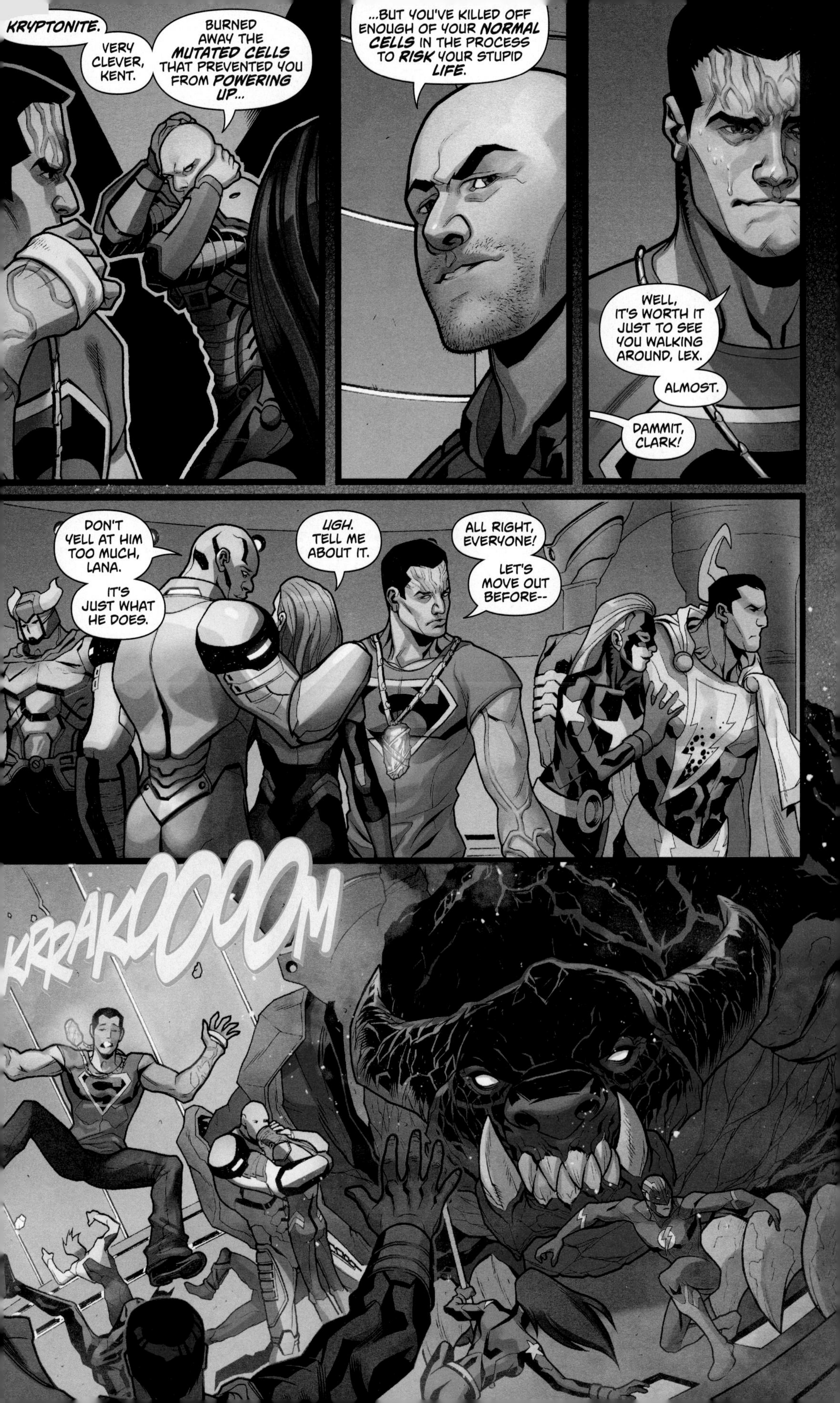
KRYPTONITE.
VERY CLEVER, KENT.
BURNED AWAY THE MUTATED CELLS THAT PREVENTED YOU FROM POWERING UP...
...BUT YOU'VE KILLED OFF ENOUGH OF YOUR NORMAL CELLS IN THE PROCESS TO RISK YOUR STUPID LIFE.
WELL, IT'S WORTH IT JUST TO SEE YOU WALKING AROUND, LEX.
ALMOST.
DAMMIT, CLARK!
DON'T YELL AT HIM TOO MUCH, LANA.
IT'S JUST WHAT HE DOES.
UGH. TELL ME ABOUT IT.
ALL RIGHT, EVERYONE!
LET'S MOVE OUT BEFORE--
KRRAKOOOOM

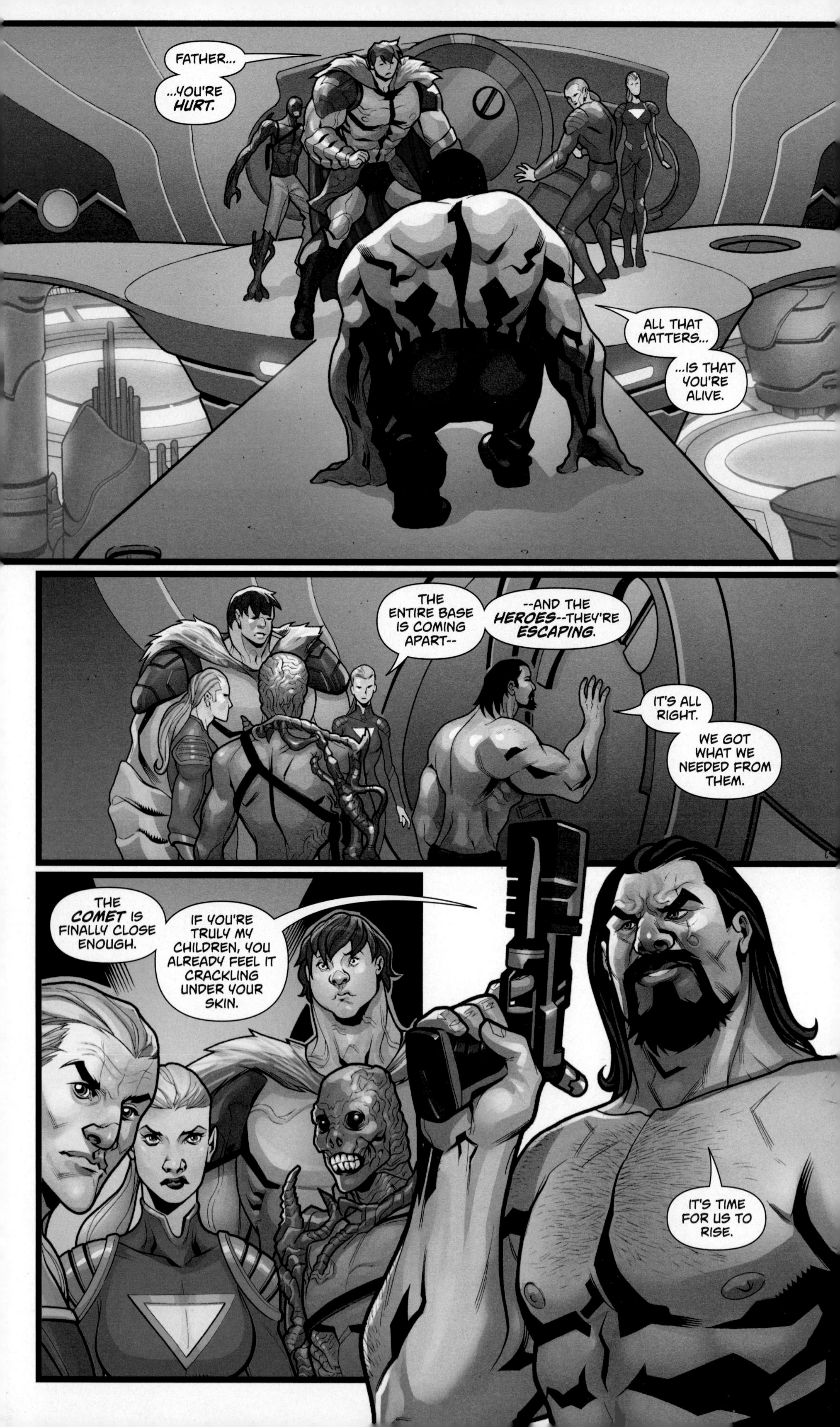
FATHER...
...YOU'RE HURT.
ALL THAT MATTERS...
...IS THAT YOU'RE ALIVE.
THE ENTIRE BASE IS COMING APART--
--AND THE HEROES--THEY'RE ESCAPING.
IT'S ALL RIGHT.
WE GOT WHAT WE NEEDED FROM THEM.
THE COMET IS FINALLY CLOSE ENOUGH.
IF YOU'RE TRULY MY CHILDREN, YOU ALREADY FEEL IT CRACKLING UNDER YOUR SKIN.
IT'S TIME FOR US TO RISE.

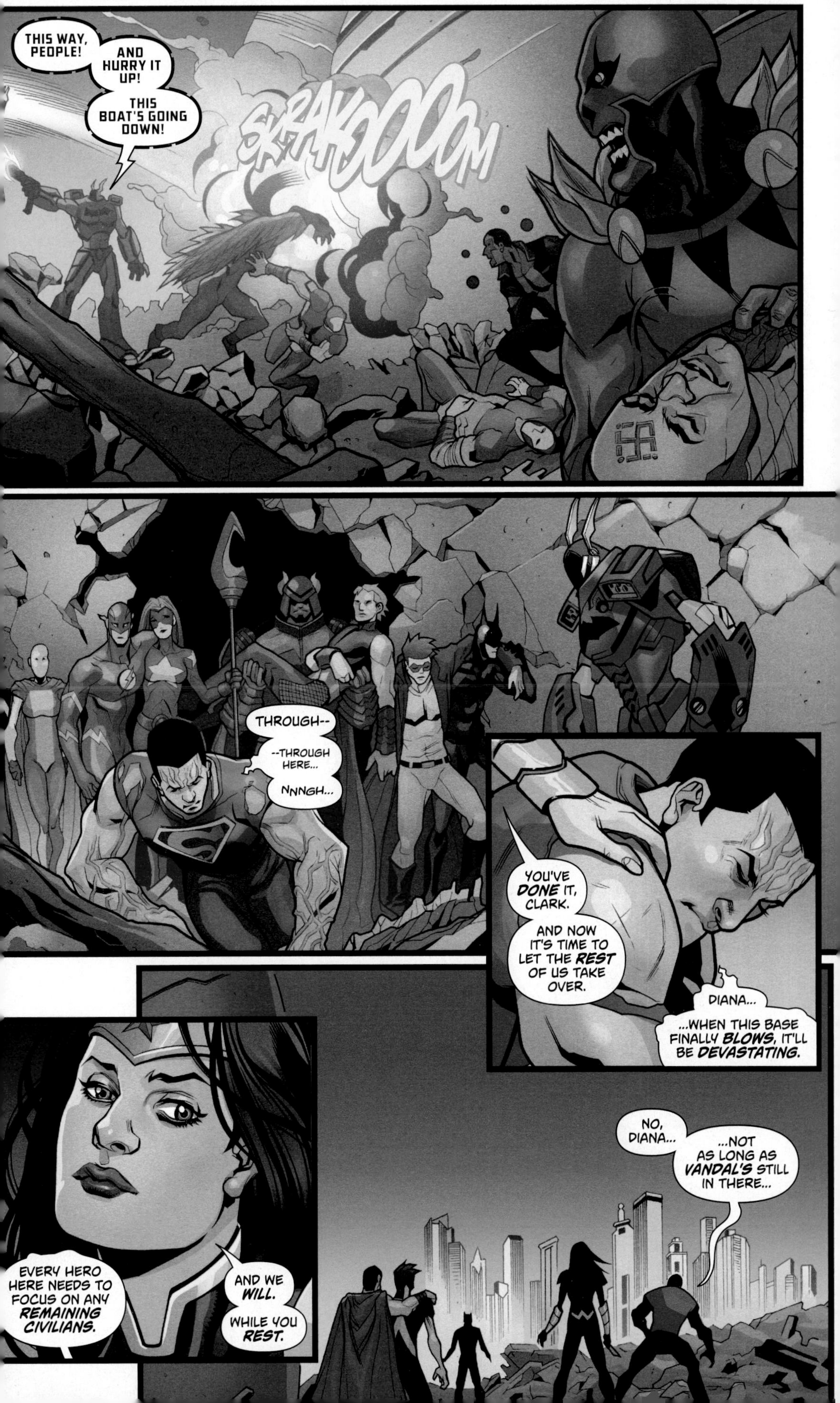
THIS WAY, PEOPLE!
AND HURRY IT UP!
THIS BOAT'S GOING DOWN!
SKRAKOOOOOM
THROUGH--
--THROUGH HERE...
NNNGH...
YOU'VE DONE IT, CLARK.
AND NOW IT'S TIME TO LET THE REST OF US TAKE OVER.
DIANA...
...WHEN THIS BASE FINALLY BLOWS, IT'LL BE DEVASTATING.
EVERY HERO HERE NEEDS TO FOCUS ON ANY REMAINING CIVILIANS.
AND WE WILL.
WHILE YOU REST.
NO, DIANA...
...NOT AS LONG AS VANDAL'S STILL IN THERE...

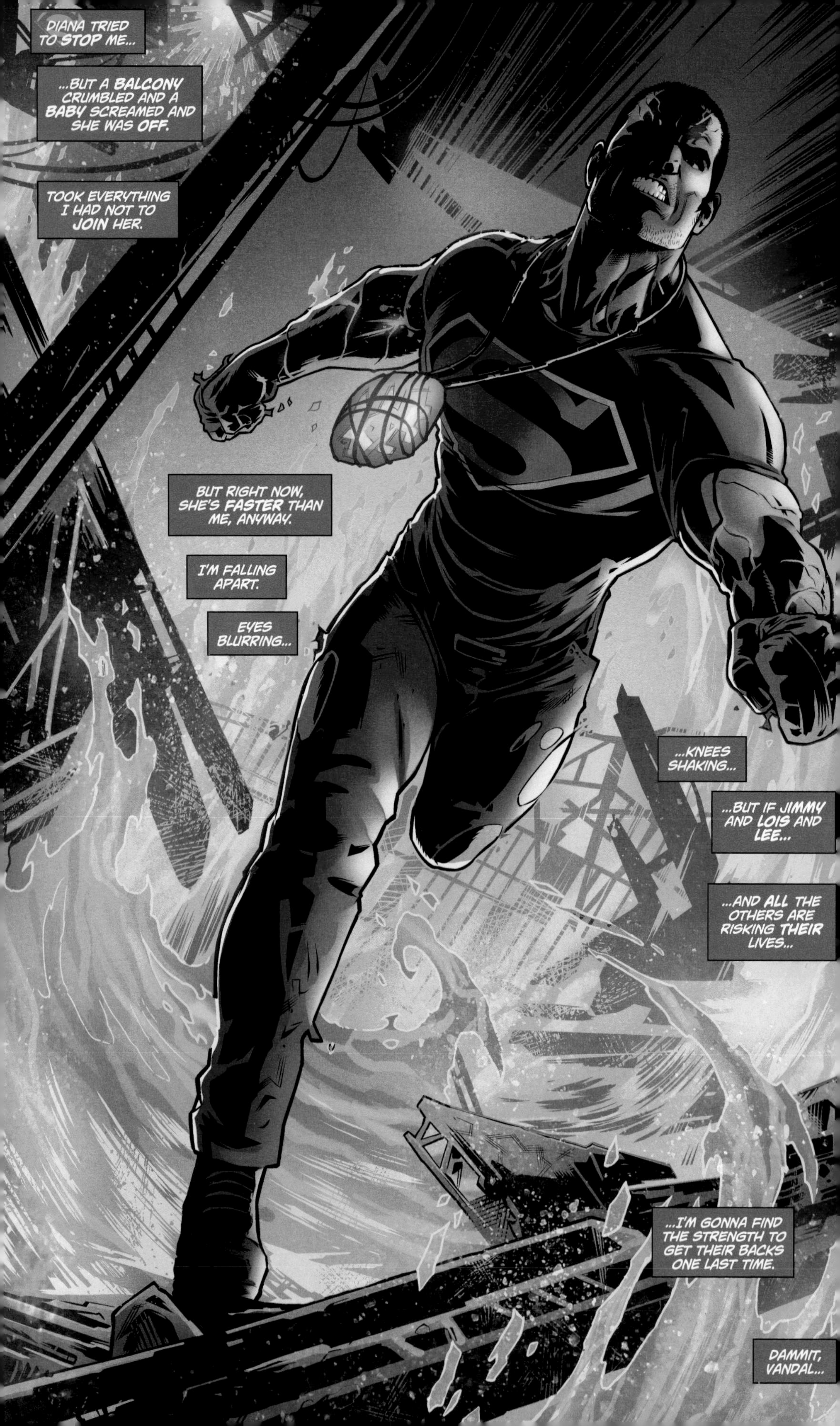
DIANA TRIED TO STOP ME...
...BUT A BALCONY CRUMBLED AND A BABY SCREAMED AND SHE WAS OFF.
TOOK EVERYTHING I HAD NOT TO JOIN HER.
BUT RIGHT NOW, SHE'S FASTER THAN ME, ANYWAY.
I'M FALLING APART.
EYES BLURRING...
...KNEES SHAKING...
...BUT IF JIMMY AND LOIS AND LEE...
...AND ALL THE OTHERS ARE RISKING THEIR LIVES...
...I'M GONNA FIND THE STRENGTH TO GET THEIR BACKS ONE LAST TIME.
DAMMIT, VANDAL...

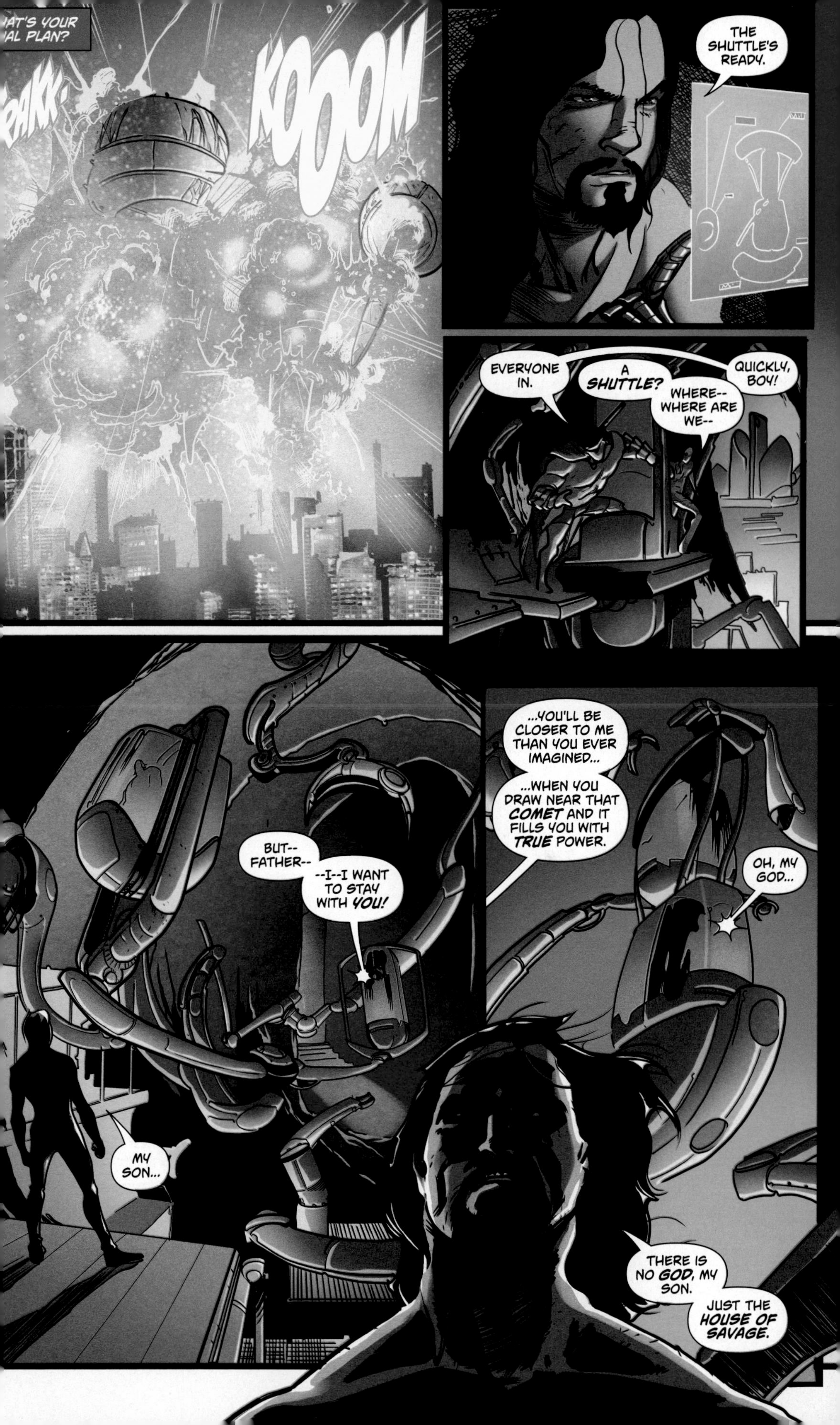

AT'S YOUR
AL PLAN?
RAKK-
KOOOM
THE SHUTTLE'S READY.
EVERYONE IN.
A SHUTTLE?
QUICKLY, BOY!
WHERE-- WHERE ARE WE--
BUT-- FATHER--
--I--I WANT TO STAY WITH YOU!
MY SON...
...YOU'LL BE CLOSER TO ME THAN YOU EVER IMAGINED...
...WHEN YOU DRAW NEAR THAT COMET AND IT FILLS YOU WITH TRUE POWER.
OH, MY GOD...
THERE IS NO GOD, MY SON.
JUST THE HOUSE OF SAVAGE.

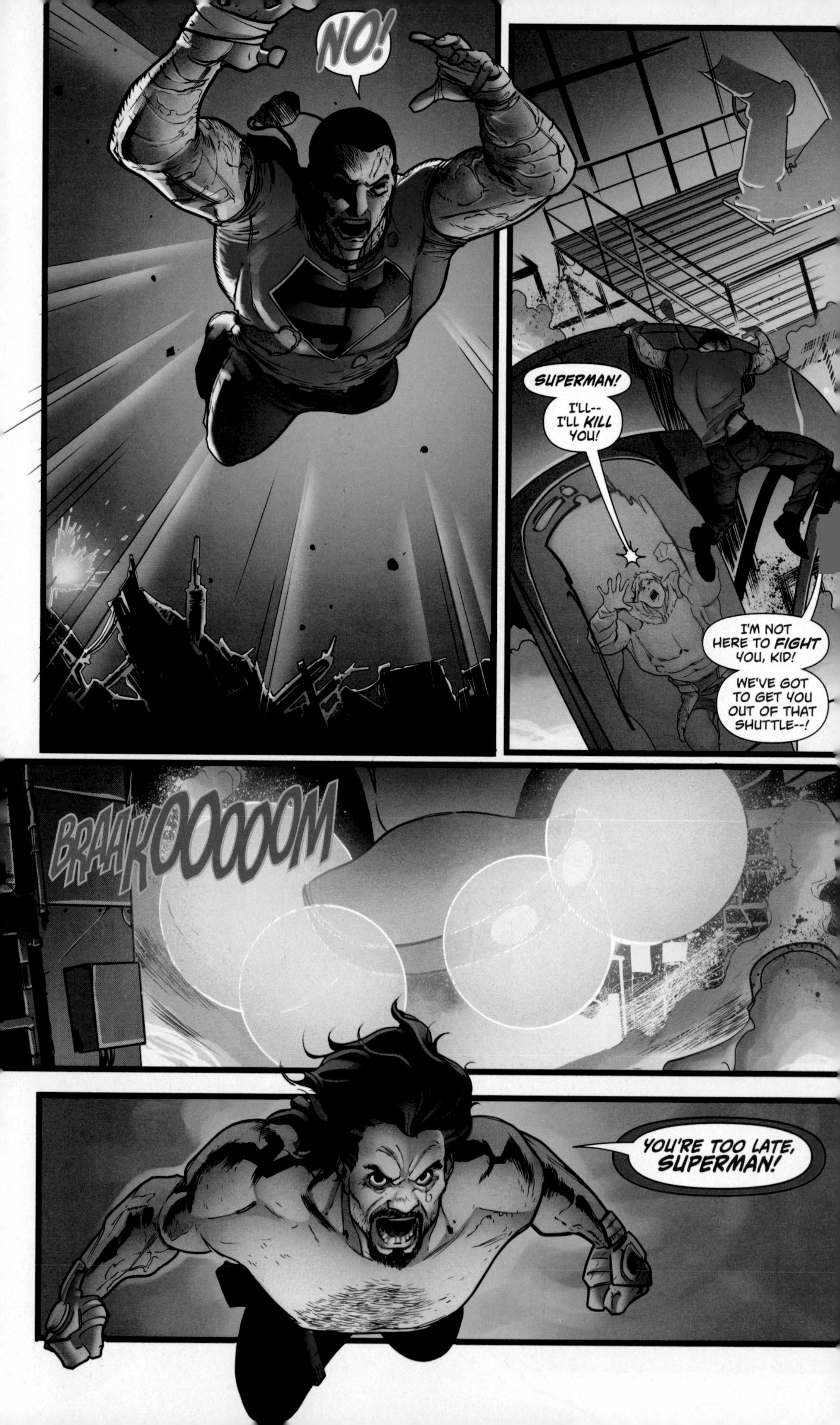
NO!
SUPERMAN!
I'LL-- I'LL KILL YOU!
I'M NOT HERE TO FIGHT YOU, KID!
WE'VE GOT TO GET YOU OUT OF THAT SHUTTLE--!
BRAAKOOOOOM
YOU'RE TOO LATE, SUPERMAN!

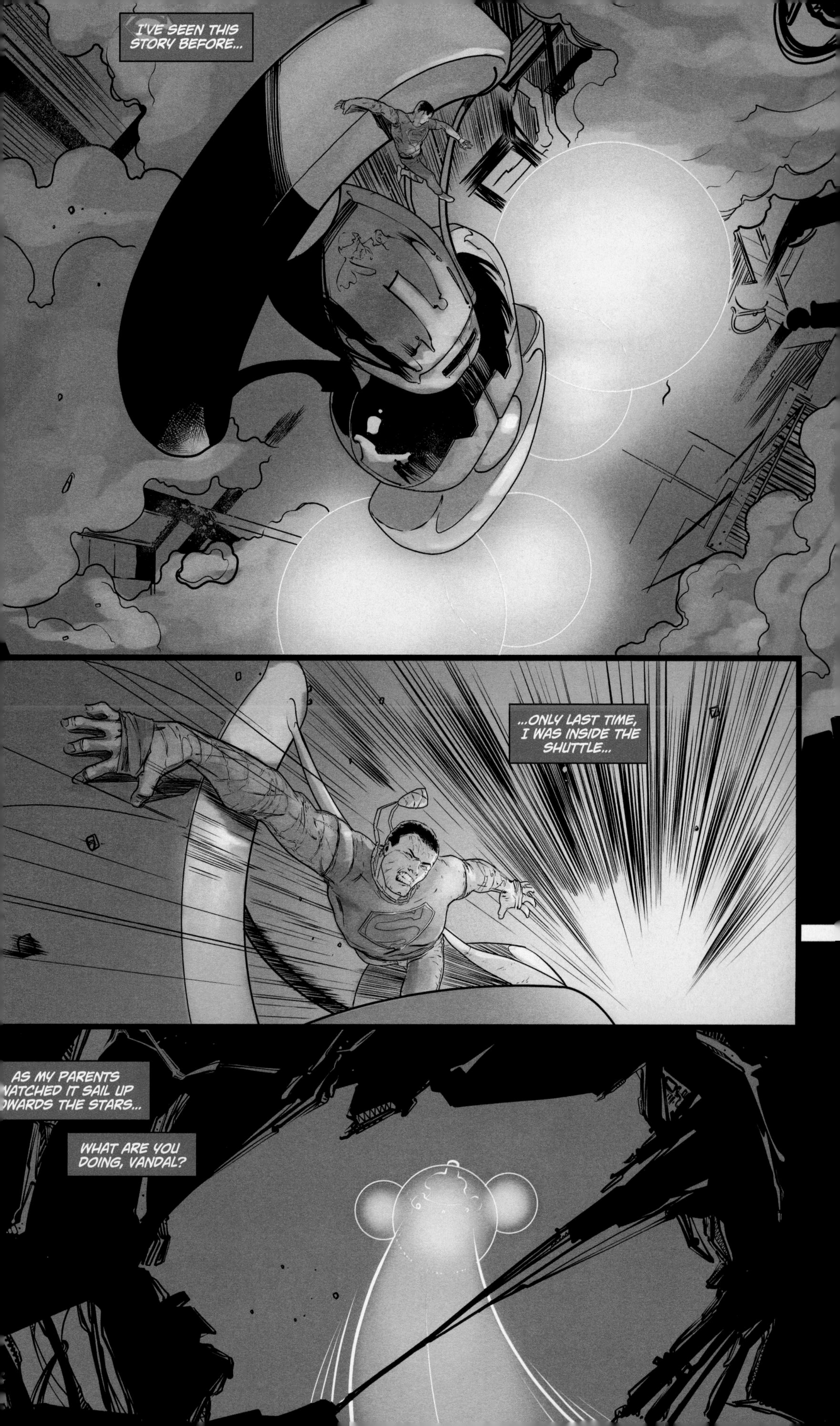
I'VE SEEN THIS STORY BEFORE...
...ONLY LAST TIME, I WAS INSIDE THE SHUTTLE...
AS MY PARENTS WATCHED IT SAIL UP OWARDS THE STARS...
WHAT ARE YOU DOING, VANDAL?

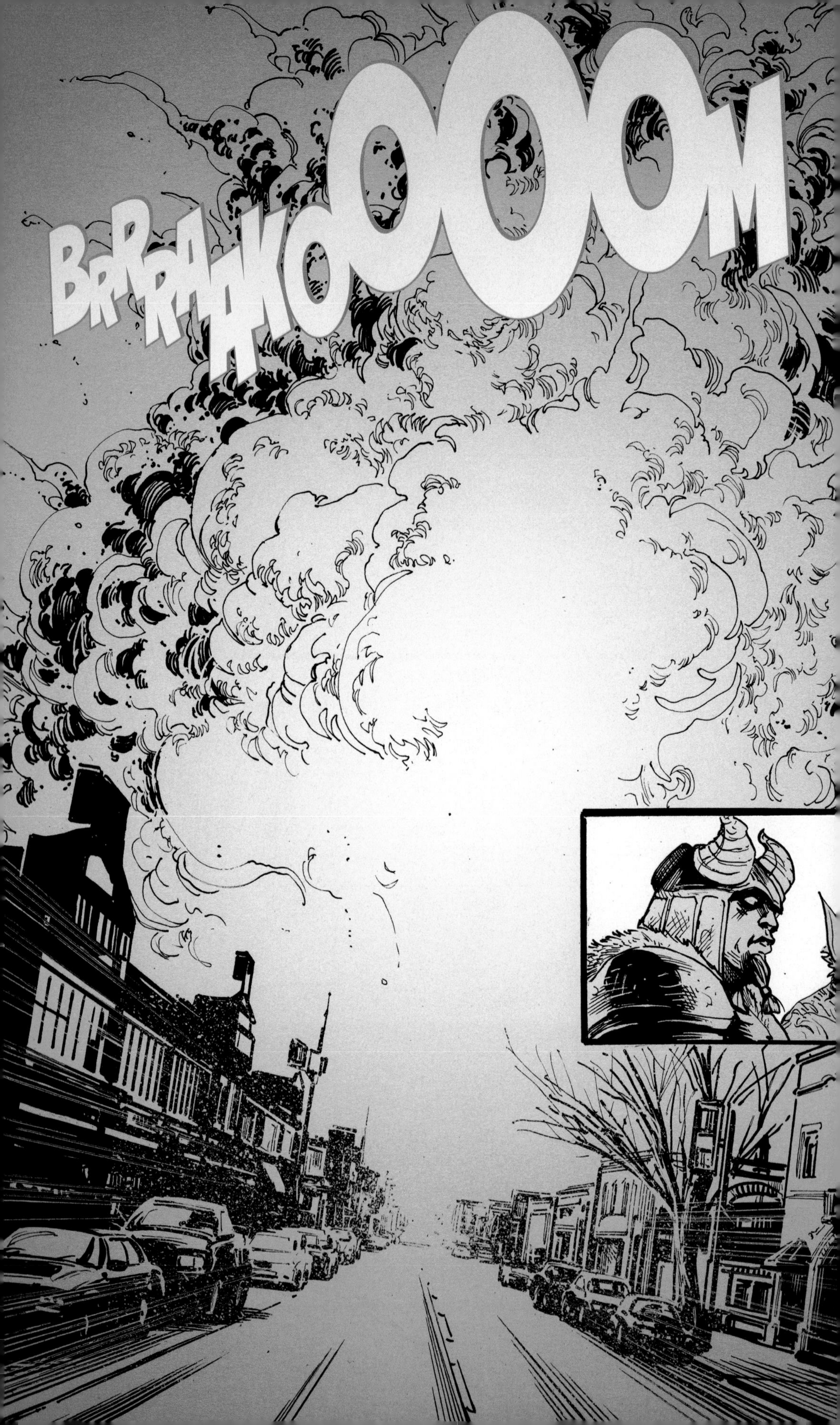
BRRRAAKOOOOM

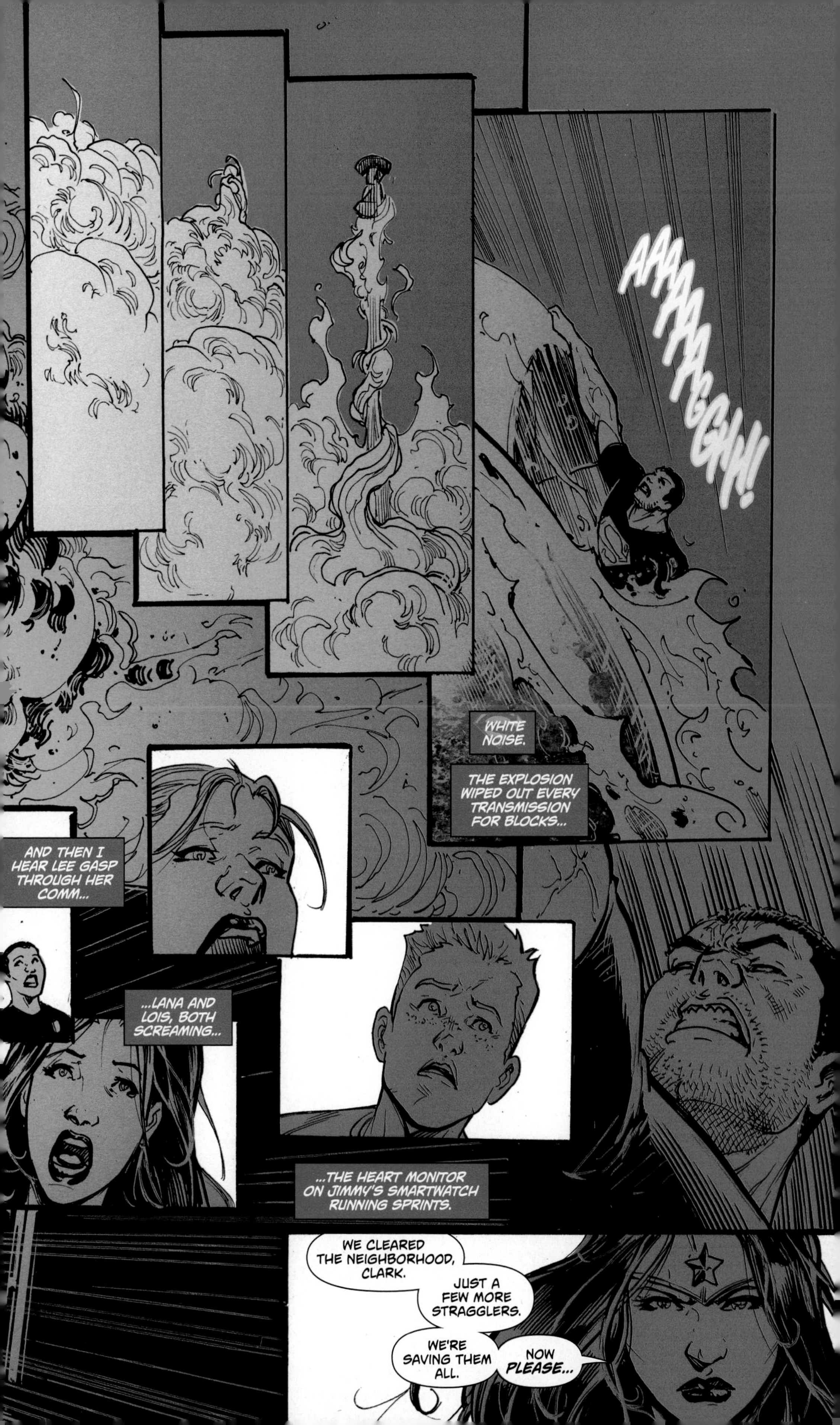
AAAAAAGGHH!
WHITE NOISE.
THE EXPLOSION WIPED OUT EVERY TRANSMISSION FOR BLOCKS...
AND THEN I HEAR LEE GASP THROUGH HER COMM...
...LANA AND LOIS, BOTH SCREAMING...
...THE HEART MONITOR ON JIMMY'S SMARTWATCH RUNNING SPRINTS.
WE CLEARED THE NEIGHBORHOOD, CLARK.
JUST A FEW MORE STRAGGLERS.
WE'RE SAVING THEM ALL.
NOW *PLEASE*...

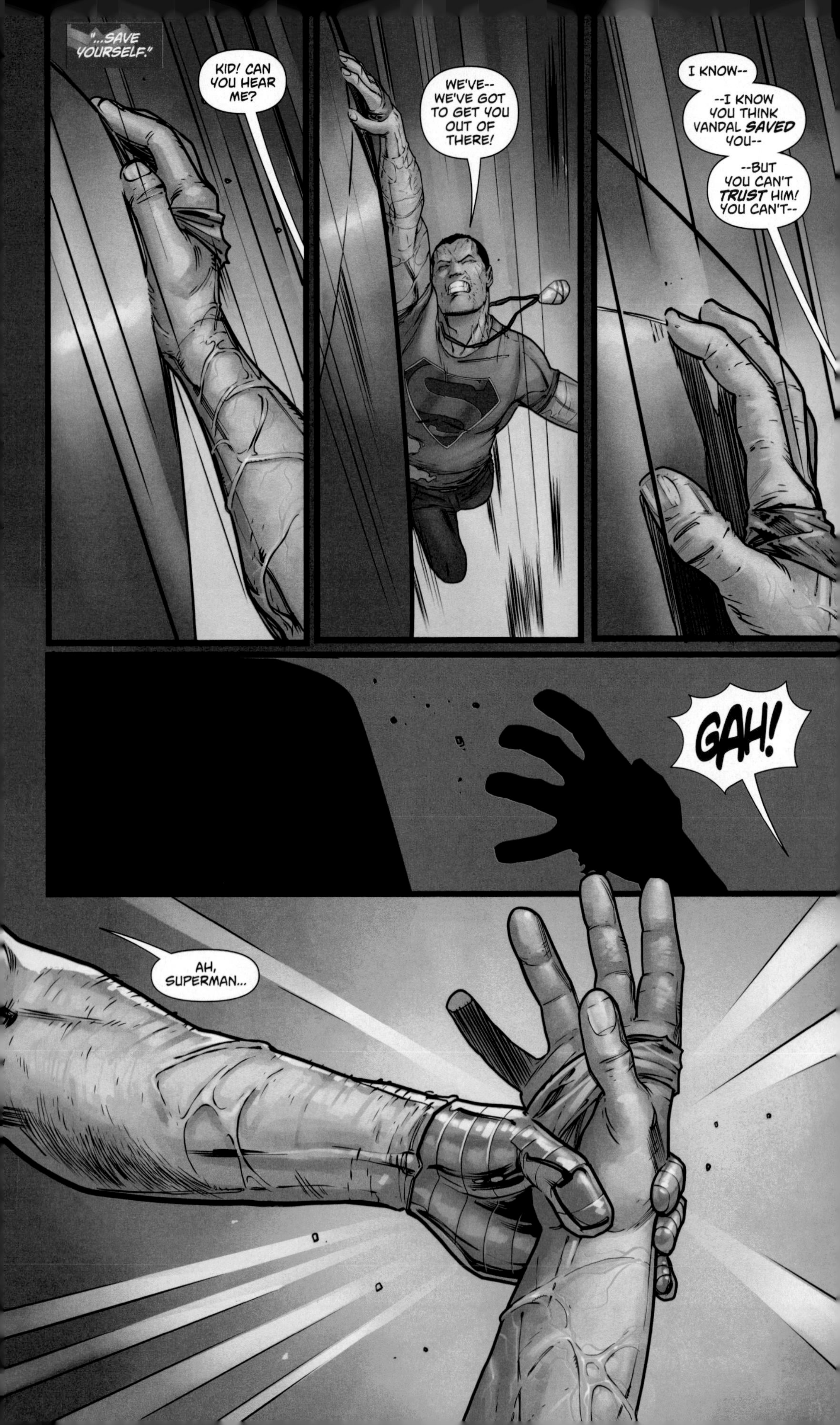
"...SAVE YOURSELF."
KID! CAN YOU HEAR ME?
WE'VE-- WE'VE GOT TO GET YOU OUT OF THERE!
I KNOW--
--I KNOW YOU THINK VANDAL SAVED YOU--
--BUT YOU CAN'T TRUST HIM! YOU CAN'T--
GAH!
AH, SUPERMAN...

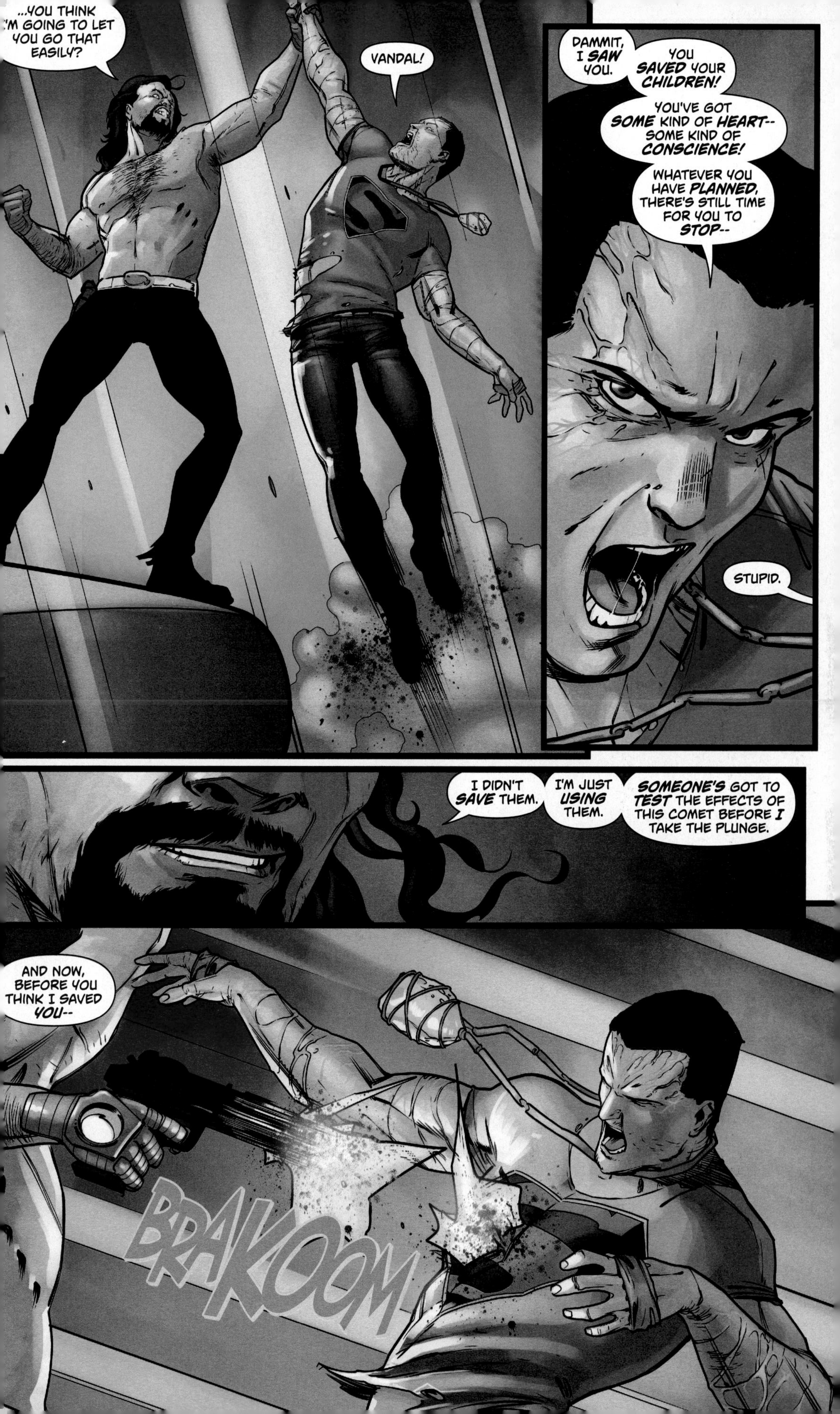
...YOU THINK I'M GOING TO LET YOU GO THAT EASILY?
VANDAL!
DAMMIT, I SAW YOU.
YOU SAVED YOUR CHILDREN!
YOU'VE GOT SOME KIND OF HEART-- SOME KIND OF CONSCIENCE!
WHATEVER YOU HAVE PLANNED, THERE'S STILL TIME FOR YOU TO STOP--
STUPID.
I DIDN'T SAVE THEM.
I'M JUST USING THEM.
SOMEONE'S GOT TO TEST THE EFFECTS OF THIS COMET BEFORE I TAKE THE PLUNGE.
AND NOW, BEFORE YOU THINK I SAVED YOU--
BRAKOOM

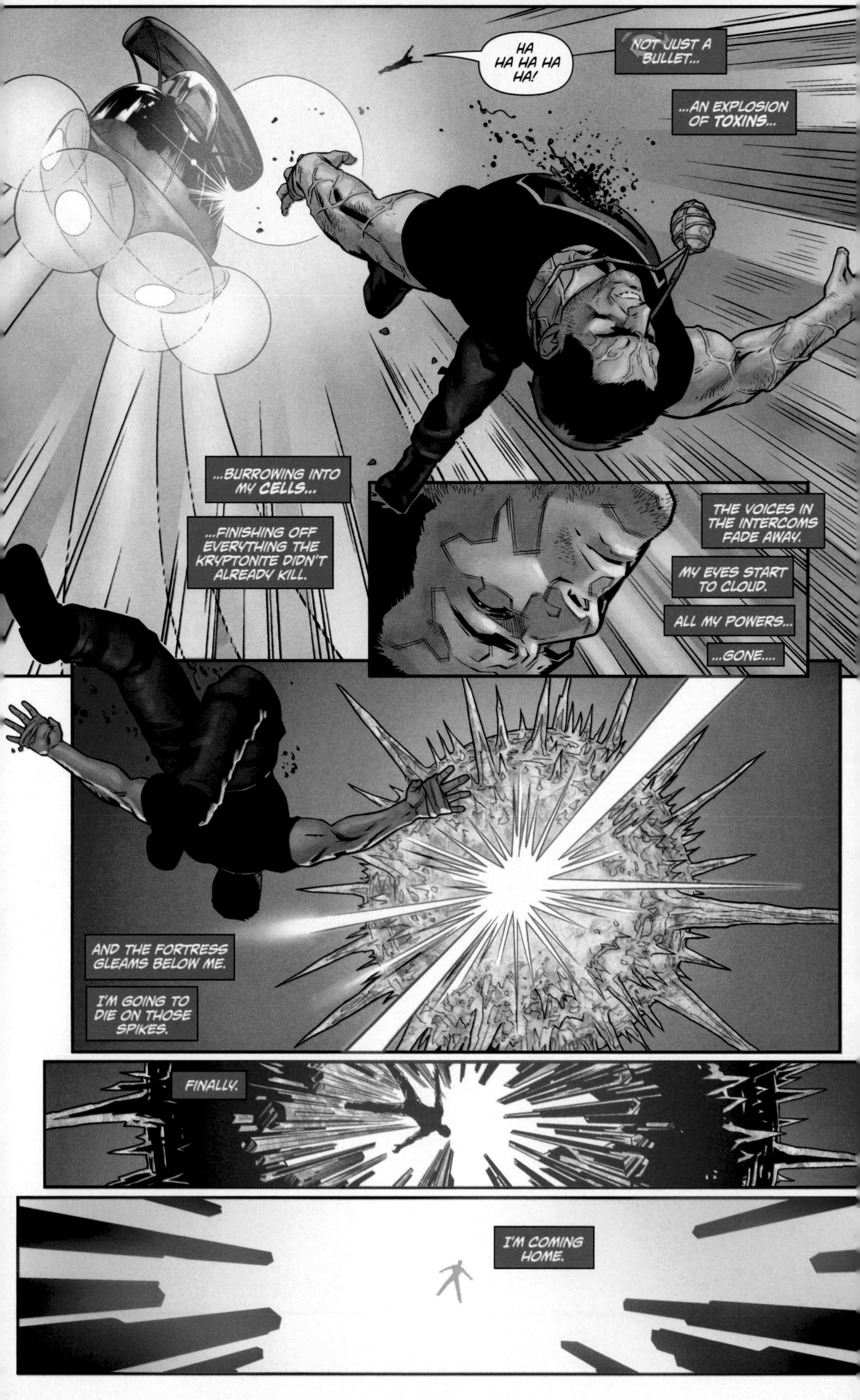
HA HA HA HA HA!
NOT JUST A BULLET...
...AN EXPLOSION OF TOXINS...
...BURROWING INTO MY CELLS...
...FINISHING OFF EVERYTHING THE KRYPTONITE DIDN'T ALREADY KILL.
THE VOICES IN THE INTERCOMS FADE AWAY.
MY EYES START TO CLOUD.
ALL MY POWERS...
...GONE....
AND THE FORTRESS GLEAMS BELOW ME.
I'M GOING TO DIE ON THOSE SPIKES.
FINALLY.
I'M COMING HOME.

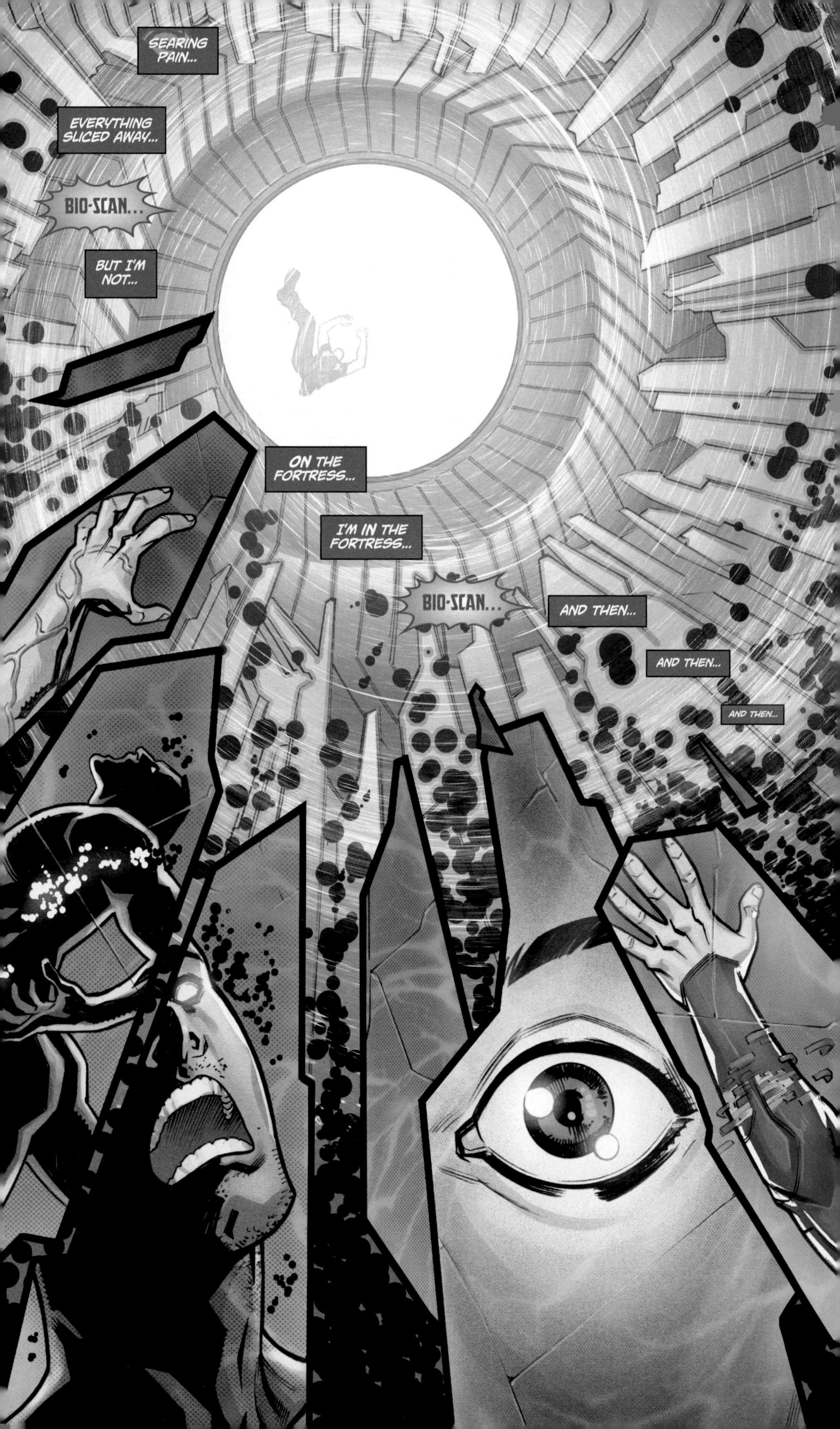
SEARING PAIN...
EVERYTHING SLICED AWAY...
BIO-SCAN...
BUT I'M NOT...
ON THE FORTRESS...
I'M IN THE FORTRESS...
BIO-SCAN...
AND THEN...
AND THEN...
AND THEN...

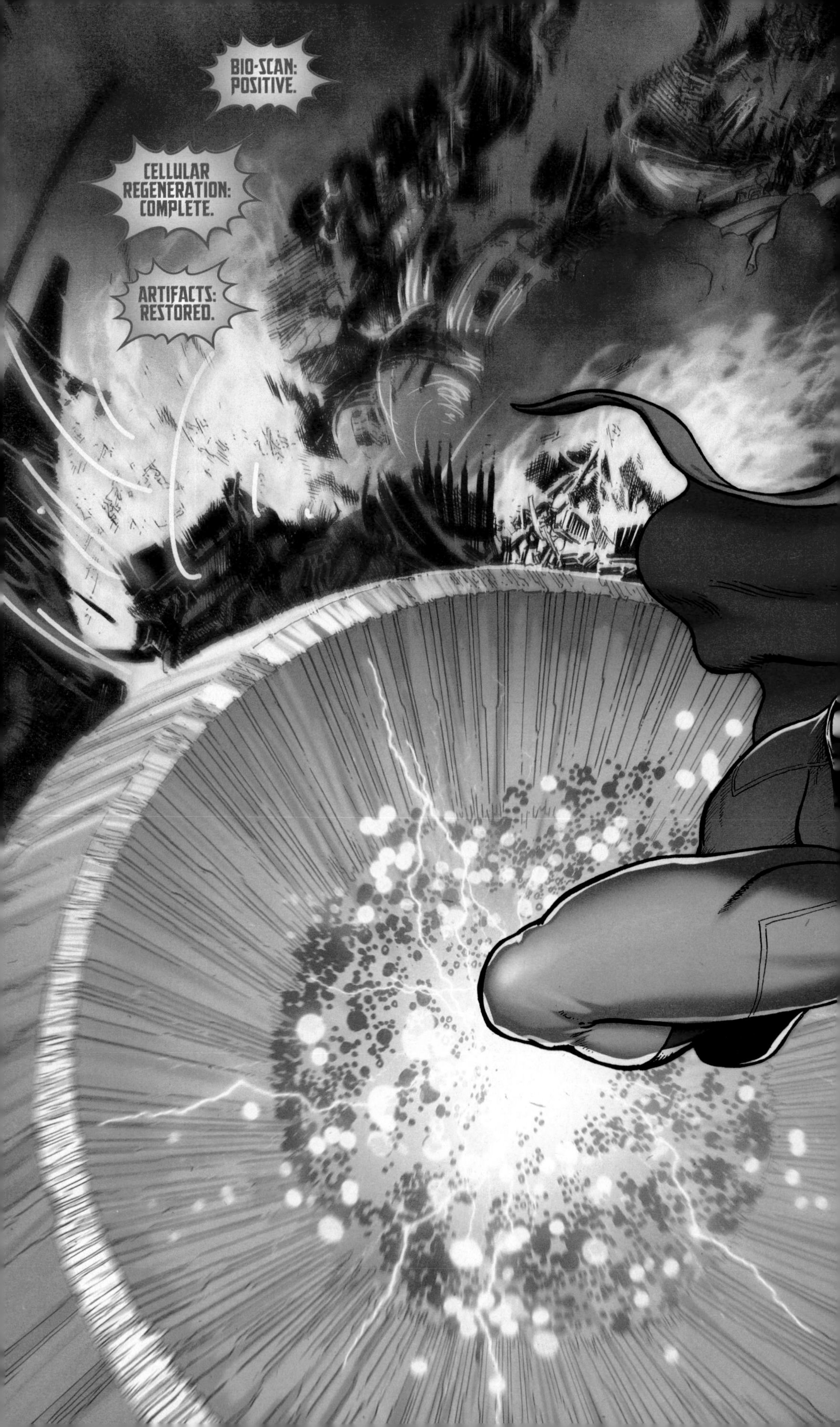
BIO-SCAN: POSITIVE.
CELLULAR REGENERATION: COMPLETE.
ARTIFACTS: RESTORED.

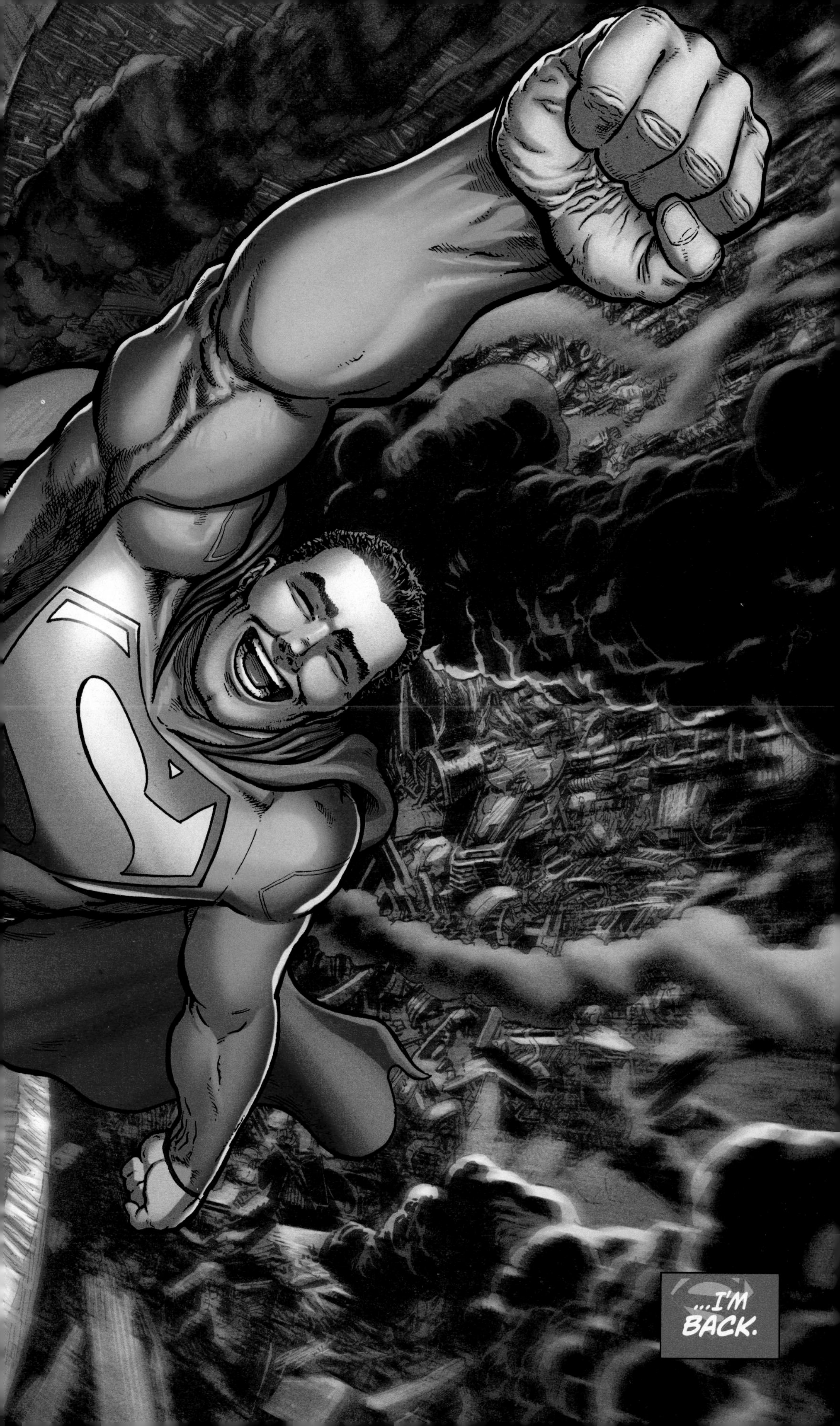
...I'M
BACK.

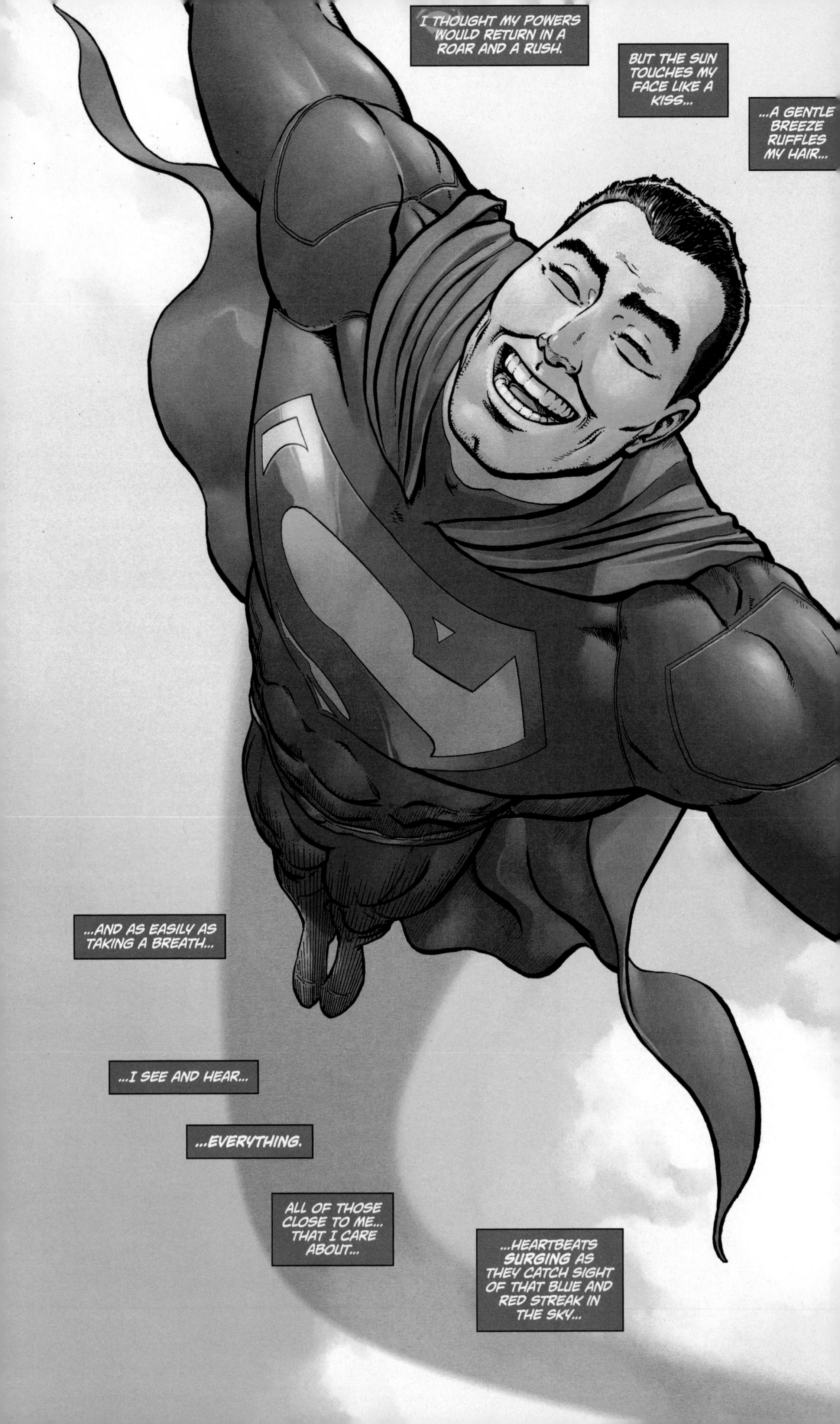
I THOUGHT MY POWERS WOULD RETURN IN A ROAR AND A RUSH.
BUT THE SUN TOUCHES MY FACE LIKE A KISS...
...A GENTLE BREEZE RUFFLES MY HAIR...
...AND AS EASILY AS TAKING A BREATH...
...I SEE AND HEAR...
...EVERYTHING.
ALL OF THOSE CLOSE TO ME... THAT I CARE ABOUT...
...HEARTBEATS SURGING AS THEY CATCH SIGHT OF THAT BLUE AND RED STREAK IN THE SKY...

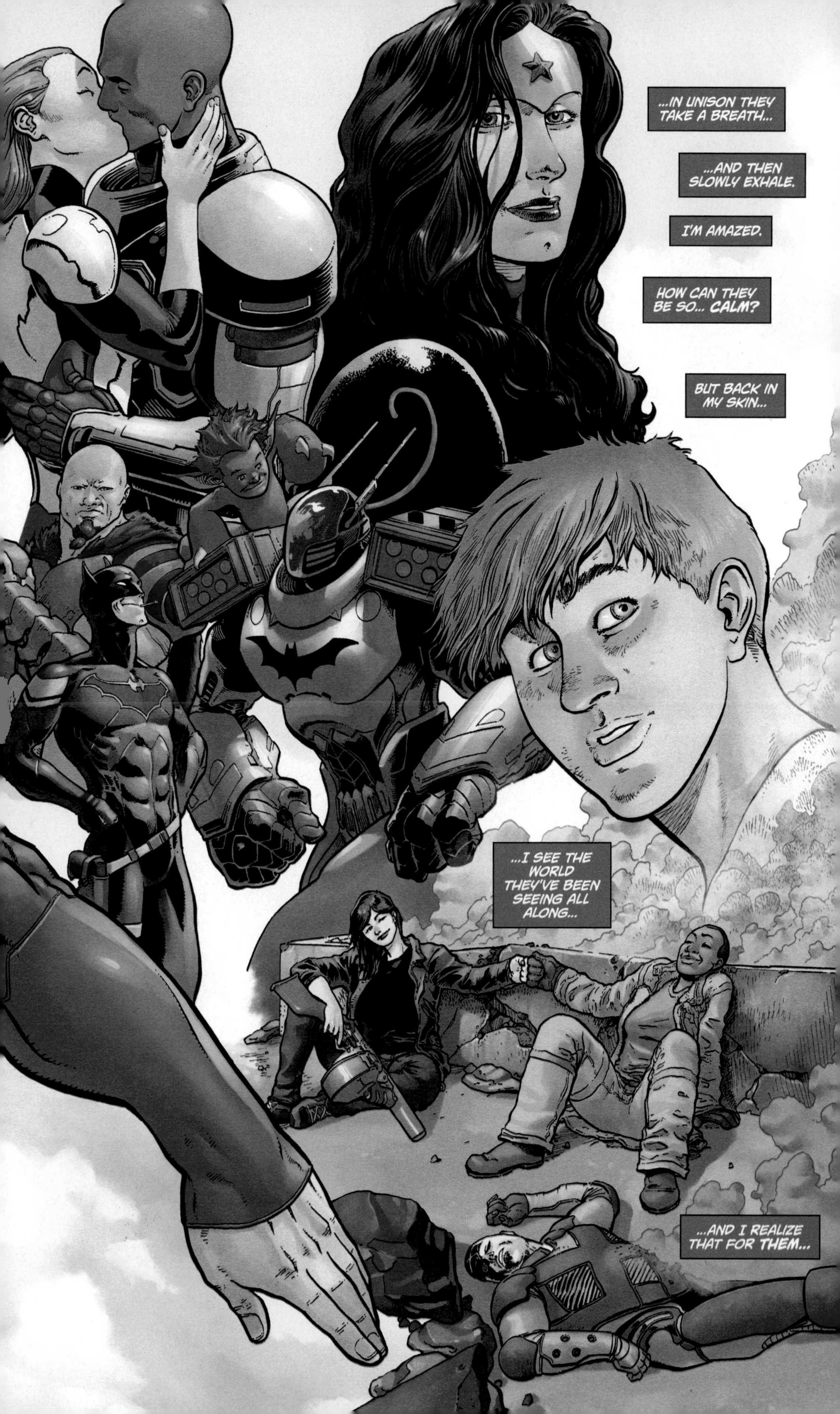
...IN UNISON THEY TAKE A BREATH...
...AND THEN SLOWLY EXHALE.
I'M AMAZED.
HOW CAN THEY BE SO... CALM?
BUT BACK IN MY SKIN...
...I SEE THE WORLD THEY'VE BEEN SEEING ALL ALONG...
...AND I REALIZE THAT FOR THEM...

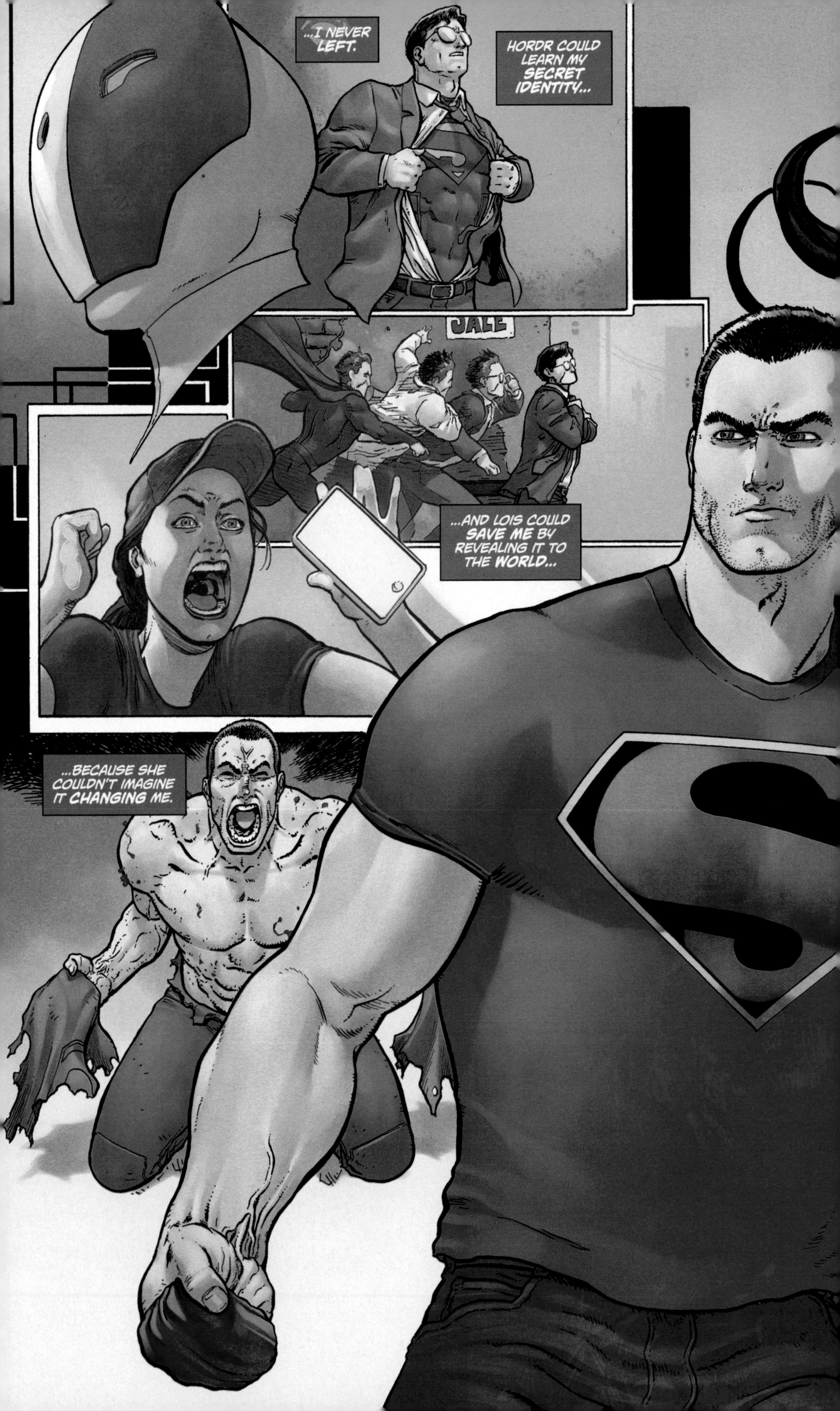
...I NEVER LEFT.
HORDR COULD LEARN MY SECRET IDENTITY...
SALE
...AND LOIS COULD SAVE ME BY REVEALING IT TO THE WORLD...
...BECAUSE SHE COULDN'T IMAGINE IT CHANGING ME.

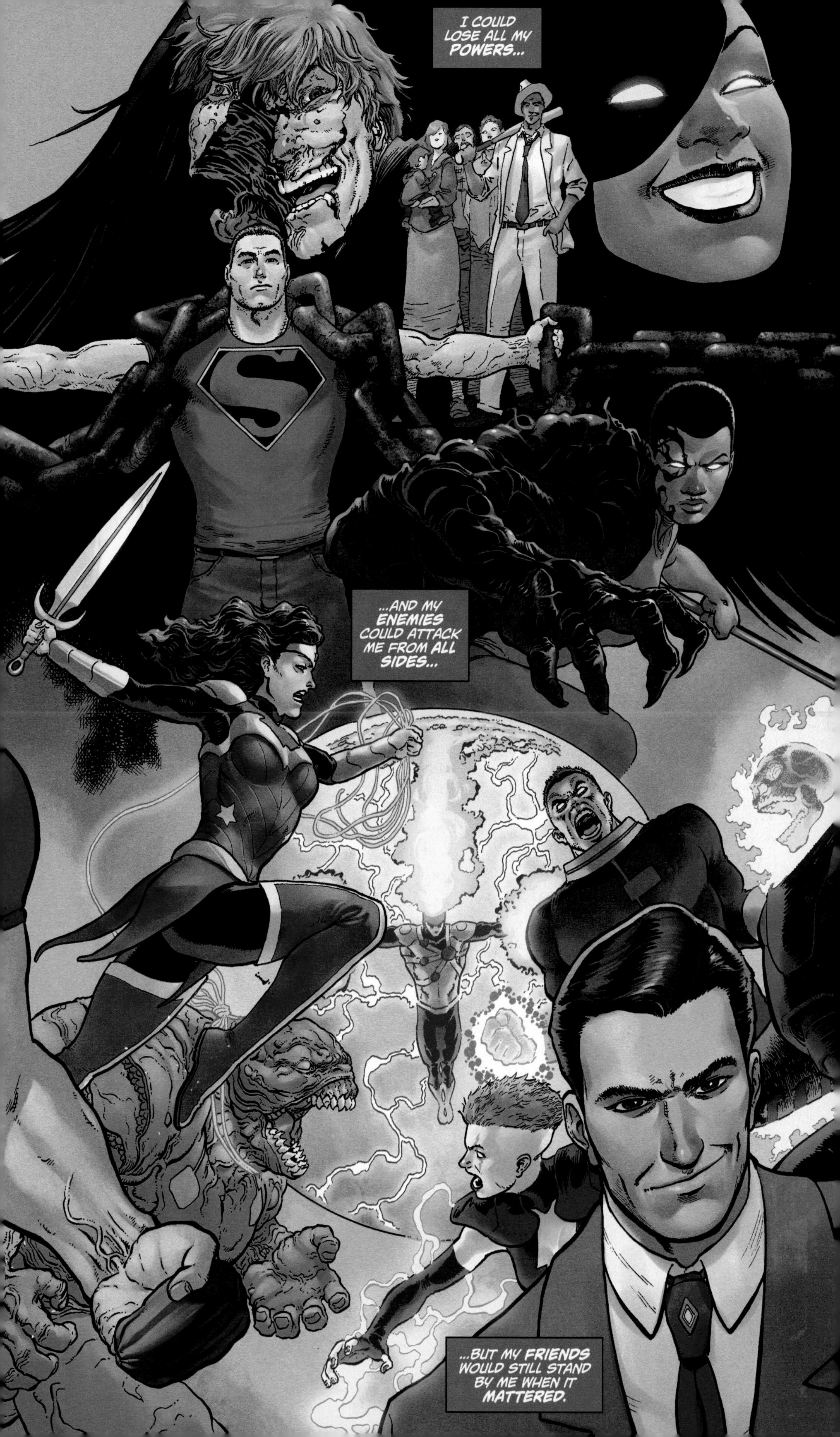
I COULD LOSE ALL MY POWERS...
...AND MY ENEMIES COULD ATTACK ME FROM ALL SIDES...
...BUT MY FRIENDS WOULD STILL STAND BY ME WHEN IT MATTERED.

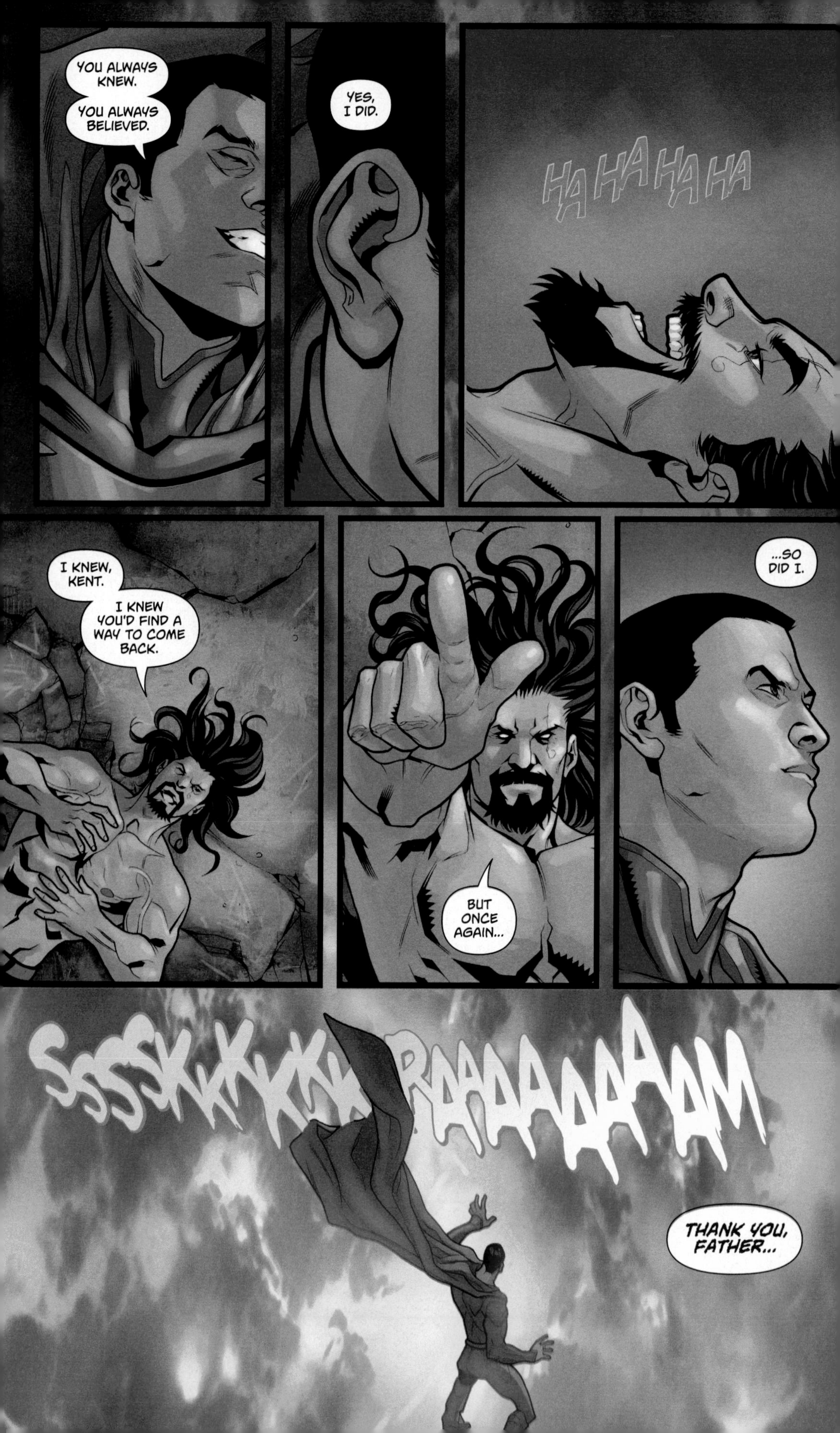
YOU ALWAYS KNEW.
YOU ALWAYS BELIEVED.
YES, I DID.
HA HA HA HA HA HA
I KNEW, KENT.
I KNEW YOU'D FIND A WAY TO COME BACK.
BUT ONCE AGAIN...
...SO DID I.
SSSSKKKKKRAAAAAAAAAM
THANK YOU, FATHER...

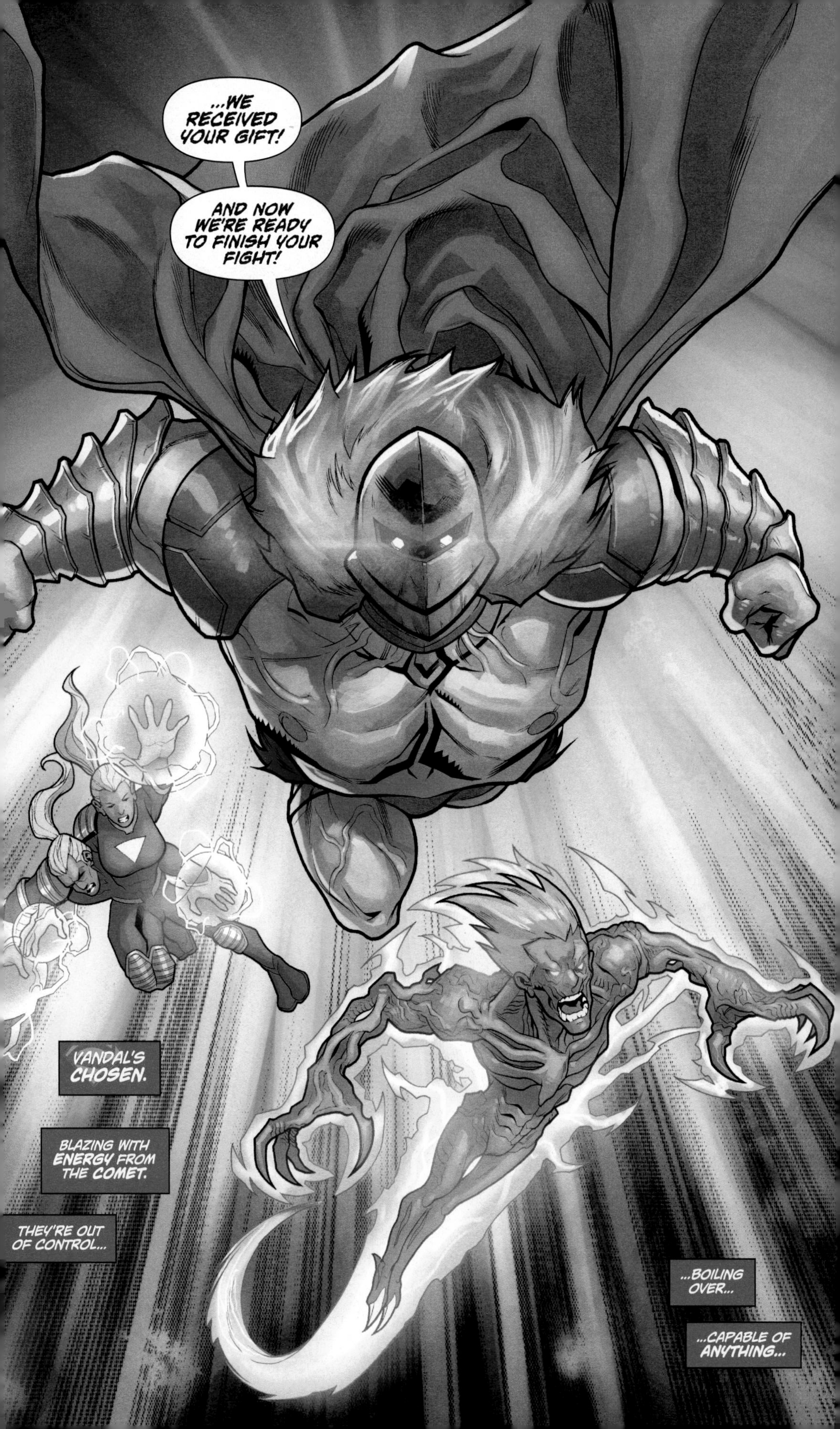
...WE RECEIVED YOUR GIFT!
AND NOW WE'RE READY TO FINISH YOUR FIGHT!
VANDAL'S CHOSEN.
BLAZING WITH ENERGY FROM THE COMET.
THEY'RE OUT OF CONTROL...
...BOILING OVER...
...CAPABLE OF ANYTHING...

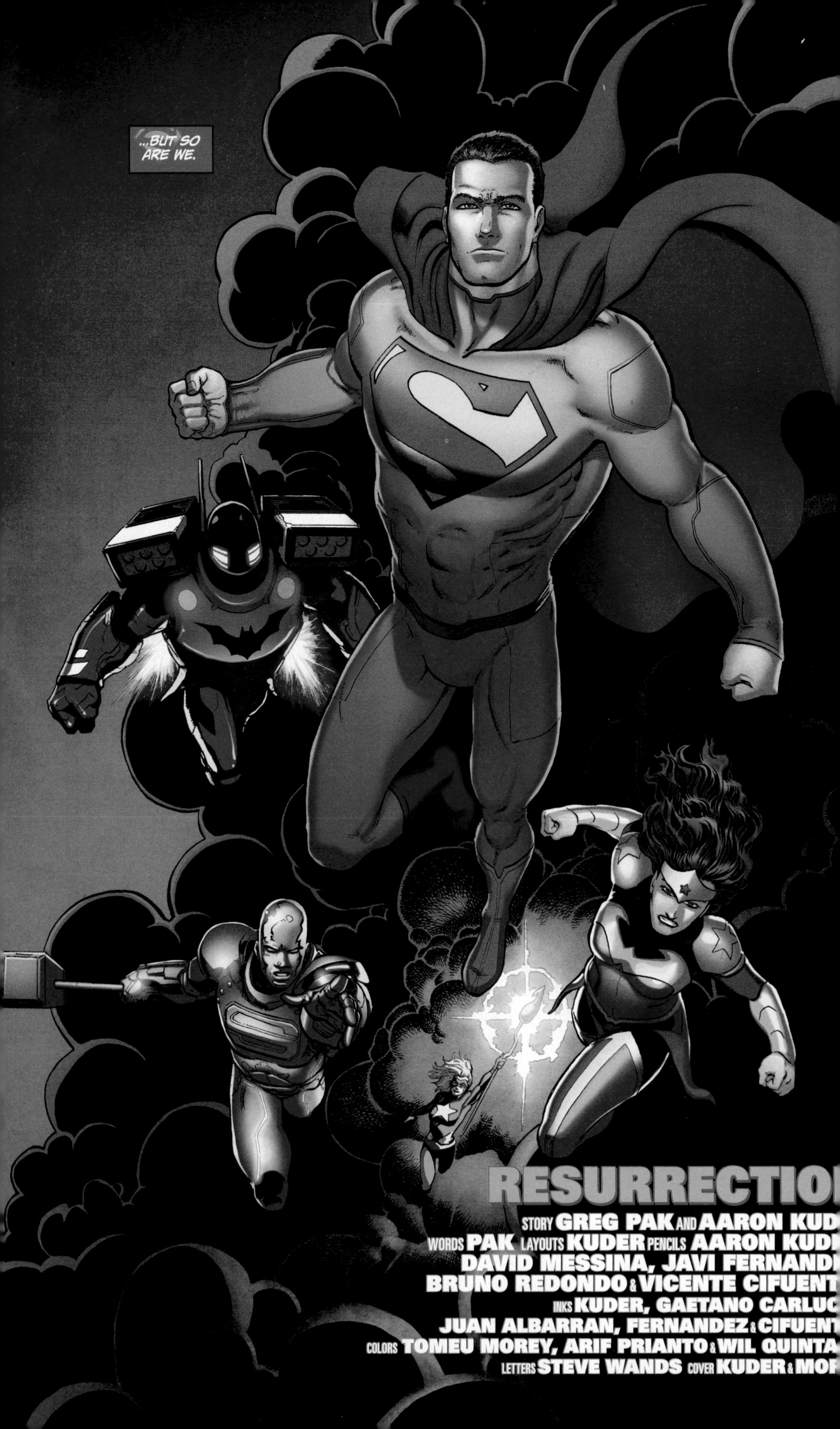
...BUT SO ARE WE.
RESURRECTIO
STORY GREG PAK AND AARON KUD
WORDS PAK LAYOUTS KUDER PENCILS AARON KUD
DAVID MESSINA, JAVI FERNAND
BRUNO REDONDO & VICENTE CIFUENT
INKS KUDER, GAETANO CARLUC
JUAN ALBARRAN, FERNANDEZ & CIFUENT
COLORS TOMEU MOREY, ARIF PRIANTO & WIL QUINTA
LETTERS STEVE WANDS COVER KUDER & MO

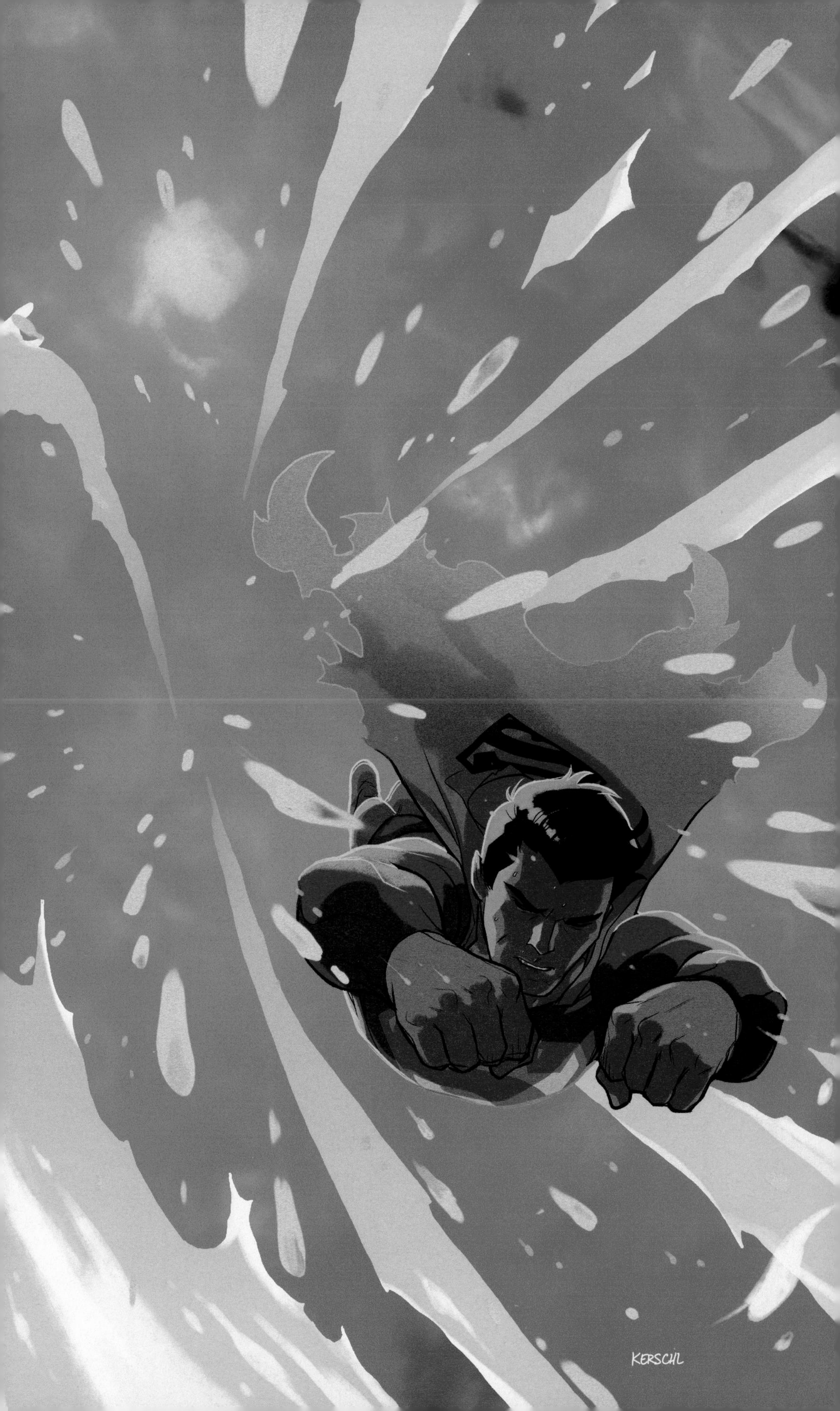
KERSCHL

Previously,
in SUPERMAN/WONDER WOMAN #28,
SUPERMAN #50-51 and BATMAN/SUPERMAN #31...

Shortly after the comet's incredible energies cause Vandal Savage's hyper-powered offspring to burn up while battling Wonder Woman and the Justice League, Superman destroys the source of the immortal's eternal power, and in the process sends Savage hurtling out into space. Unfortunately, in the midst of his greatest victory, Kal-El learns that his repeated exposure to Kryptonite of late, plus recent battles inside Apokolips' fire pits and against the Kryptonian deity Rao, have taken a toll: the Last Son of Krypton is dying.

While Superman starts sharing his terminal diagnosis with loved ones, his residual solar energy flares become the source of mysterious tests conducted in China by Dr. Omen, as well as the unexpected catalyst that transforms fleeing convict Danny Swan into a "Solar-Superman." Believing himself to be the Man of Steel and Clark Kent, Swan comes unhinged and even begins taking lives until he is subdued by Lois Lane.

The real Superman, meanwhile, travels to New York City with Batman after asking the Dark Knight to help him locate his missing cousin, Kara. During their investigation, they're attacked by monstrous incarnations of the Chinese Zodiac, one of which manages to draw Superman's blood before teleporting away. With the immediate threat ended, Superman and Batman resume their search for Supergirl, and their next stop is National City...

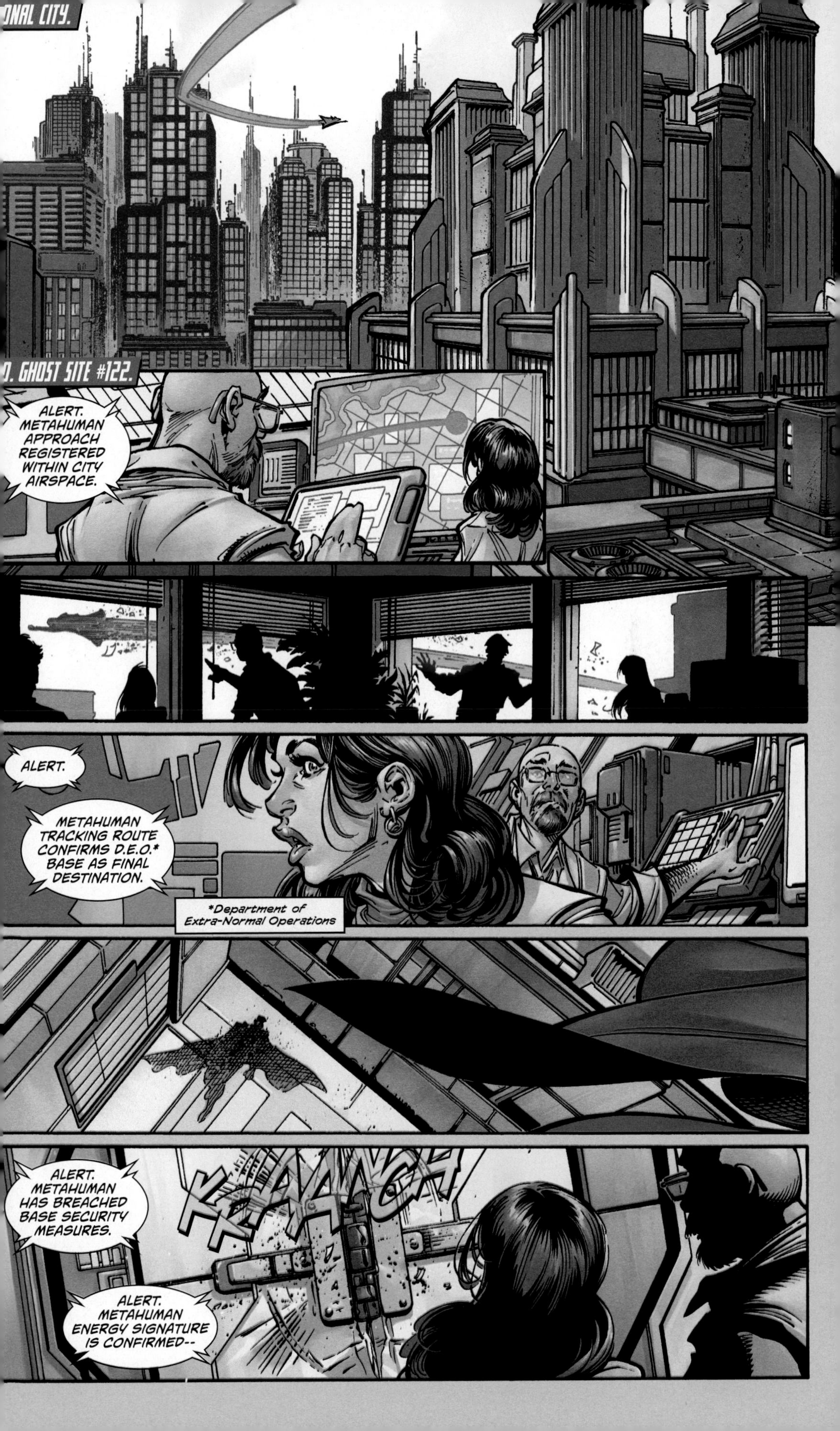

ONAL CITY.
D. GHOST SITE #122.
ALERT. METAHUMAN APPROACH REGISTERED WITHIN CITY AIRSPACE.
ALERT.
METAHUMAN TRACKING ROUTE CONFIRMS D.E.O.* BASE AS FINAL DESTINATION.
*Department of Extra-Normal Operations
KRAAAACH
ALERT. METAHUMAN HAS BREACHED BASE SECURITY MEASURES.
ALERT. METAHUMAN ENERGY SIGNATURE IS CONFIRMED--

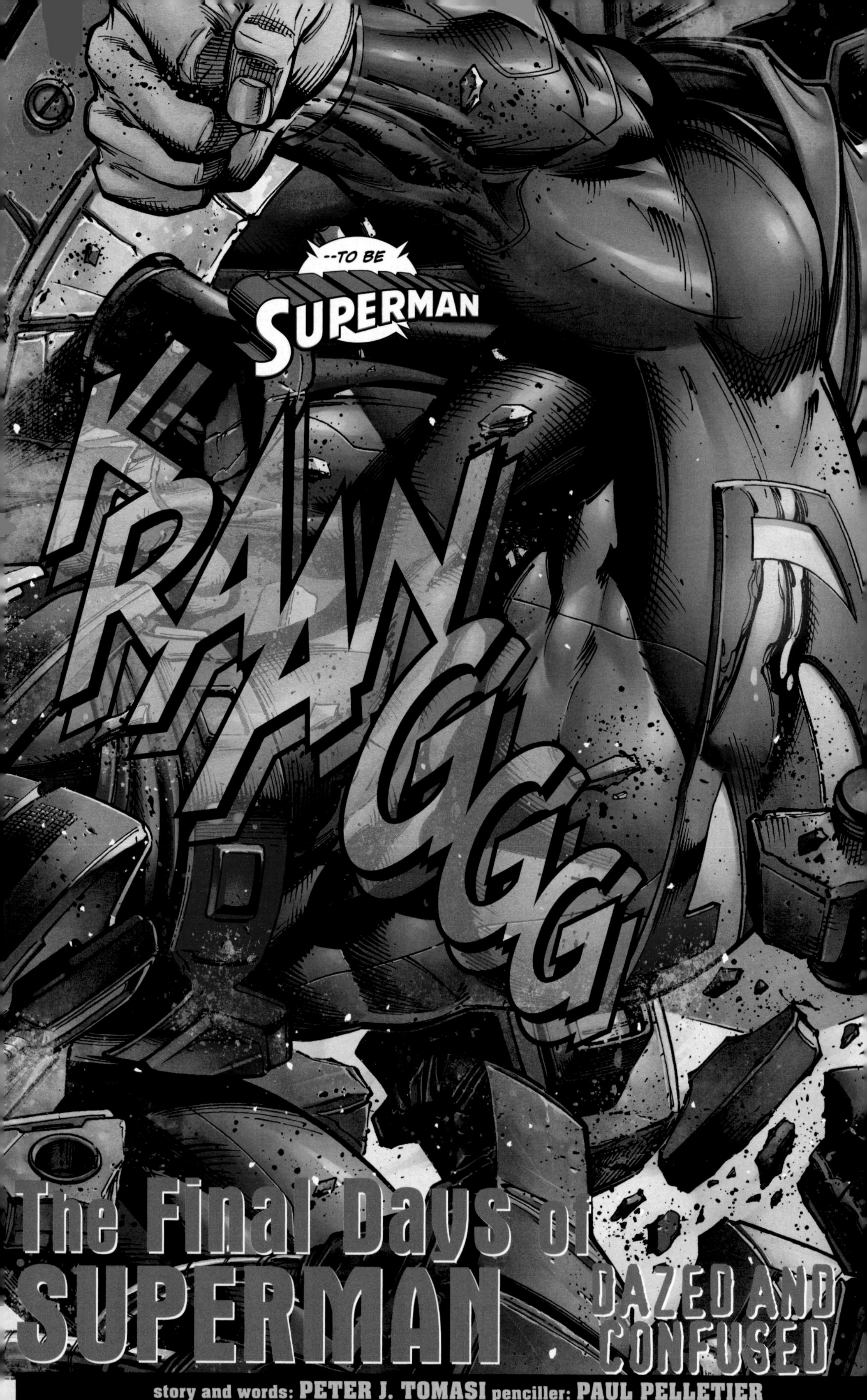
--TO BE
SUPERMAN
The Final Days of
SUPERMAN
DAZED AND
CONFUSED

story and words: PETER J. TOMASI penciller: PAUL PELLETIER
inker: SANDRA HOPE ARCHER colors: TOMEU MOREY letters: ROB LEIGH cover: KARL KERSC

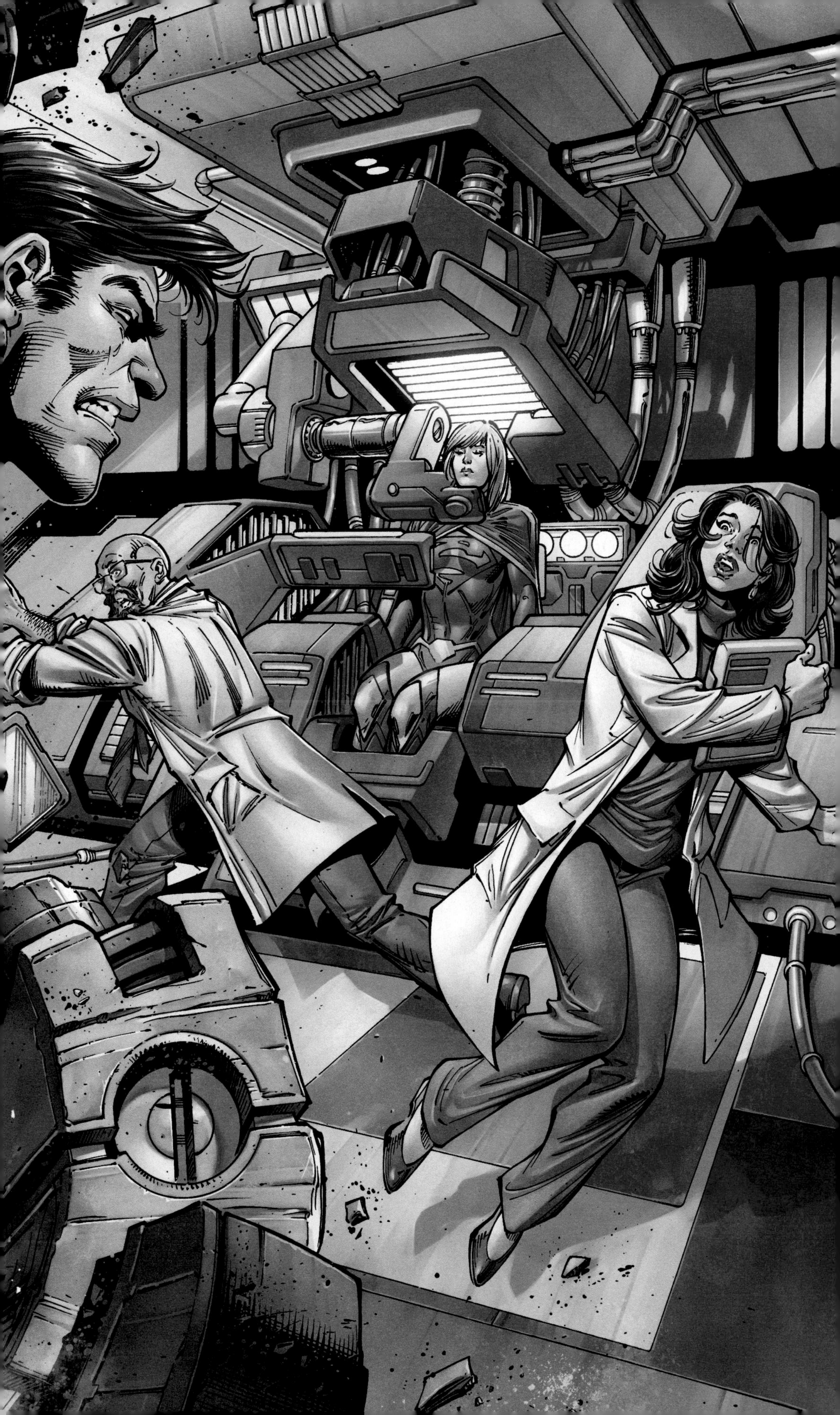

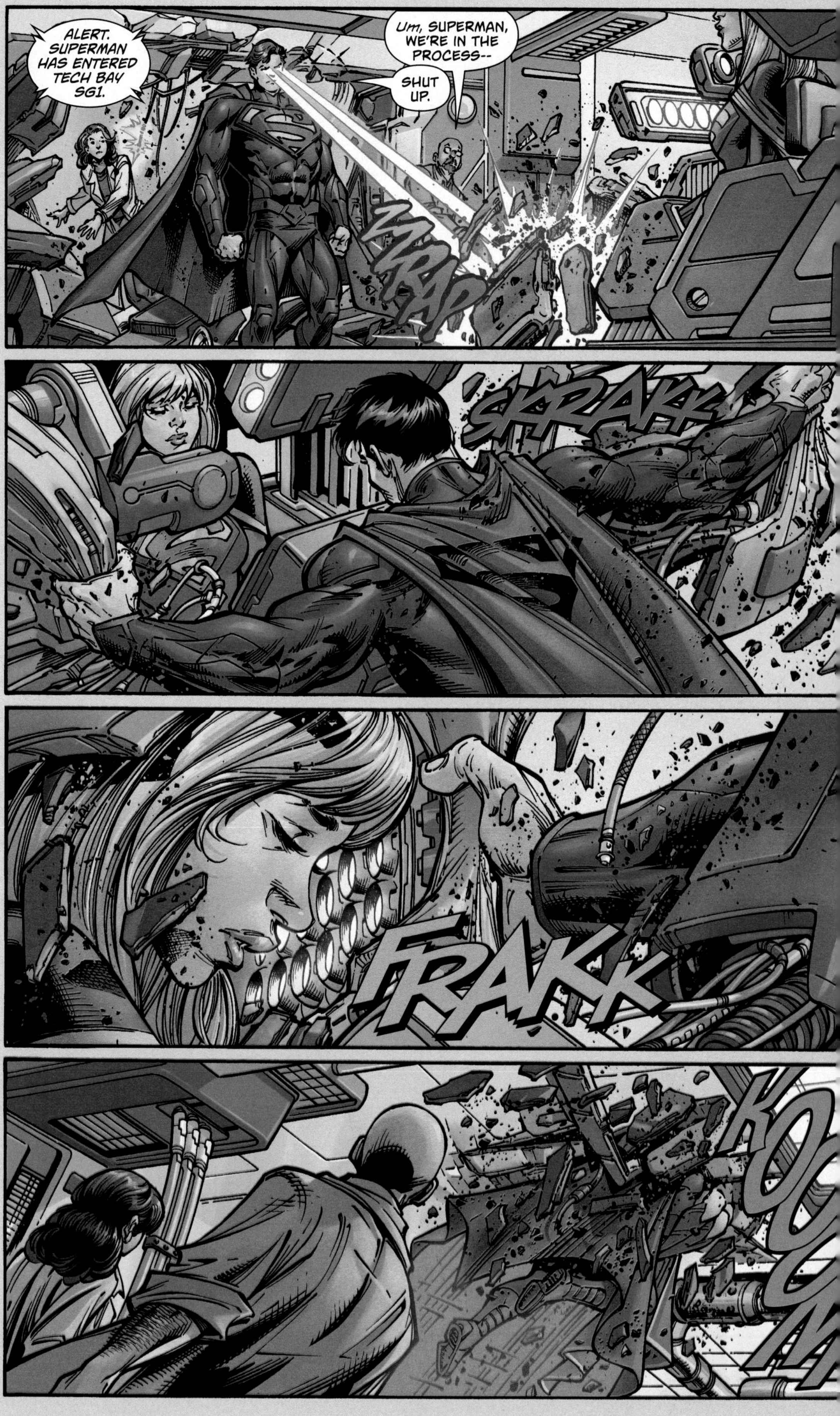
ALERT. SUPERMAN HAS ENTERED TECH BAY SG1.
Um, SUPERMAN, WE'RE IN THE PROCESS--
SHUT UP.
SKRAKK
FRAKK

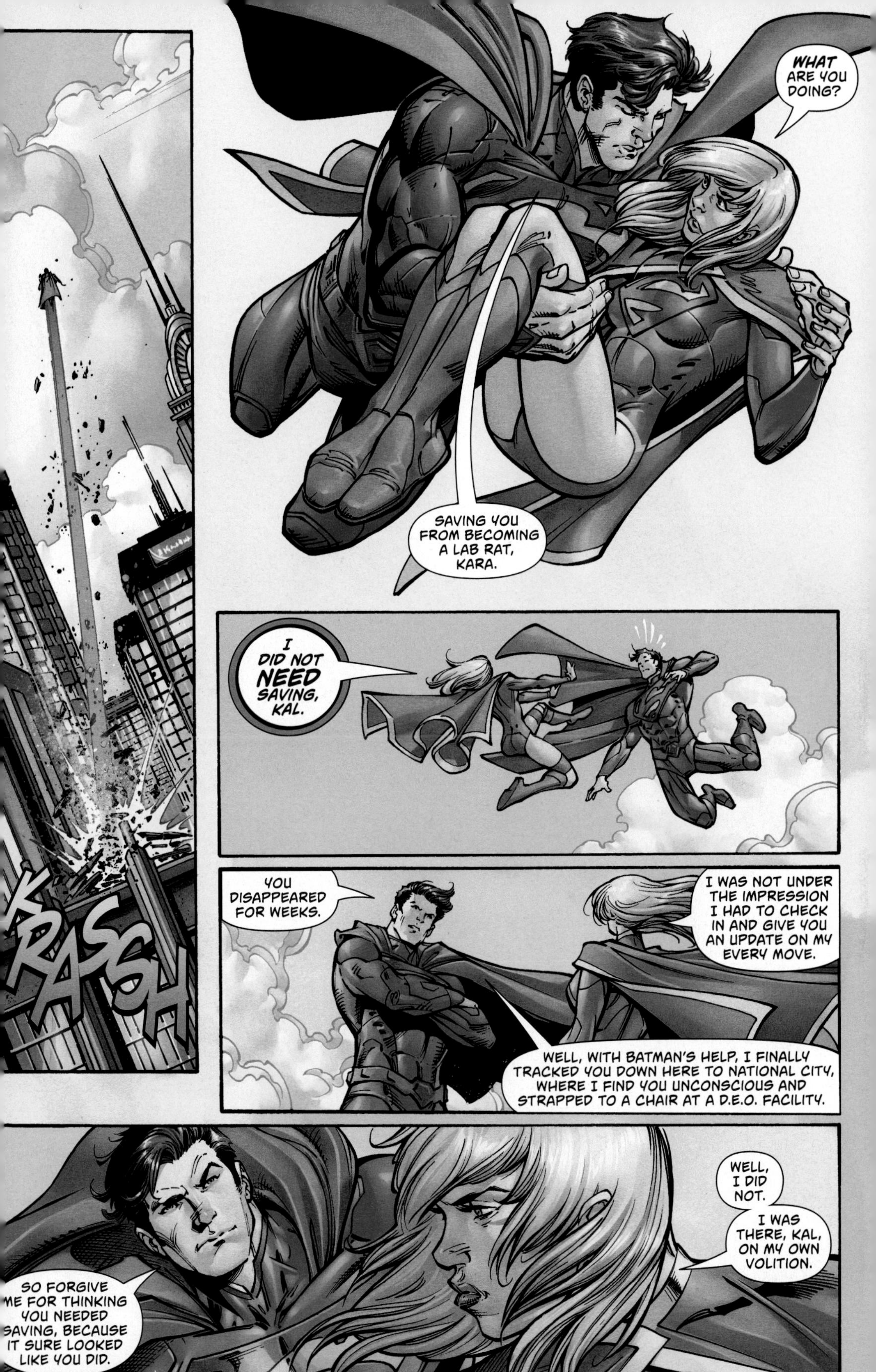
KRASH
WHAT ARE YOU DOING?
SAVING YOU FROM BECOMING A LAB RAT, KARA.
I DID NOT NEED SAVING, KAL.
YOU DISAPPEARED FOR WEEKS.
I WAS NOT UNDER THE IMPRESSION I HAD TO CHECK IN AND GIVE YOU AN UPDATE ON MY EVERY MOVE.
WELL, WITH BATMAN'S HELP, I FINALLY TRACKED YOU DOWN HERE TO NATIONAL CITY, WHERE I FIND YOU UNCONSCIOUS AND STRAPPED TO A CHAIR AT A D.E.O. FACILITY.
SO FORGIVE ME FOR THINKING YOU NEEDED SAVING, BECAUSE IT SURE LOOKED LIKE YOU DID.
WELL, I DID NOT.
I WAS THERE, KAL, ON MY OWN VOLITION.

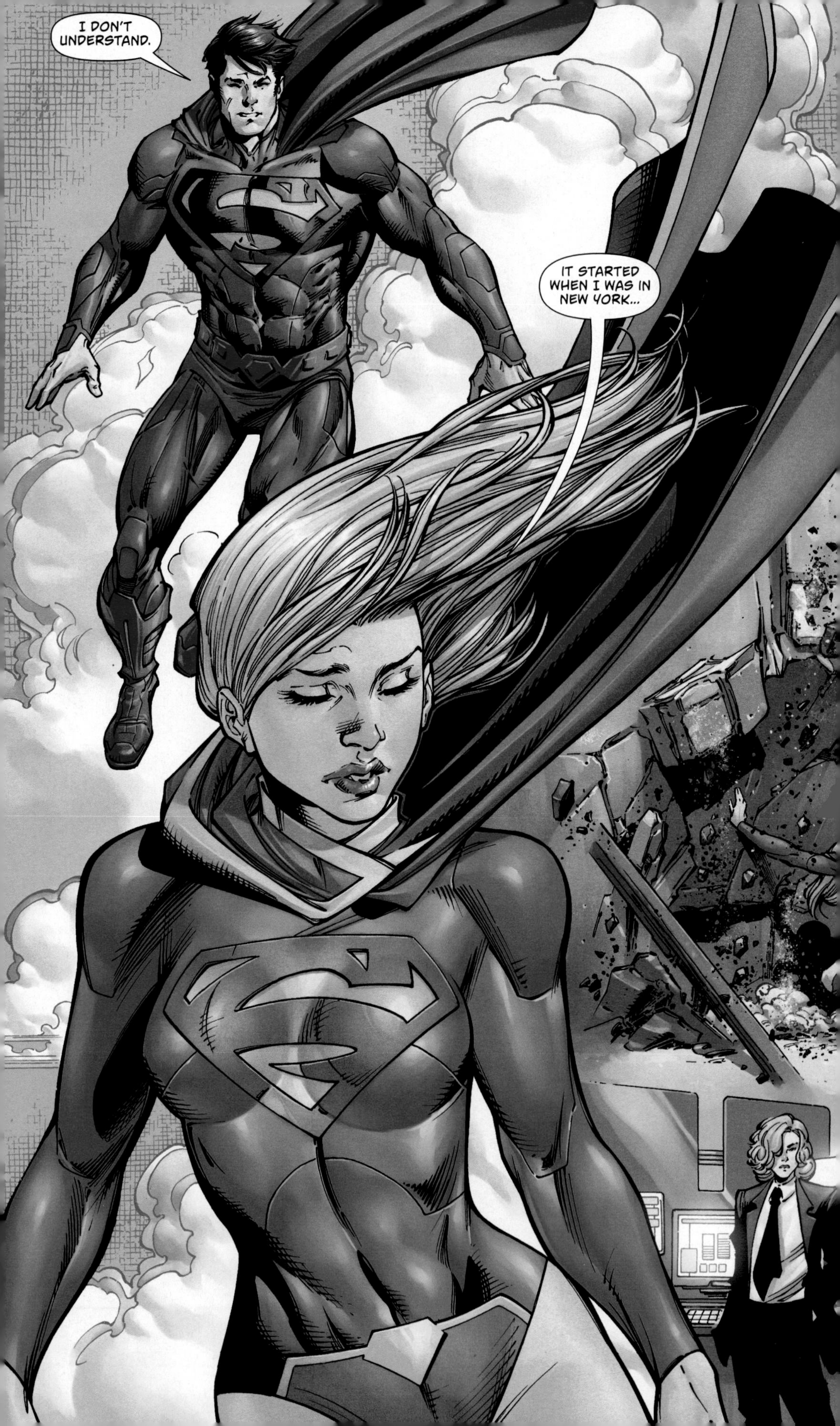
I DON'T UNDERSTAND.
IT STARTED WHEN I WAS IN NEW YORK...

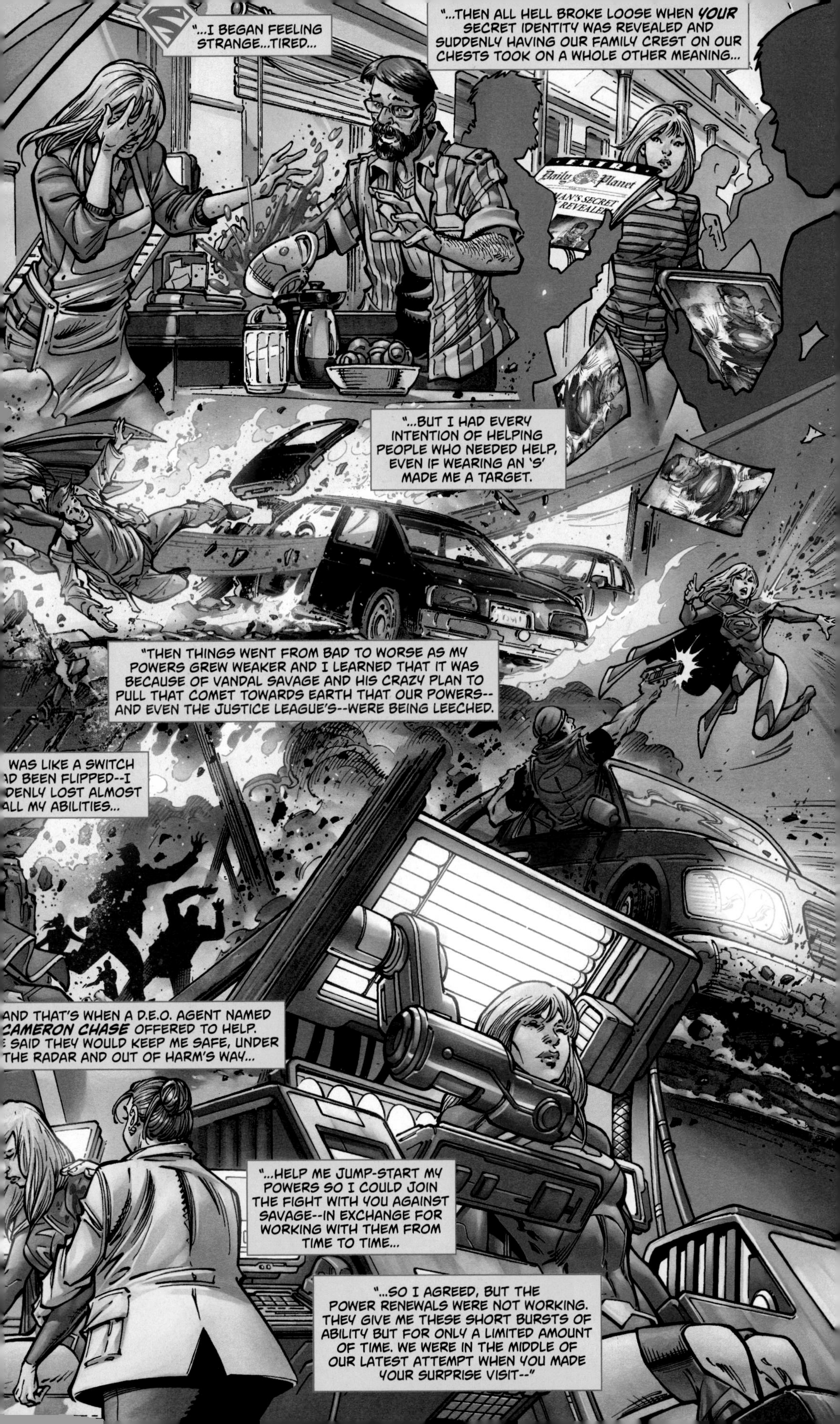
"...I BEGAN FEELING STRANGE...TIRED...
"...THEN ALL HELL BROKE LOOSE WHEN YOUR SECRET IDENTITY WAS REVEALED AND SUDDENLY HAVING OUR FAMILY CREST ON OUR CHESTS TOOK ON A WHOLE OTHER MEANING...
EXTRA
Daily Planet
"...BUT I HAD EVERY INTENTION OF HELPING PEOPLE WHO NEEDED HELP, EVEN IF WEARING AN 'S' MADE ME A TARGET.
"THEN THINGS WENT FROM BAD TO WORSE AS MY POWERS GREW WEAKER AND I LEARNED THAT IT WAS BECAUSE OF VANDAL SAVAGE AND HIS CRAZY PLAN TO PULL THAT COMET TOWARDS EARTH THAT OUR POWERS--AND EVEN THE JUSTICE LEAGUE'S--WERE BEING LEECHED.
WAS LIKE A SWITCH AD BEEN FLIPPED--I DENLY LOST ALMOST ALL MY ABILITIES...
AND THAT'S WHEN A D.E.O. AGENT NAMED CAMERON CHASE OFFERED TO HELP. SAID THEY WOULD KEEP ME SAFE, UNDER THE RADAR AND OUT OF HARM'S WAY...
"...HELP ME JUMP-START MY POWERS SO I COULD JOIN THE FIGHT WITH YOU AGAINST SAVAGE--IN EXCHANGE FOR WORKING WITH THEM FROM TIME TO TIME...
"...SO I AGREED, BUT THE POWER RENEWALS WERE NOT WORKING. THEY GIVE ME THESE SHORT BURSTS OF ABILITY BUT FOR ONLY A LIMITED AMOUNT OF TIME. WE WERE IN THE MIDDLE OF OUR LATEST ATTEMPT WHEN YOU MADE YOUR SURPRISE VISIT--"

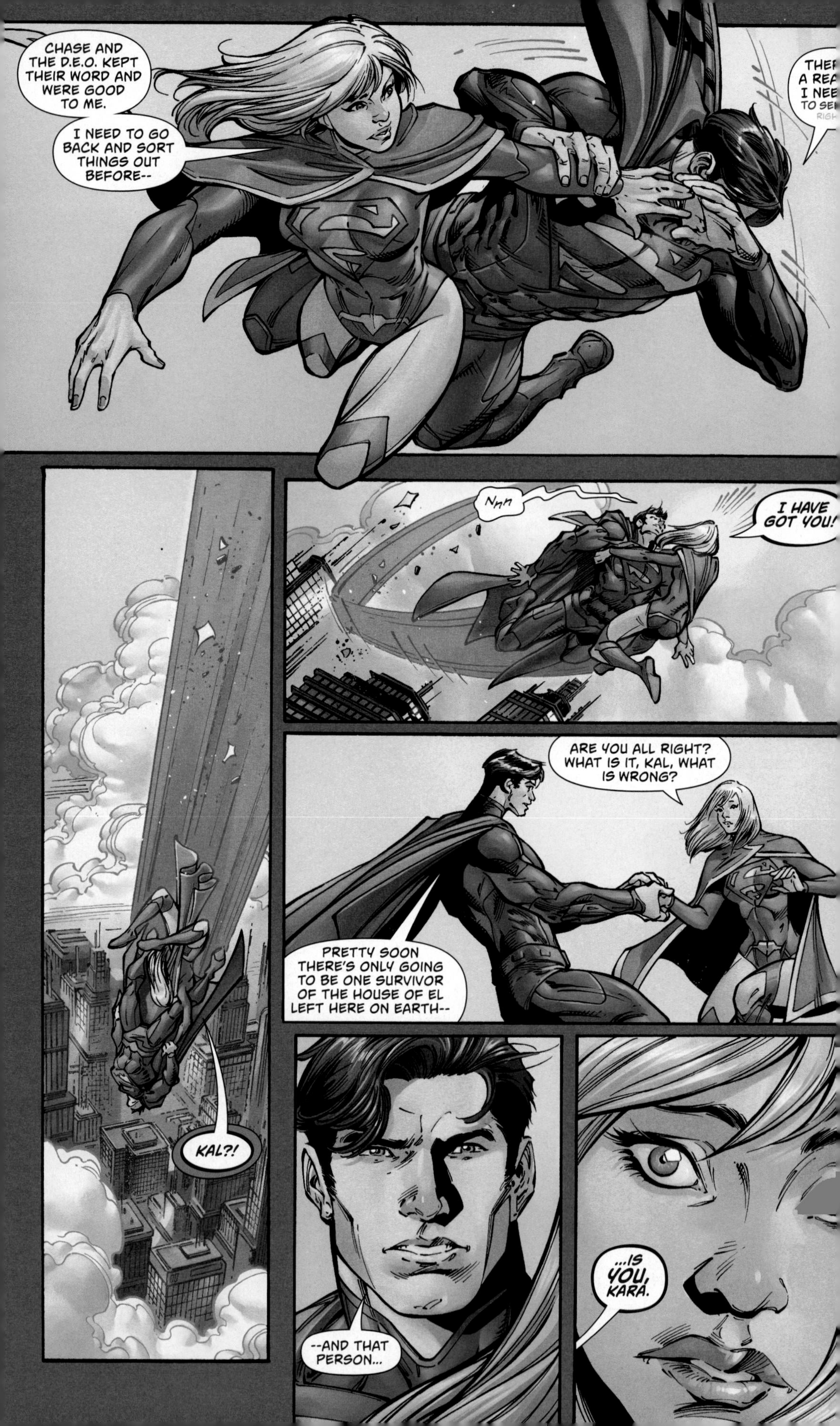
CHASE AND THE D.E.O. KEPT THEIR WORD AND WERE GOOD TO ME.
I NEED TO GO BACK AND SORT THINGS OUT BEFORE--
KAL?!
Nnn
I HAVE GOT YOU!
ARE YOU ALL RIGHT? WHAT IS IT, KAL, WHAT IS WRONG?
PRETTY SOON THERE'S ONLY GOING TO BE ONE SURVIVOR OF THE HOUSE OF EL LEFT HERE ON EARTH--
--AND THAT PERSON...
...IS YOU, KARA.

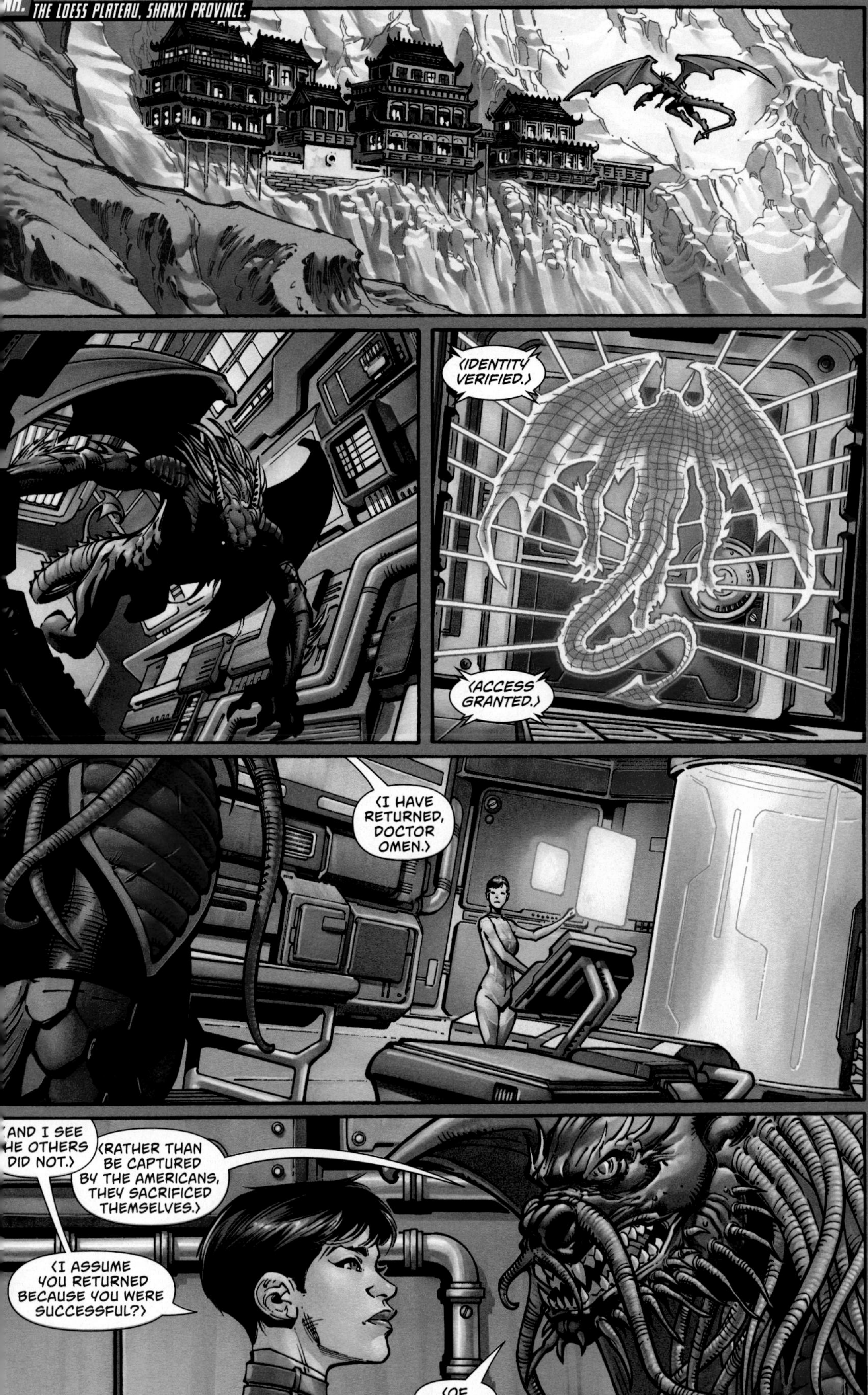

...NA. THE LOESS PLATEAU, SHANXI PROVINCE.
‹IDENTITY VERIFIED.›
‹ACCESS GRANTED.›
‹I HAVE RETURNED, DOCTOR OMEN.›
‹AND I SEE THE OTHERS DID NOT.›
‹RATHER THAN BE CAPTURED BY THE AMERICANS, THEY SACRIFICED THEMSELVES.›
‹I ASSUME YOU RETURNED BECAUSE YOU WERE SUCCESSFUL?›
‹OF COURSE.›

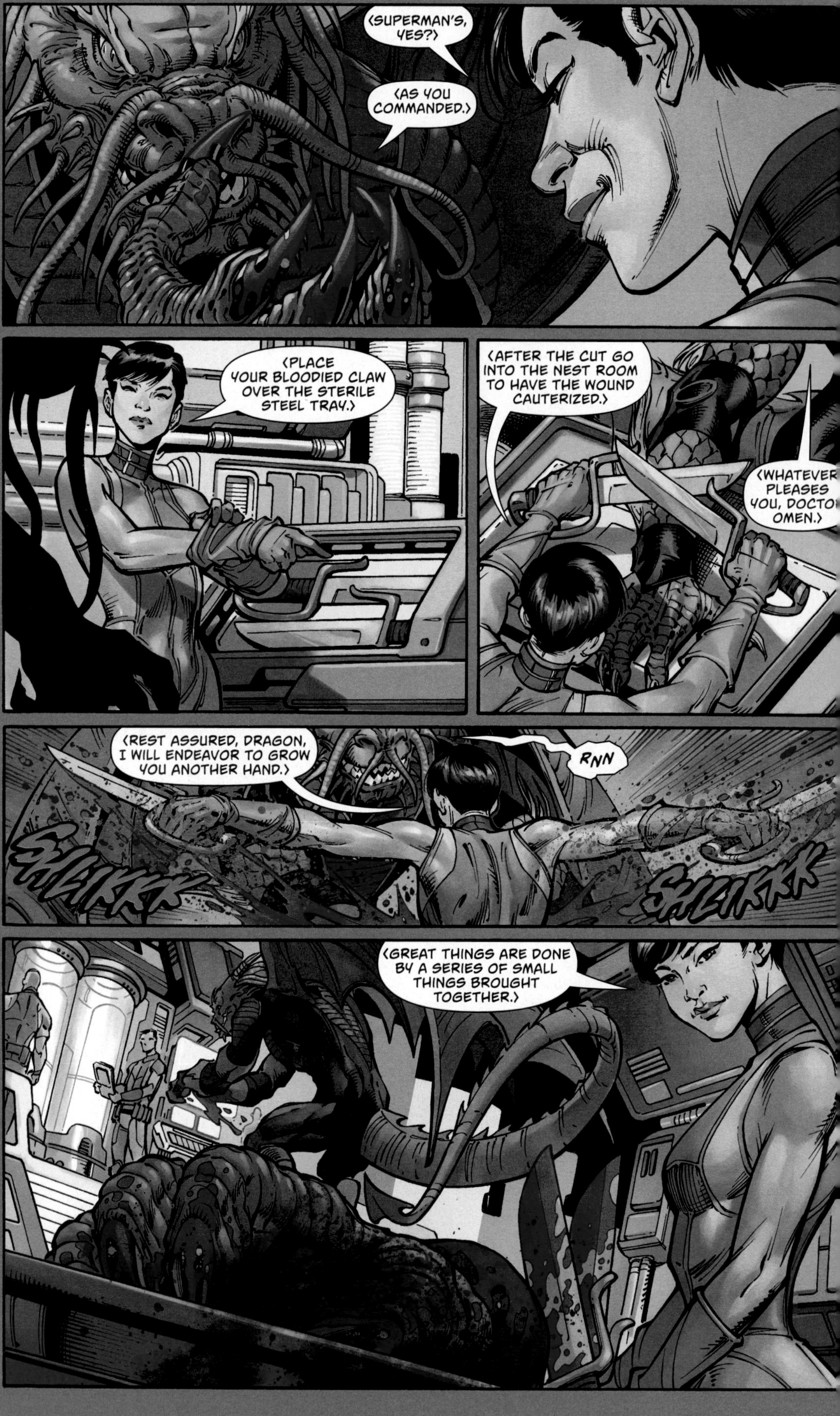

‹SUPERMAN'S, YES?›
‹AS YOU COMMANDED.›
‹PLACE YOUR BLOODIED CLAW OVER THE STERILE STEEL TRAY.›
‹AFTER THE CUT GO INTO THE NEST ROOM TO HAVE THE WOUND CAUTERIZED.›
‹WHATEVER PLEASES YOU, DOCTO OMEN.›
‹REST ASSURED, DRAGON, I WILL ENDEAVOR TO GROW YOU ANOTHER HAND.›
RNN
SHLIKKK
SHLIKKK
‹GREAT THINGS ARE DONE BY A SERIES OF SMALL THINGS BROUGHT TOGETHER.›

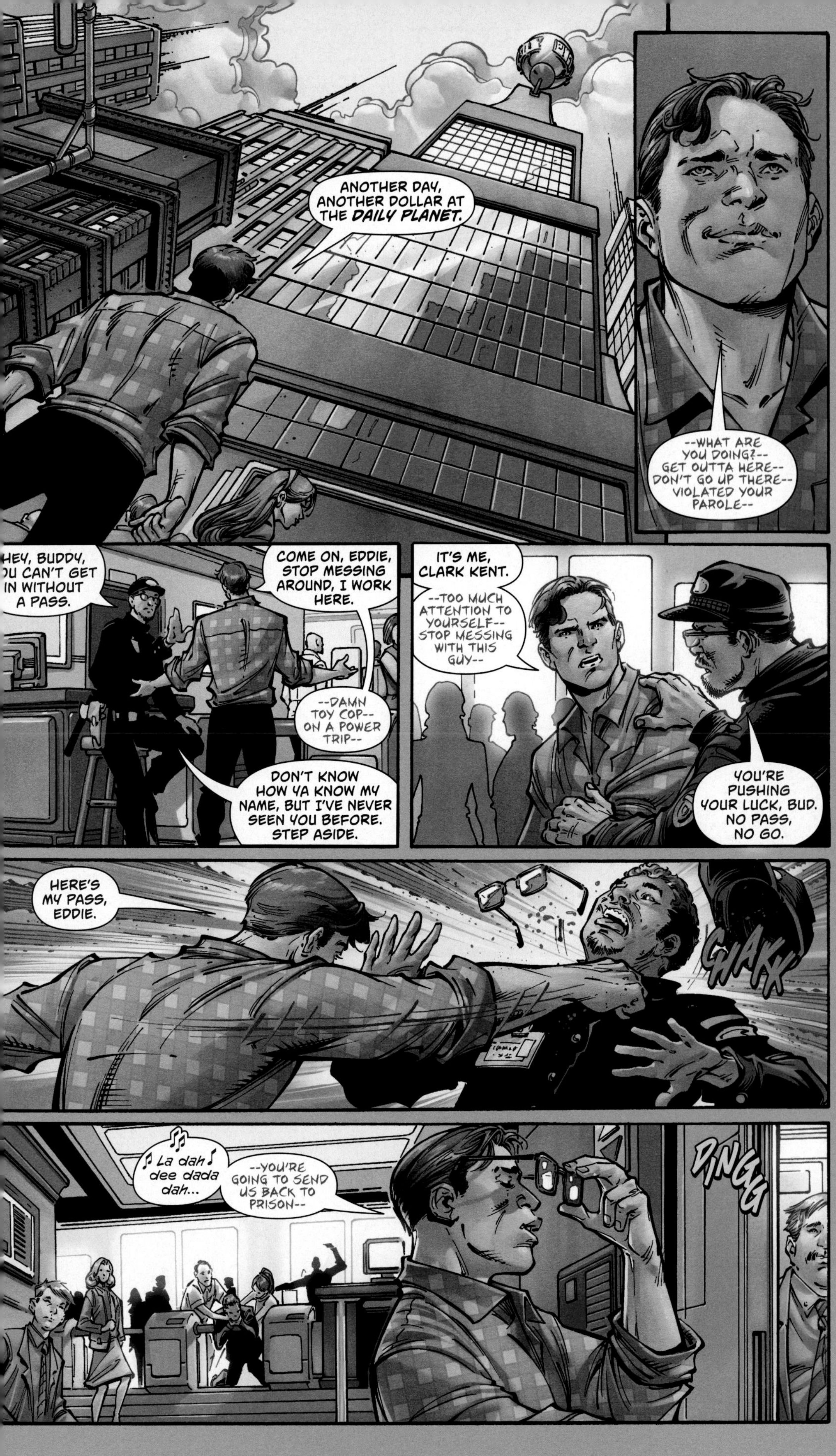

ANOTHER DAY, ANOTHER DOLLAR AT THE *DAILY PLANET*.
--WHAT ARE YOU DOING?-- GET OUTTA HERE-- DON'T GO UP THERE-- VIOLATED YOUR PAROLE--
HEY, BUDDY, YOU CAN'T GET IN WITHOUT A PASS.
COME ON, EDDIE, STOP MESSING AROUND, I WORK HERE.
--DAMN TOY COP-- ON A POWER TRIP--
DON'T KNOW HOW YA KNOW MY NAME, BUT I'VE NEVER SEEN YOU BEFORE. STEP ASIDE.
IT'S ME, CLARK KENT.
--TOO MUCH ATTENTION TO YOURSELF-- STOP MESSING WITH THIS GUY--
YOU'RE PUSHING YOUR LUCK, BUD. NO PASS, NO GO.
HERE'S MY PASS, EDDIE.
GHAKK
♪ La dah ♪ dee dada dah...
--YOU'RE GOING TO SEND US BACK TO PRISON--
DINGG

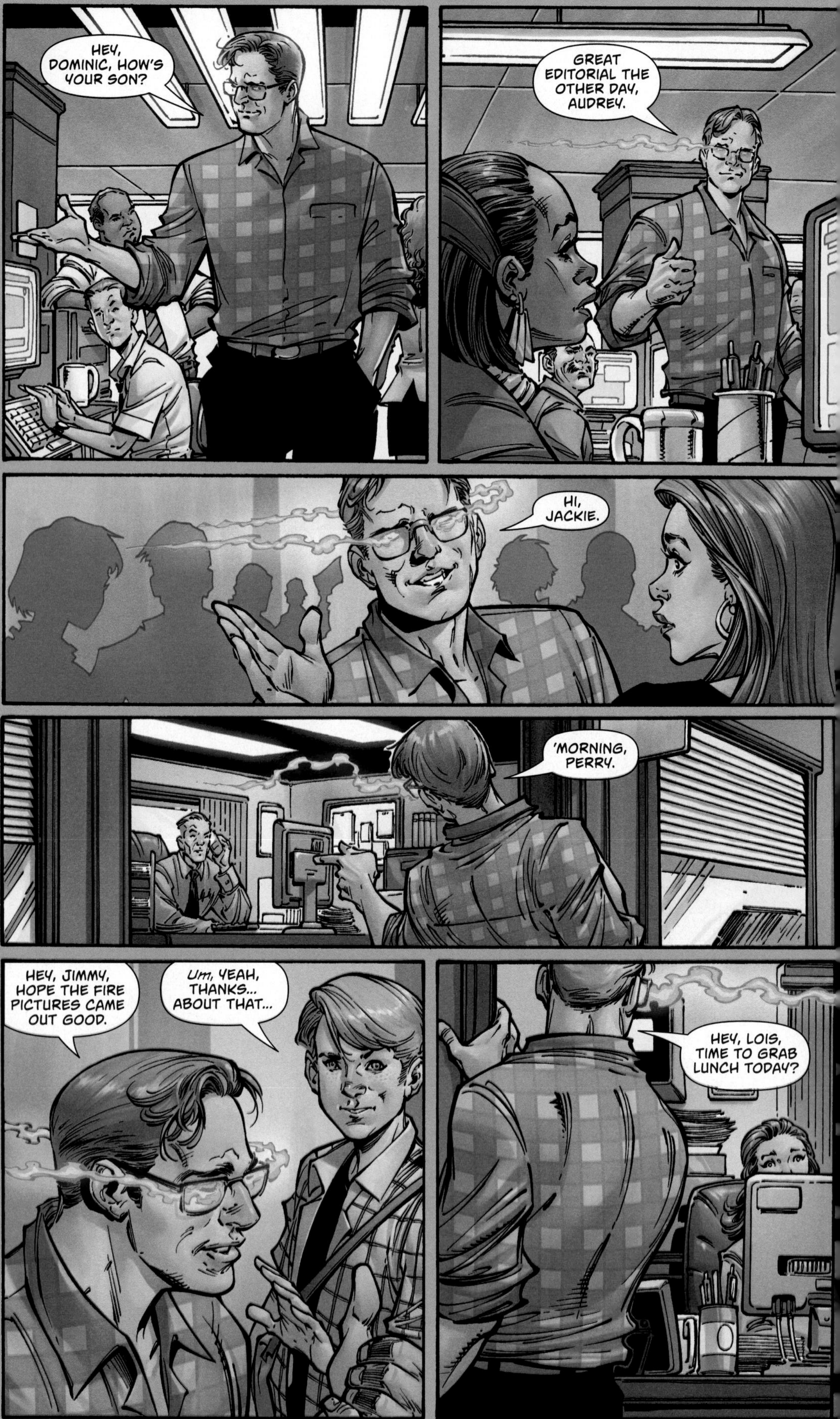
HEY, DOMINIC, HOW'S YOUR SON?
GREAT EDITORIAL THE OTHER DAY, AUDREY.
HI, JACKIE.
'MORNING, PERRY.
HEY, JIMMY, HOPE THE FIRE PICTURES CAME OUT GOOD.
Um, YEAH, THANKS... ABOUT THAT...
HEY, LOIS, TIME TO GRAB LUNCH TODAY?

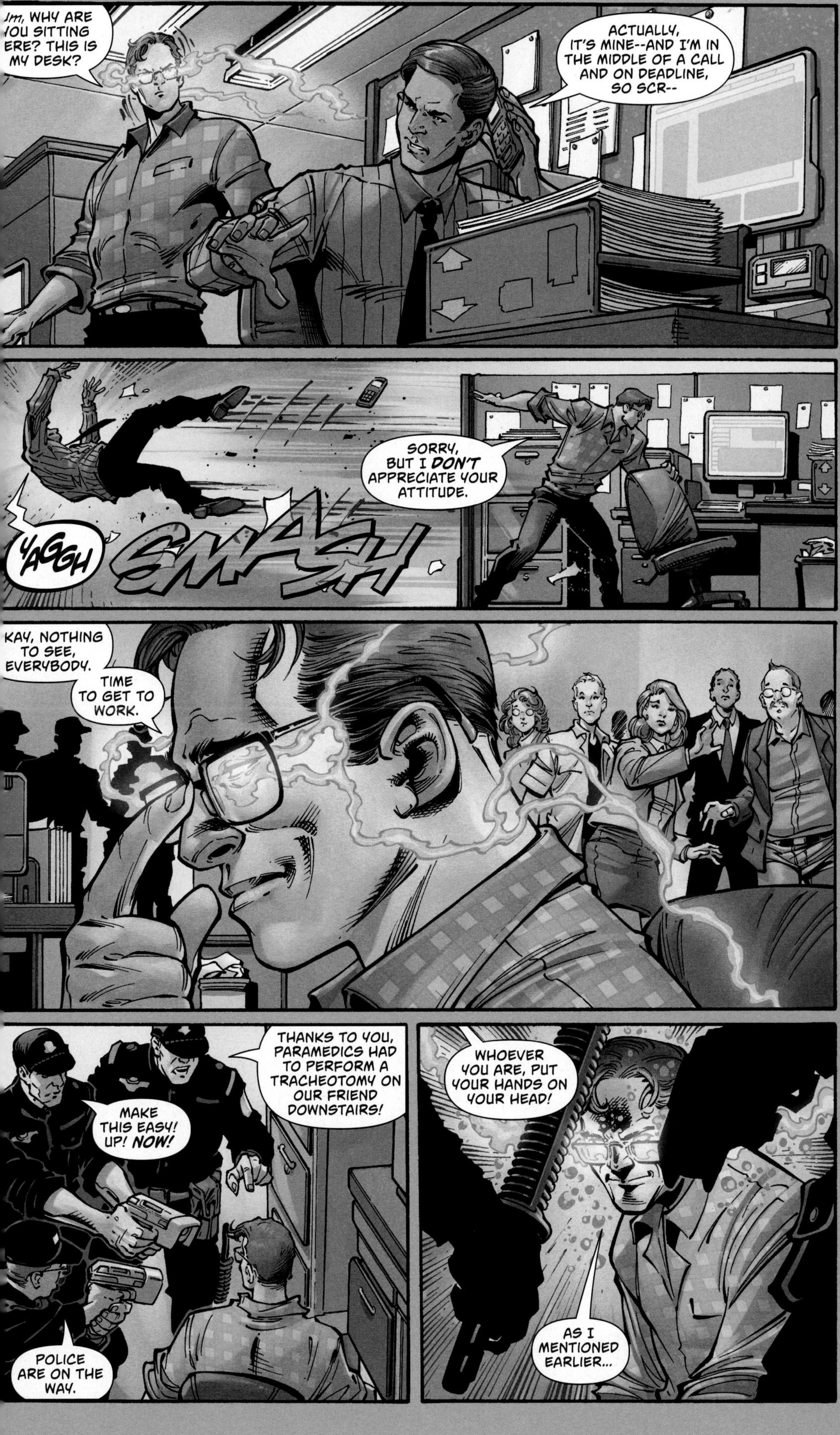

...M, WHY ARE YOU SITTING ...ERE? THIS IS MY DESK?
ACTUALLY, IT'S MINE--AND I'M IN THE MIDDLE OF A CALL AND ON DEADLINE, SO SCR--
YAGGH
SMASH
SORRY, BUT I DON'T APPRECIATE YOUR ATTITUDE.
...KAY, NOTHING TO SEE, EVERYBODY.
TIME TO GET TO WORK.
THANKS TO YOU, PARAMEDICS HAD TO PERFORM A TRACHEOTOMY ON OUR FRIEND DOWNSTAIRS!
MAKE THIS EASY! UP! NOW!
POLICE ARE ON THE WAY.
WHOEVER YOU ARE, PUT YOUR HANDS ON YOUR HEAD!
AS I MENTIONED EARLIER...

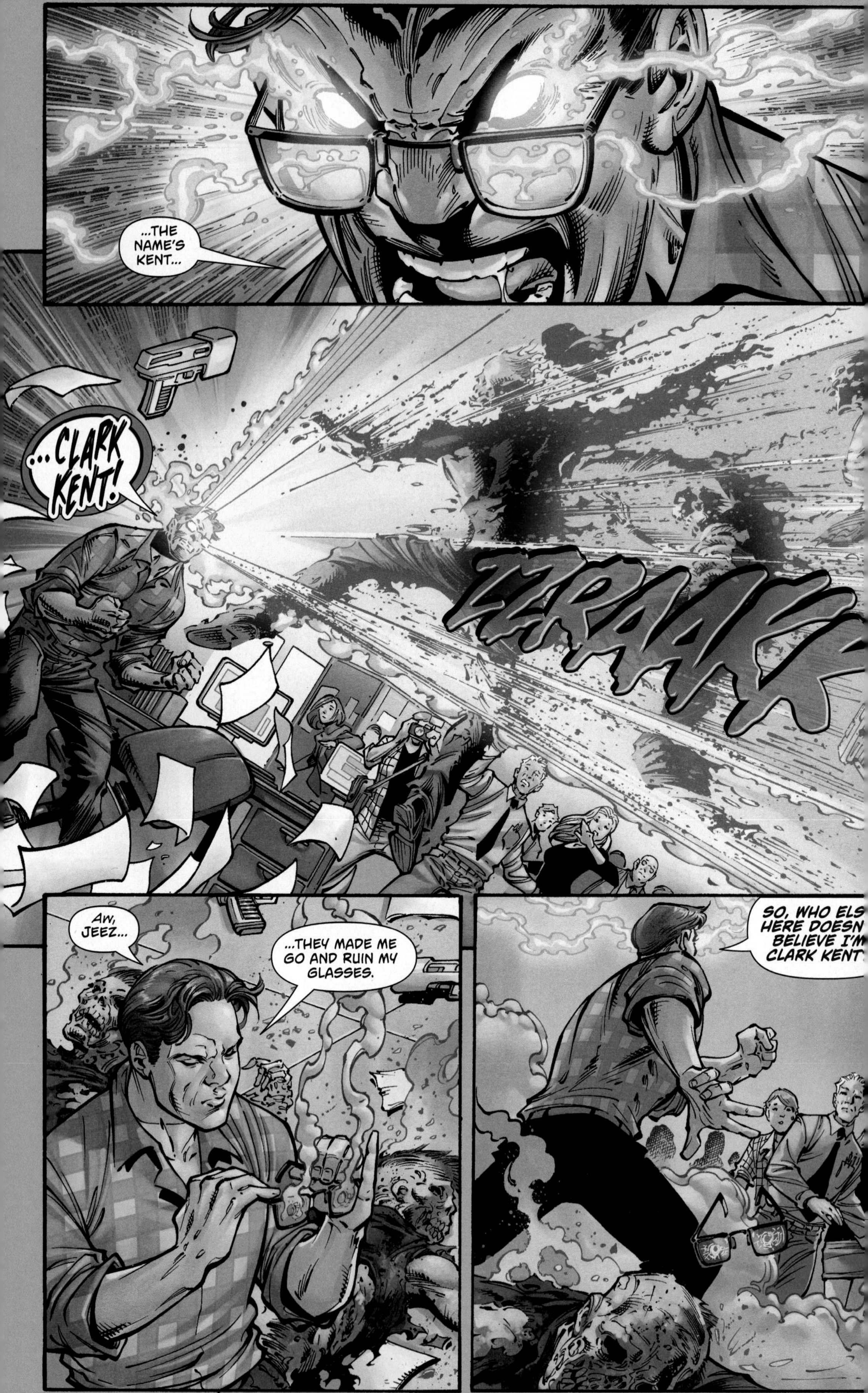

...THE NAME'S KENT...
...CLARK KENT!
ZZRAAKK
AW, JEEZ...
...THEY MADE ME GO AND RUIN MY GLASSES.
SO, WHO ELS HERE DOESN BELIEVE I'M CLARK KENT

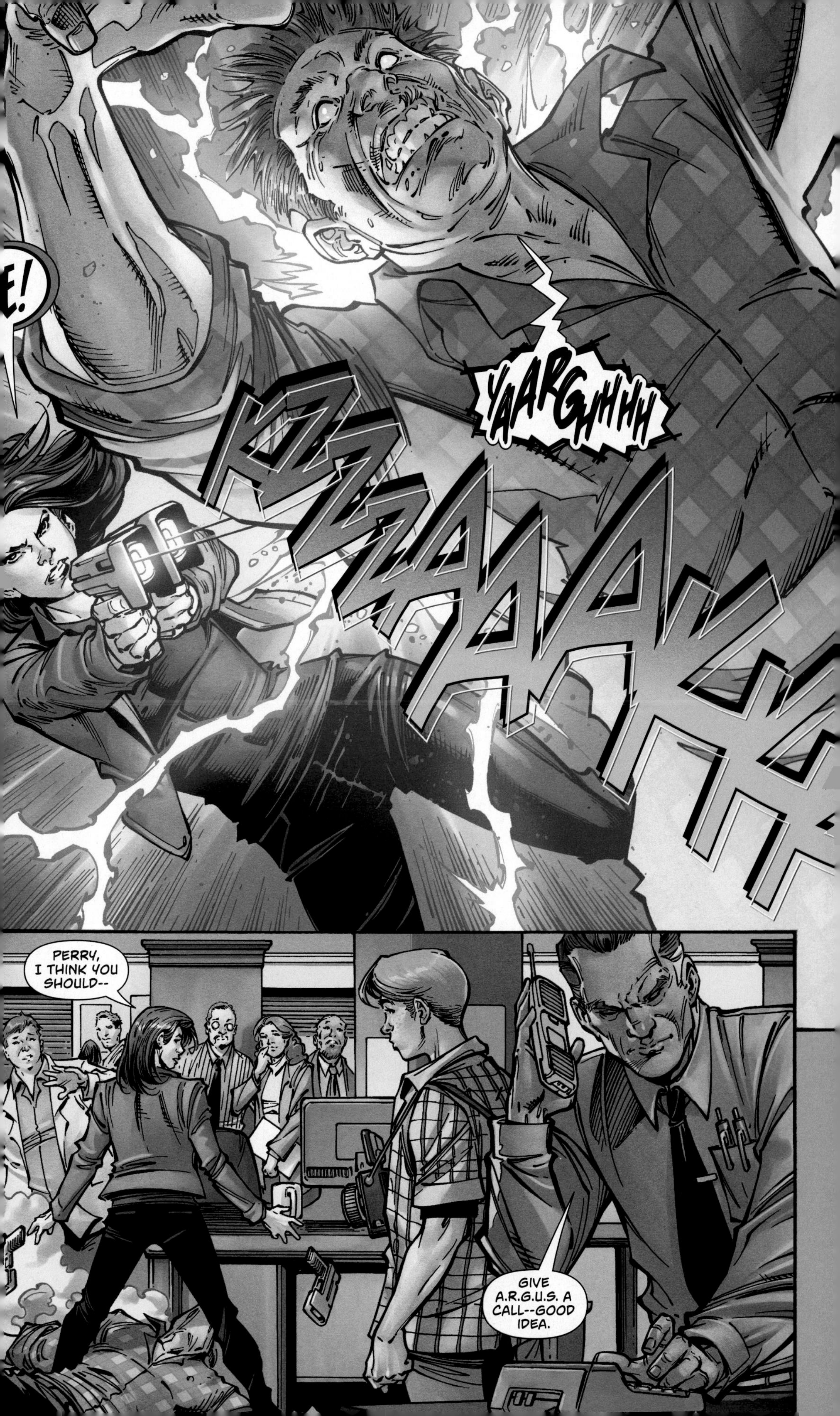
E!
YAARGHHHH
KZZZAAAAAAAKT
PERRY, I THINK YOU SHOULD--
GIVE A.R.G.U.S. A CALL--GOOD IDEA.

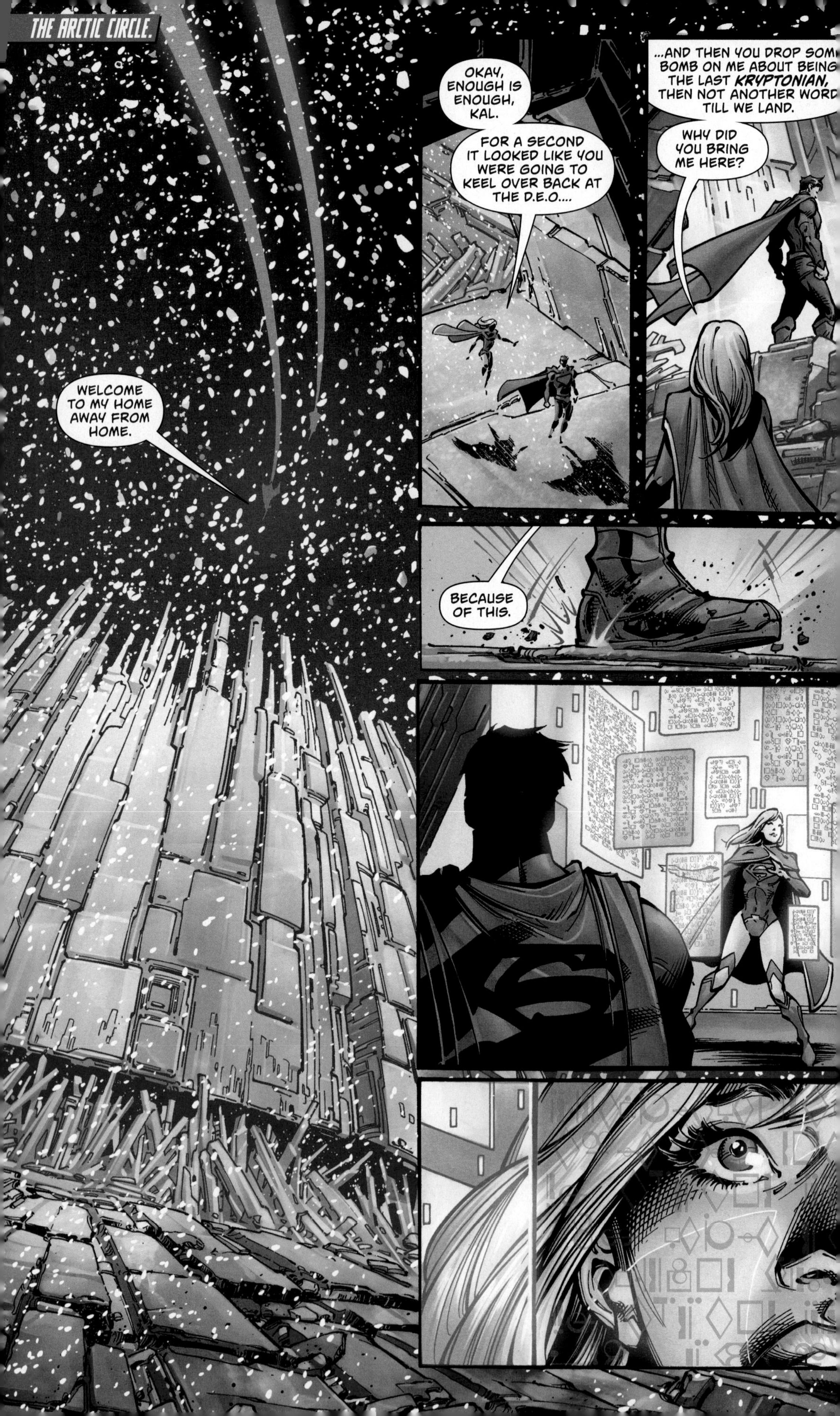
THE ARCTIC CIRCLE.
WELCOME TO MY HOME AWAY FROM HOME.
OKAY, ENOUGH IS ENOUGH, KAL.
FOR A SECOND IT LOOKED LIKE YOU WERE GOING TO KEEL OVER BACK AT THE D.E.O....
...AND THEN YOU DROP SOM BOMB ON ME ABOUT BEING THE LAST KRYPTONIAN, THEN NOT ANOTHER WORD TILL WE LAND.
WHY DID YOU BRING ME HERE?
BECAUSE OF THIS.

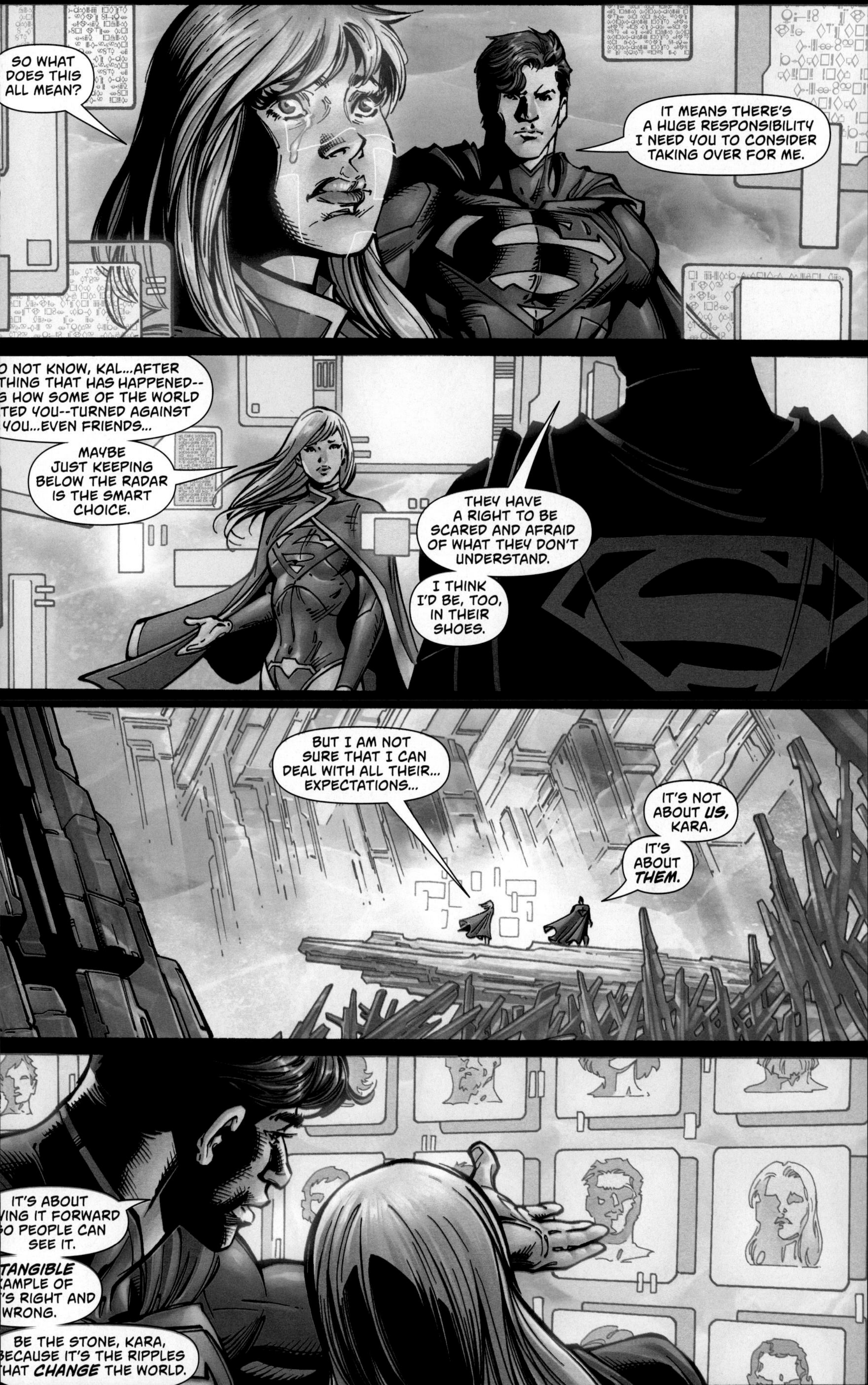
SO WHAT DOES THIS ALL MEAN?
IT MEANS THERE'S A HUGE RESPONSIBILITY I NEED YOU TO CONSIDER TAKING OVER FOR ME.
O NOT KNOW, KAL...AFTER THING THAT HAS HAPPENED-- S HOW SOME OF THE WORLD TED YOU--TURNED AGAINST YOU...EVEN FRIENDS...
MAYBE JUST KEEPING BELOW THE RADAR IS THE SMART CHOICE.
THEY HAVE A RIGHT TO BE SCARED AND AFRAID OF WHAT THEY DON'T UNDERSTAND.
I THINK I'D BE, TOO, IN THEIR SHOES.
BUT I AM NOT SURE THAT I CAN DEAL WITH ALL THEIR... EXPECTATIONS...
IT'S NOT ABOUT *US,* KARA.
IT'S ABOUT *THEM.*
IT'S ABOUT VING IT FORWARD O PEOPLE CAN SEE IT.
TANGIBLE AMPLE OF 'S RIGHT AND WRONG.
BE THE STONE, KARA, BECAUSE IT'S THE RIPPLES THAT *CHANGE* THE WORLD.

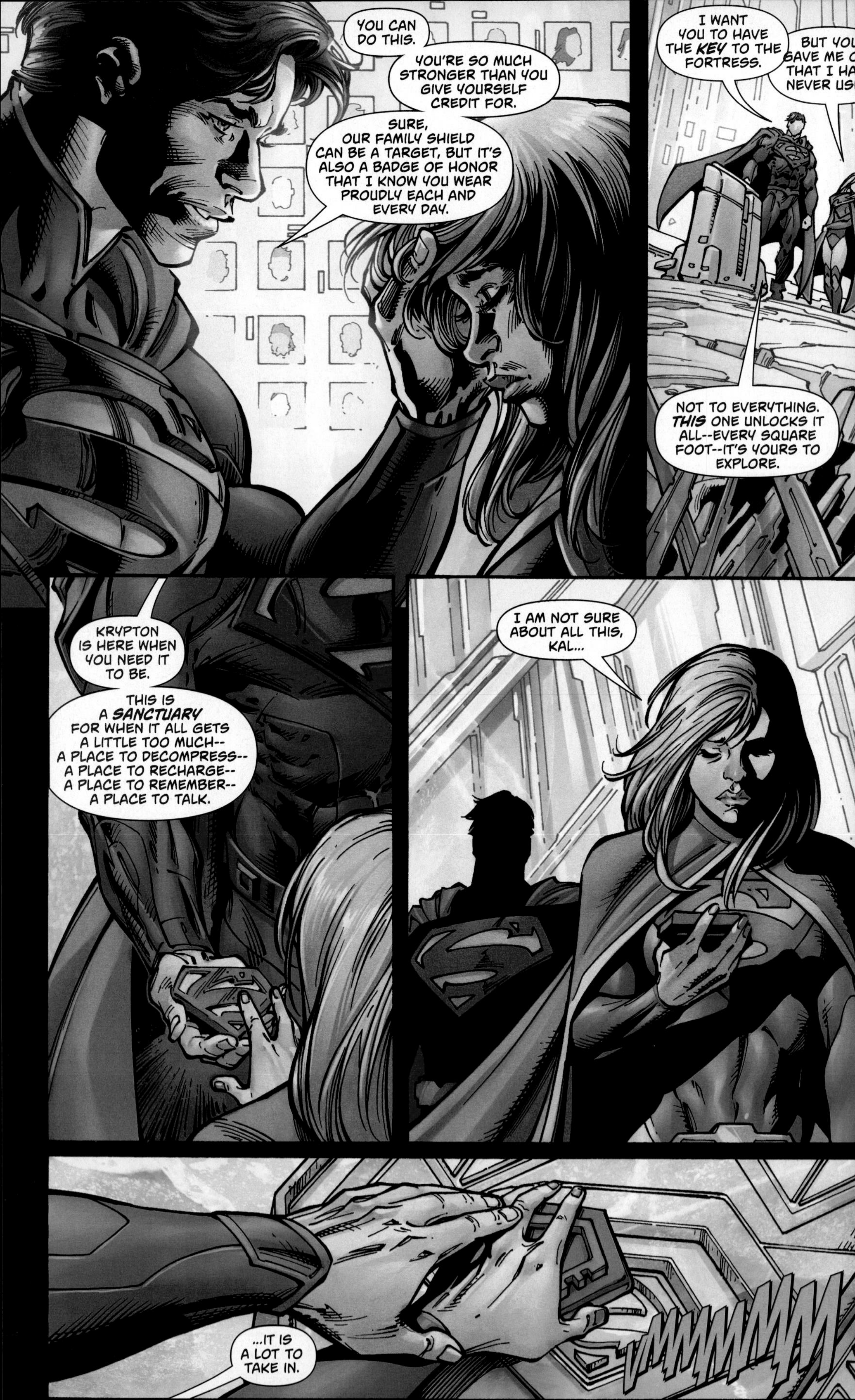
YOU CAN DO THIS.
YOU'RE SO MUCH STRONGER THAN YOU GIVE YOURSELF CREDIT FOR.
SURE, OUR FAMILY SHIELD CAN BE A TARGET, BUT IT'S ALSO A BADGE OF HONOR THAT I KNOW YOU WEAR PROUDLY EACH AND EVERY DAY.
I WANT YOU TO HAVE THE *KEY* TO THE FORTRESS.
NOT TO EVERYTHING. ***THIS*** ONE UNLOCKS IT ALL--EVERY SQUARE FOOT--IT'S YOURS TO EXPLORE.
KRYPTON IS HERE WHEN YOU NEED IT TO BE.
THIS IS A ***SANCTUARY*** FOR WHEN IT ALL GETS A LITTLE TOO MUCH-- A PLACE TO DECOMPRESS-- A PLACE TO RECHARGE-- A PLACE TO REMEMBER-- A PLACE TO TALK.
I AM NOT SURE ABOUT ALL THIS, KAL...
...IT IS A LOT TO TAKE IN.

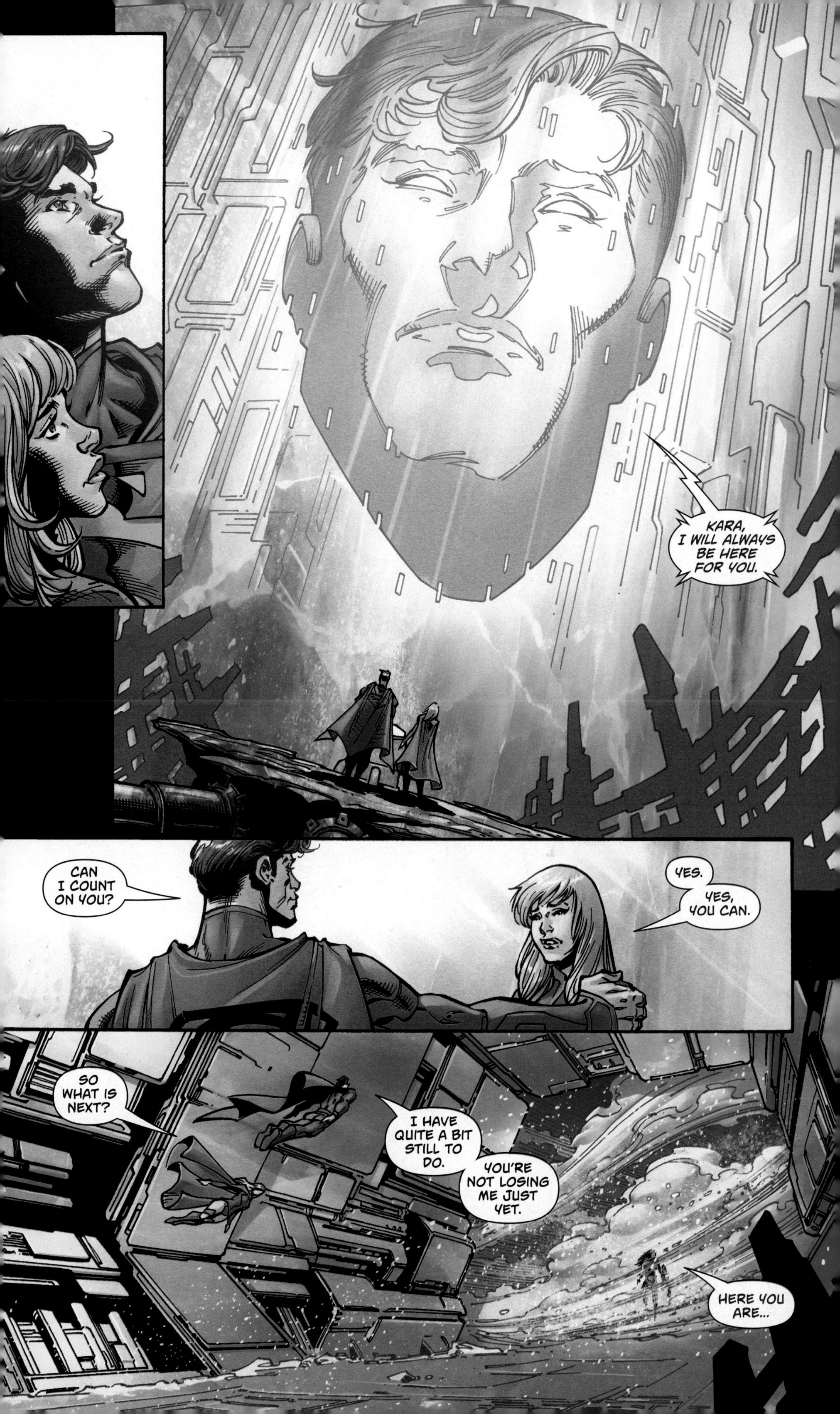
KARA, I WILL ALWAYS BE HERE FOR YOU.
CAN I COUNT ON YOU?
YES.
YES, YOU CAN.
SO WHAT IS NEXT?
I HAVE QUITE A BIT STILL TO DO.
YOU'RE NOT LOSING ME JUST YET.
HERE YOU ARE...

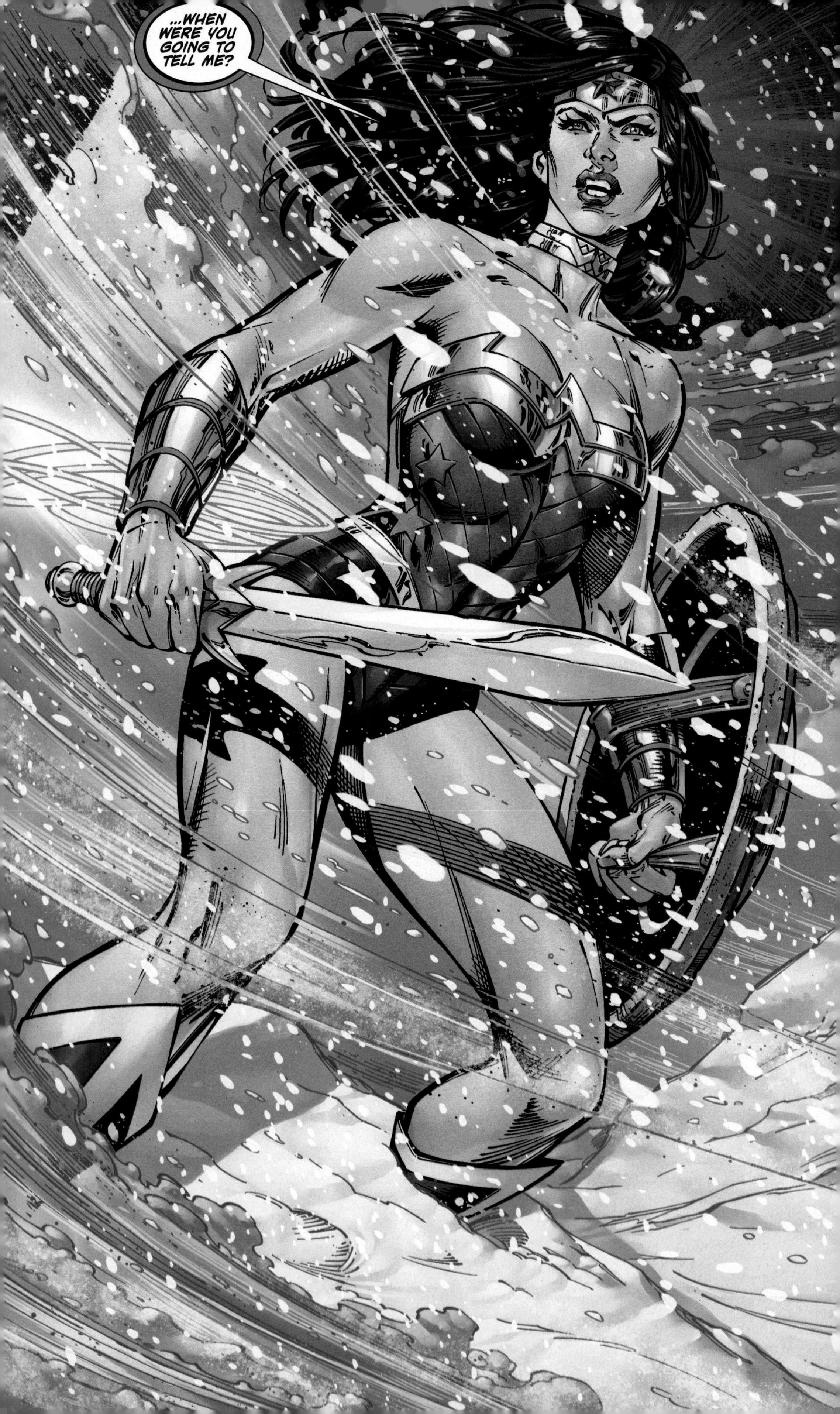
...WHEN WERE YOU GOING TO TELL ME?

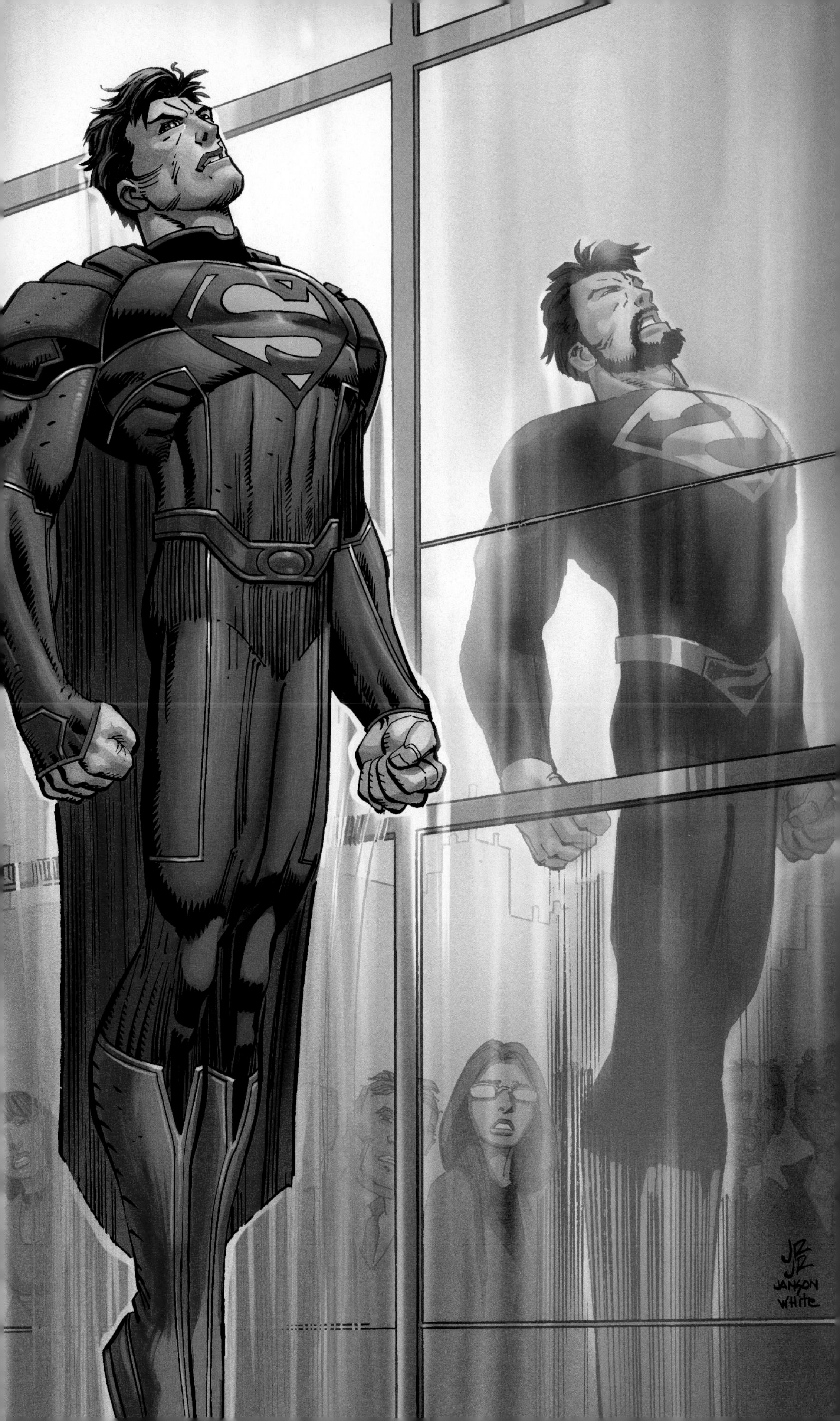
JANSON
WHITE

Previously,
in SUPERMAN/WONDER WOMAN #28
and BATMAN/SUPERMAN #32...

Tragically, it takes Superman facing his final days for him to confess that he has never stopped loving Diana, while it takes the Solar-Superman's incarceration to bring the reunited couple to A.R.G.U.S. As Superman tries to connect his unstable doppelgänger's origins to another imprisoned foe, Ulysses, the rage over seeing Diana betray him with an "impostor" Kal-El literally fuels Solar-Superman to make an explosive escape.

Rejoined by Batman, Superman and Wonder Woman trace what they believe is the Solar-Superman's energy signature to China. However, they soon discover that the signature actually belongs to Dr. Omen's genetic "Super-Functionary," created from Superman's blood and powered by his residual solar energy flares. The mysterious being is freed by its creator moments before she's arrested, forcing the trinity of heroes to leave China empty-handed. As for the Solar-Superman? He unexpectedly resurfaces in Metropolis floating just outside the balcony of the high-rise apartment where Lois Lane resides...

IT'S THESE SMALL, SILENT MOMENTS BETWEEN THE BATTLES AND THE SAVES I WISH I HAD MORE OF...

...FLYING BESIDE THE WOMAN I LOVE...

...AND THE WOMAN WHO LOVES ME...

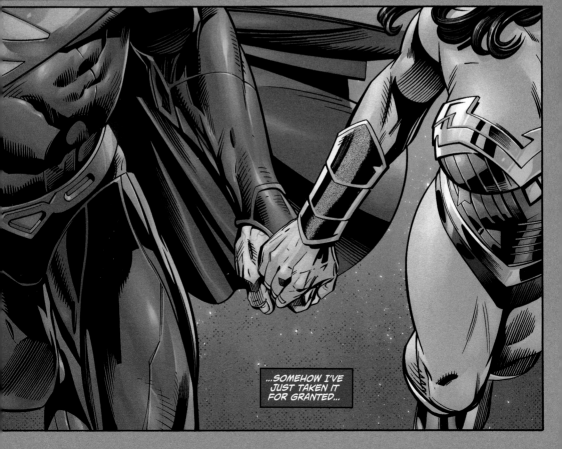

...SOMEHOW I'VE JUST TAKEN IT FOR GRANTED...

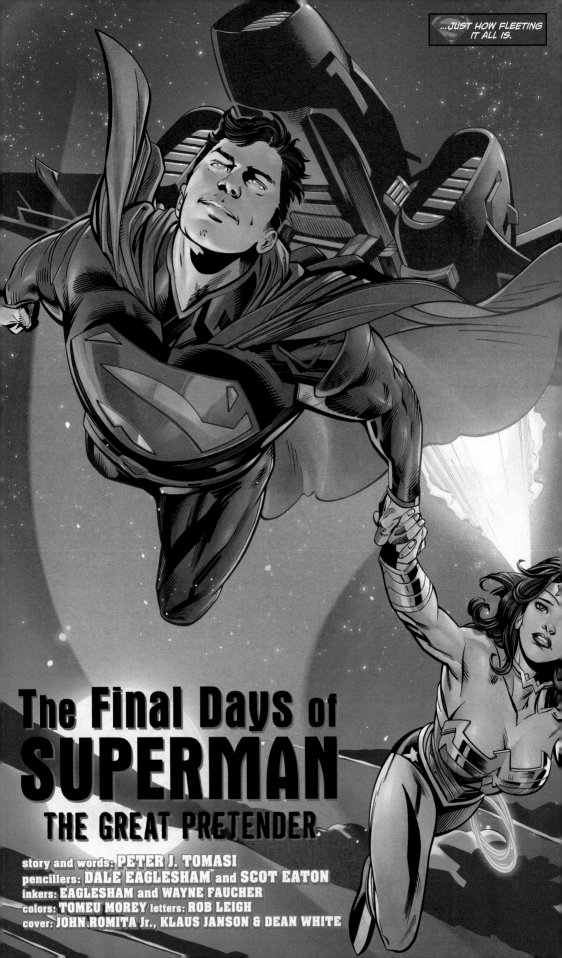

...JUST HOW FLEETING IT ALL IS.

The Final Days of SUPERMAN
THE GREAT PRETENDER

story and words: **PETER J. TOMASI**
pencillers: **DALE EAGLESHAM** and **SCOT EATON**
inkers: **EAGLESHAM** and **WAYNE FAUCHER**
colors: **TOMEU MOREY** letters: **ROB LEIGH**
cover: **JOHN ROMITA Jr., KLAUS JANSON & DEAN WHITE**

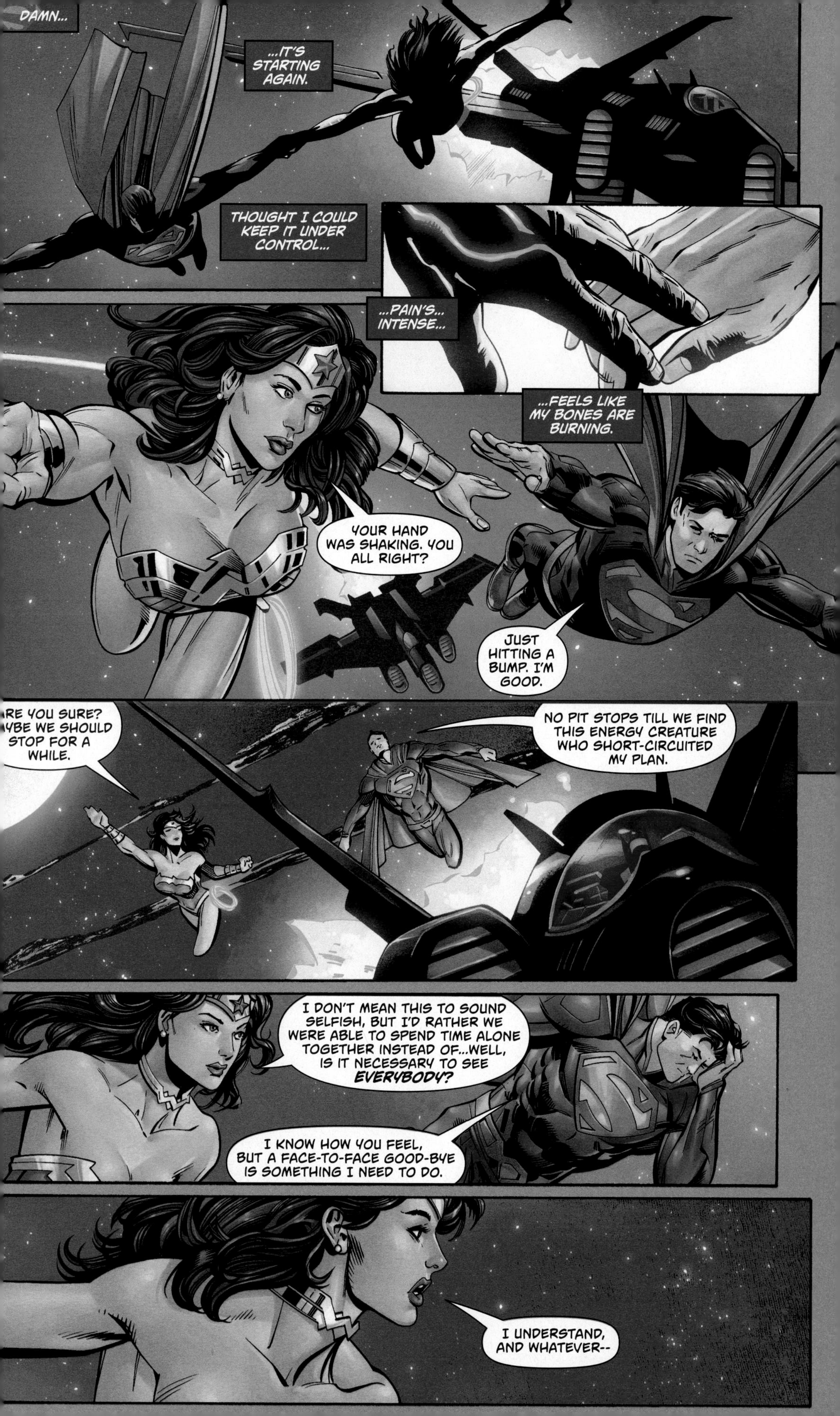
DAMN...
...IT'S STARTING AGAIN.
THOUGHT I COULD KEEP IT UNDER CONTROL...
...PAIN'S... INTENSE...
...FEELS LIKE MY BONES ARE BURNING.
YOUR HAND WAS SHAKING. YOU ALL RIGHT?
JUST HITTING A BUMP. I'M GOOD.
RE YOU SURE? YBE WE SHOULD STOP FOR A WHILE.
NO PIT STOPS TILL WE FIND THIS ENERGY CREATURE WHO SHORT-CIRCUITED MY PLAN.
I DON'T MEAN THIS TO SOUND SELFISH, BUT I'D RATHER WE WERE ABLE TO SPEND TIME ALONE TOGETHER INSTEAD OF...WELL, IS IT NECESSARY TO SEE ***EVERYBODY?***
I KNOW HOW YOU FEEL, BUT A FACE-TO-FACE GOOD-BYE IS SOMETHING I NEED TO DO.
I UNDERSTAND, AND WHATEVER--

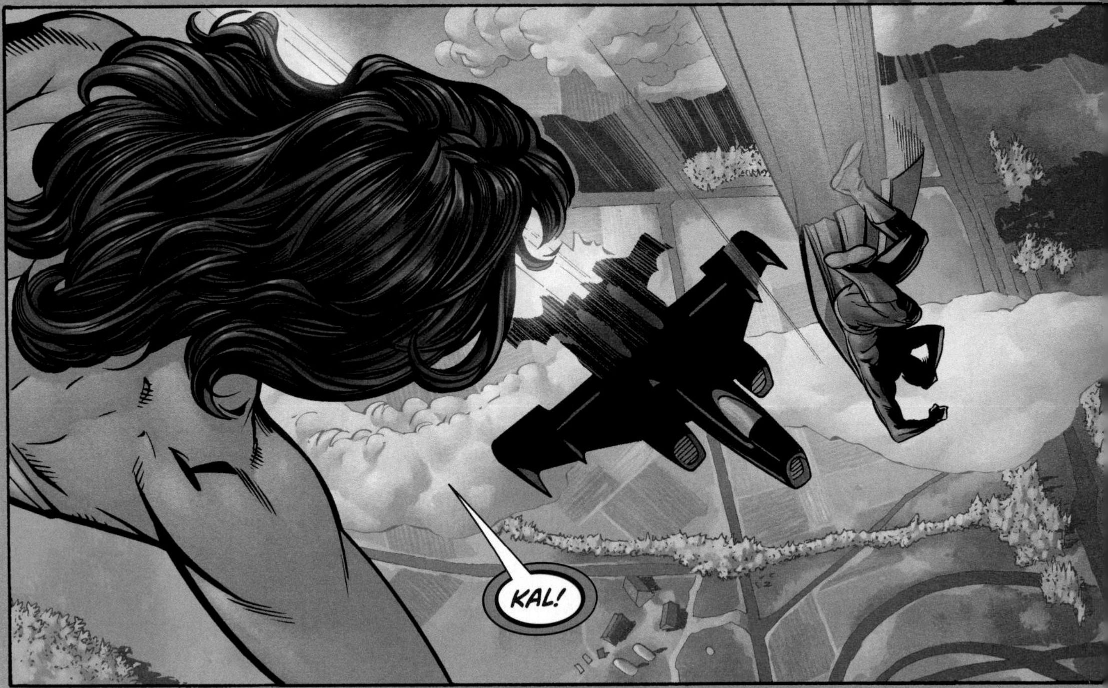
KAL!

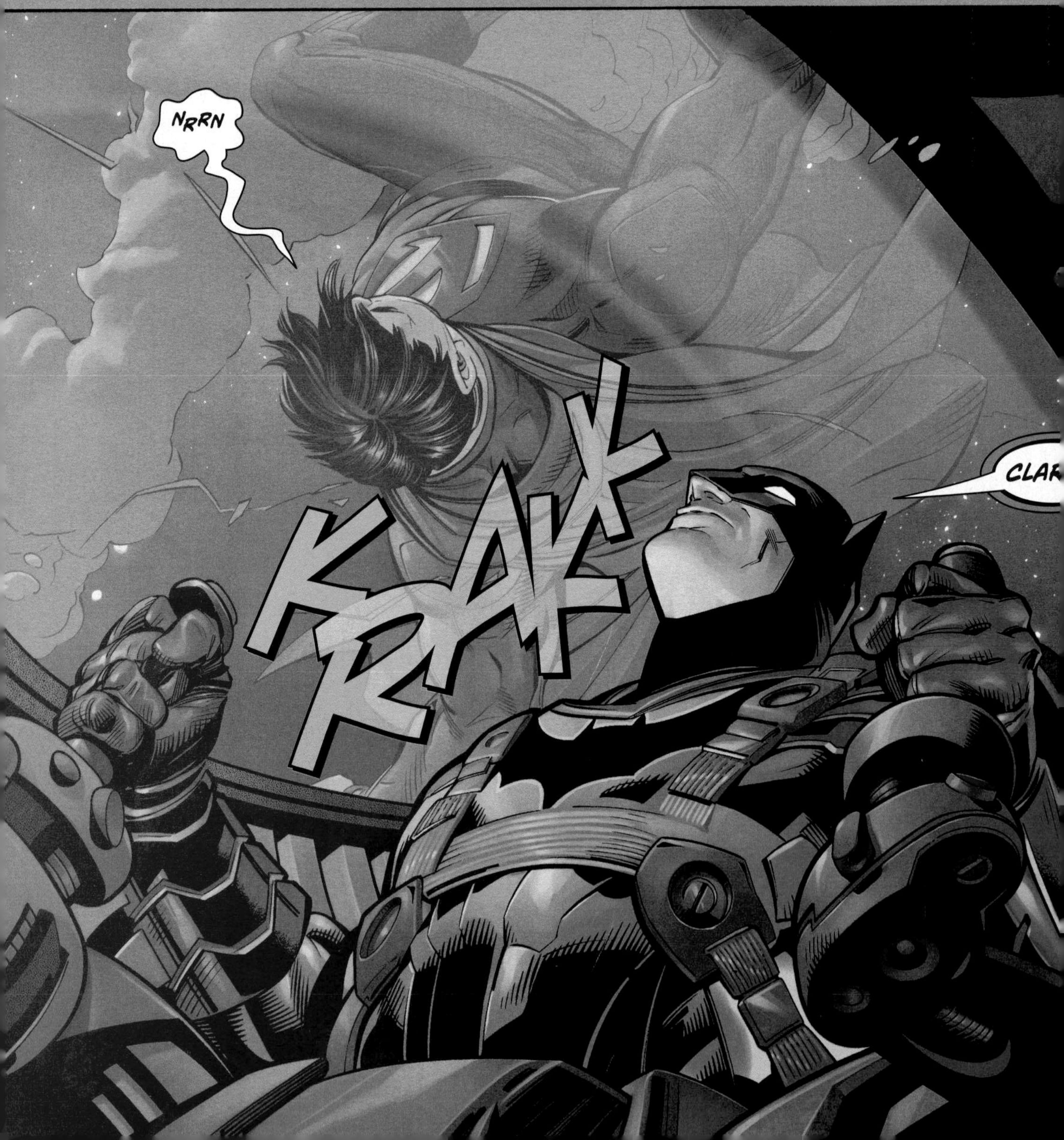
NRRN
KRAK
CLAR

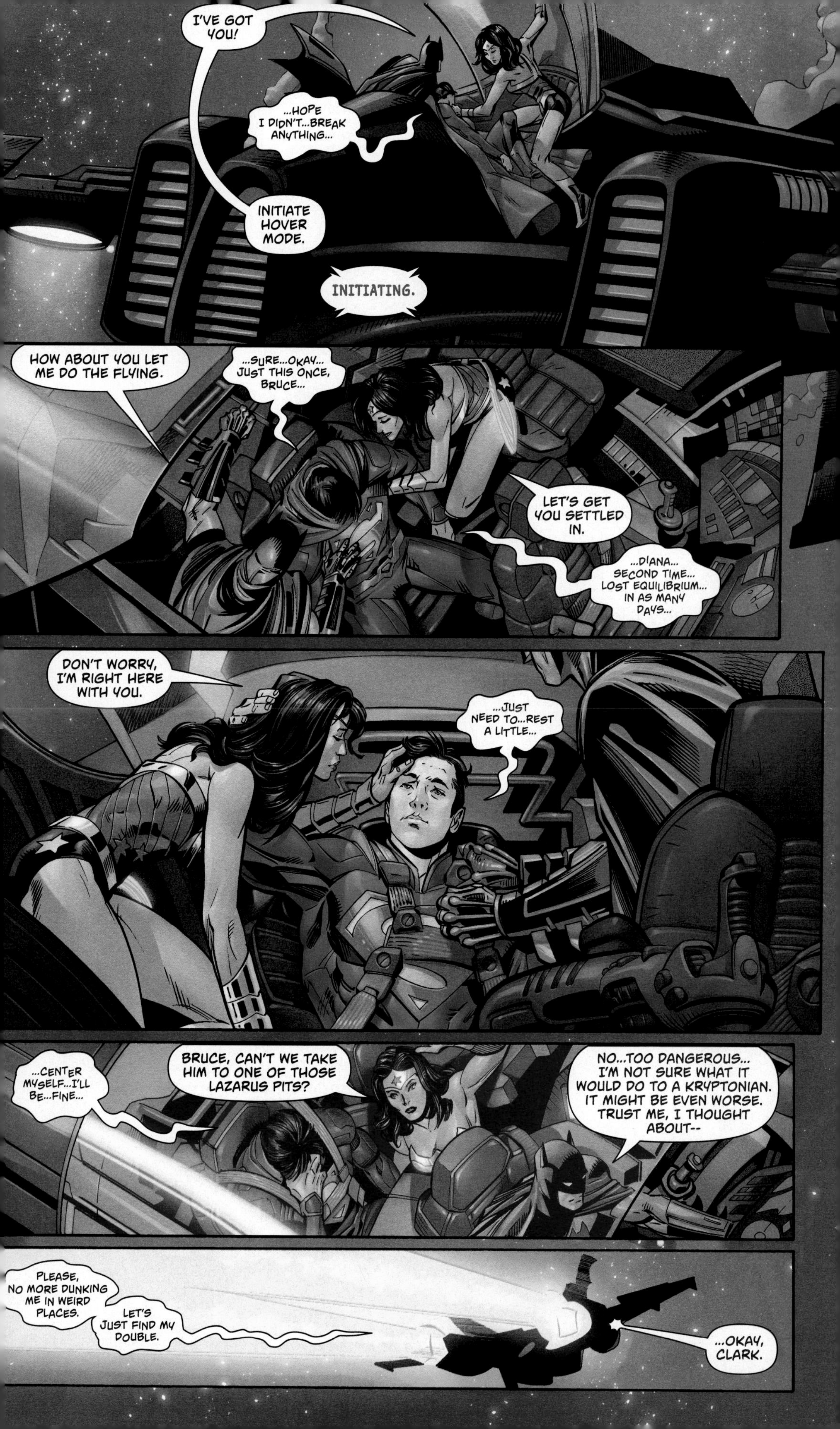
I'VE GOT YOU!
...HOPE I DIDN'T...BREAK ANYTHING...
INITIATE HOVER MODE.
INITIATING.
HOW ABOUT YOU LET ME DO THE FLYING.
...SURE...OKAY... JUST THIS ONCE, BRUCE...
LET'S GET YOU SETTLED IN.
...DIANA... SECOND TIME... LOST EQUILIBRIUM... IN AS MANY DAYS...
DON'T WORRY, I'M RIGHT HERE WITH YOU.
...JUST NEED TO...REST A LITTLE...
...CENTER MYSELF...I'LL BE...FINE...
BRUCE, CAN'T WE TAKE HIM TO ONE OF THOSE LAZARUS PITS?
NO...TOO DANGEROUS... I'M NOT SURE WHAT IT WOULD DO TO A KRYPTONIAN. IT MIGHT BE EVEN WORSE. TRUST ME, I THOUGHT ABOUT--
PLEASE, NO MORE DUNKING ME IN WEIRD PLACES.
LET'S JUST FIND MY DOUBLE.
...OKAY, CLARK.

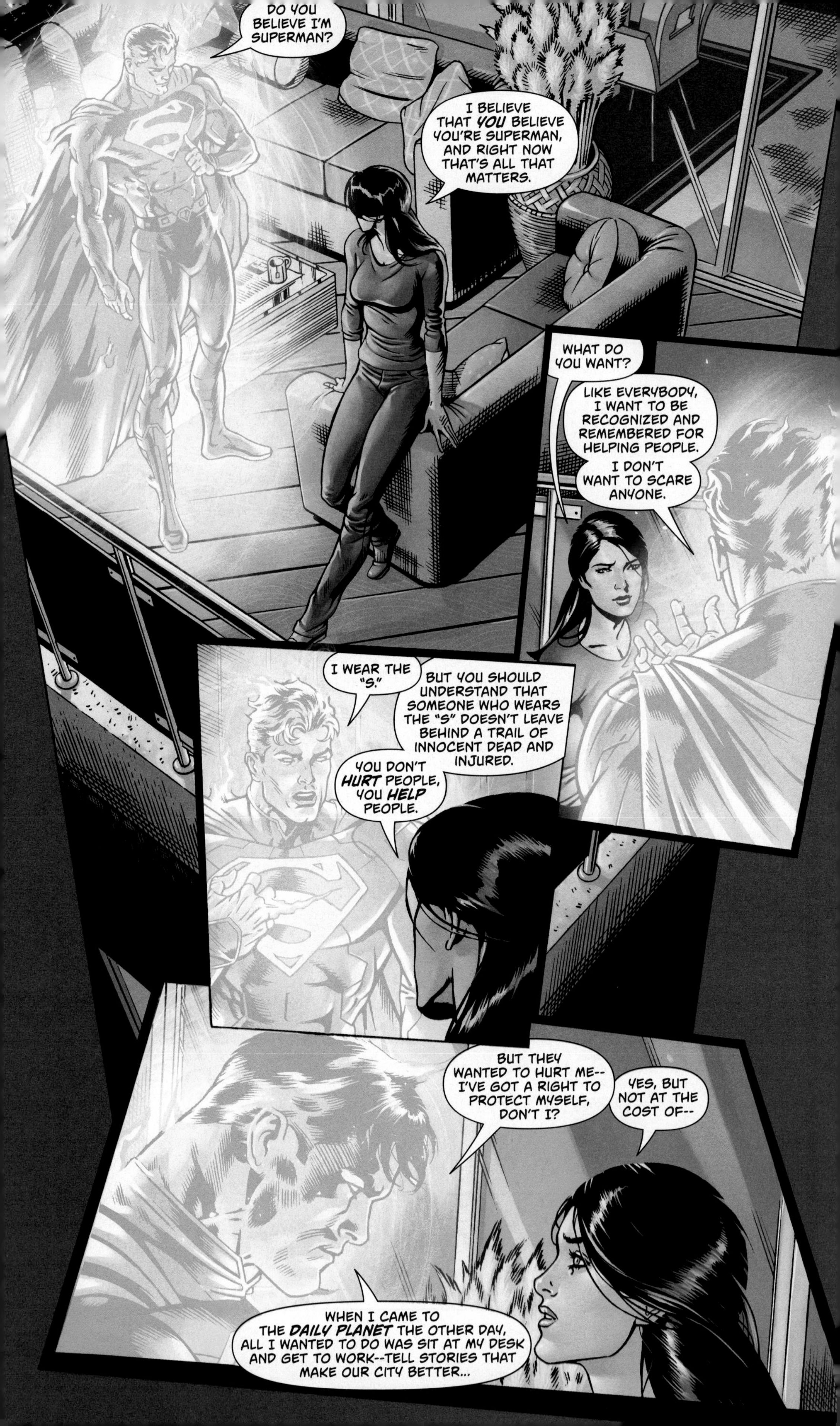
DO YOU BELIEVE I'M SUPERMAN?
I BELIEVE THAT *YOU* BELIEVE YOU'RE SUPERMAN, AND RIGHT NOW THAT'S ALL THAT MATTERS.
WHAT DO YOU WANT?
LIKE EVERYBODY, I WANT TO BE RECOGNIZED AND REMEMBERED FOR HELPING PEOPLE.
I DON'T WANT TO SCARE ANYONE.
I WEAR THE "S."
BUT YOU SHOULD UNDERSTAND THAT SOMEONE WHO WEARS THE "S" DOESN'T LEAVE BEHIND A TRAIL OF INNOCENT DEAD AND INJURED.
YOU DON'T *HURT* PEOPLE, YOU *HELP* PEOPLE.
BUT THEY WANTED TO HURT ME--I'VE GOT A RIGHT TO PROTECT MYSELF, DON'T I?
YES, BUT NOT AT THE COST OF--
WHEN I CAME TO THE *DAILY PLANET* THE OTHER DAY, ALL I WANTED TO DO WAS SIT AT MY DESK AND GET TO WORK--TELL STORIES THAT MAKE OUR CITY BETTER...

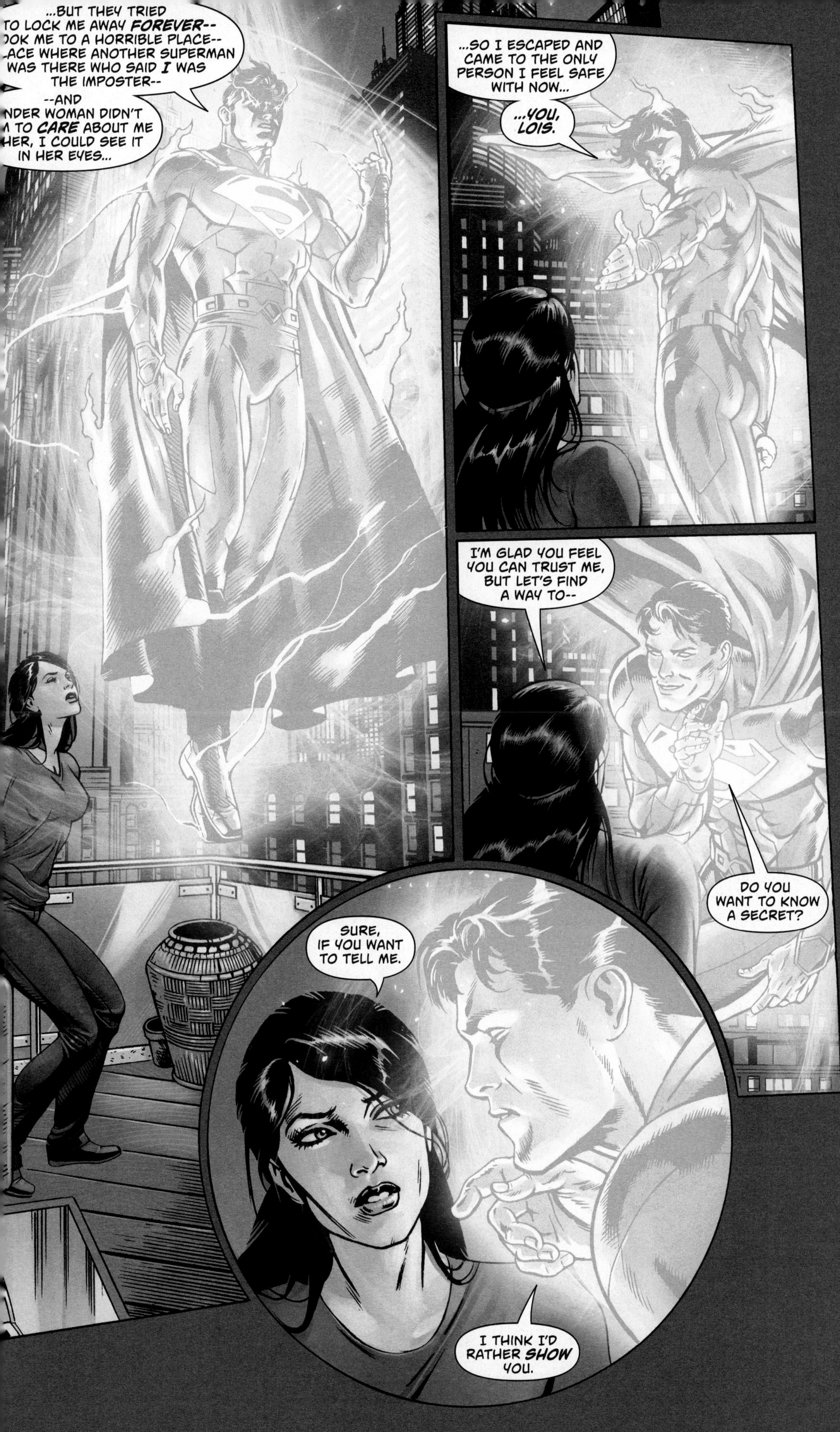
...BUT THEY TRIED TO LOCK ME AWAY FOREVER-- OOK ME TO A HORRIBLE PLACE-- ACE WHERE ANOTHER SUPERMAN WAS THERE WHO SAID I WAS THE IMPOSTER--
--AND NDER WOMAN DIDN'T TO CARE ABOUT ME HER, I COULD SEE IT IN HER EYES...
...SO I ESCAPED AND CAME TO THE ONLY PERSON I FEEL SAFE WITH NOW...
...YOU, LOIS.
I'M GLAD YOU FEEL YOU CAN TRUST ME, BUT LET'S FIND A WAY TO--
DO YOU WANT TO KNOW A SECRET?
SURE, IF YOU WANT TO TELL ME.
I THINK I'D RATHER SHOW YOU.

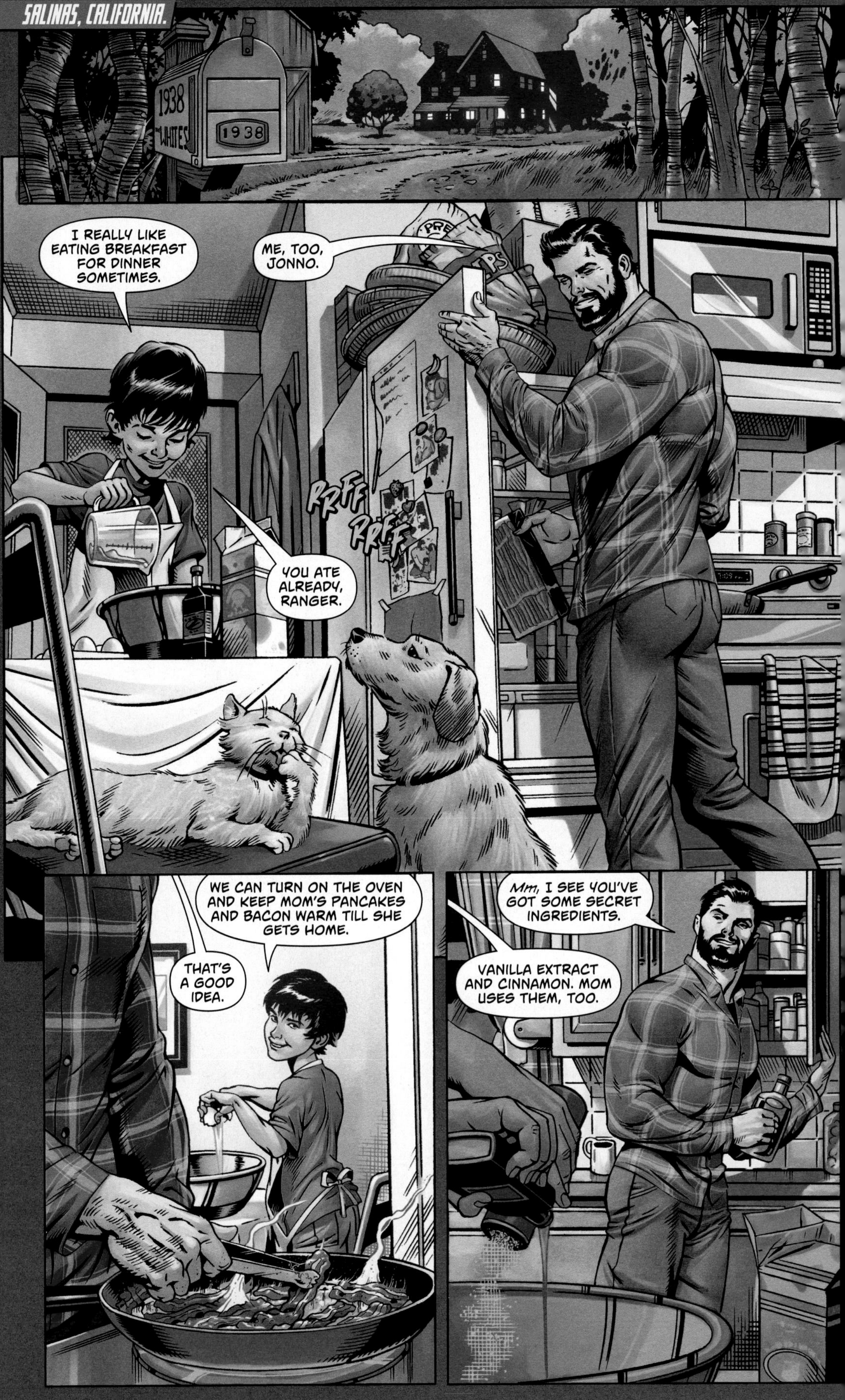
SALINAS, CALIFORNIA.
1938
WHITES
1938
I REALLY LIKE EATING BREAKFAST FOR DINNER SOMETIMES.
ME, TOO, JONNO.
RRFF RRFF
YOU ATE ALREADY, RANGER.
WE CAN TURN ON THE OVEN AND KEEP MOM'S PANCAKES AND BACON WARM TILL SHE GETS HOME.
THAT'S A GOOD IDEA.
Mm, I SEE YOU'VE GOT SOME SECRET INGREDIENTS.
VANILLA EXTRACT AND CINNAMON. MOM USES THEM, TOO.

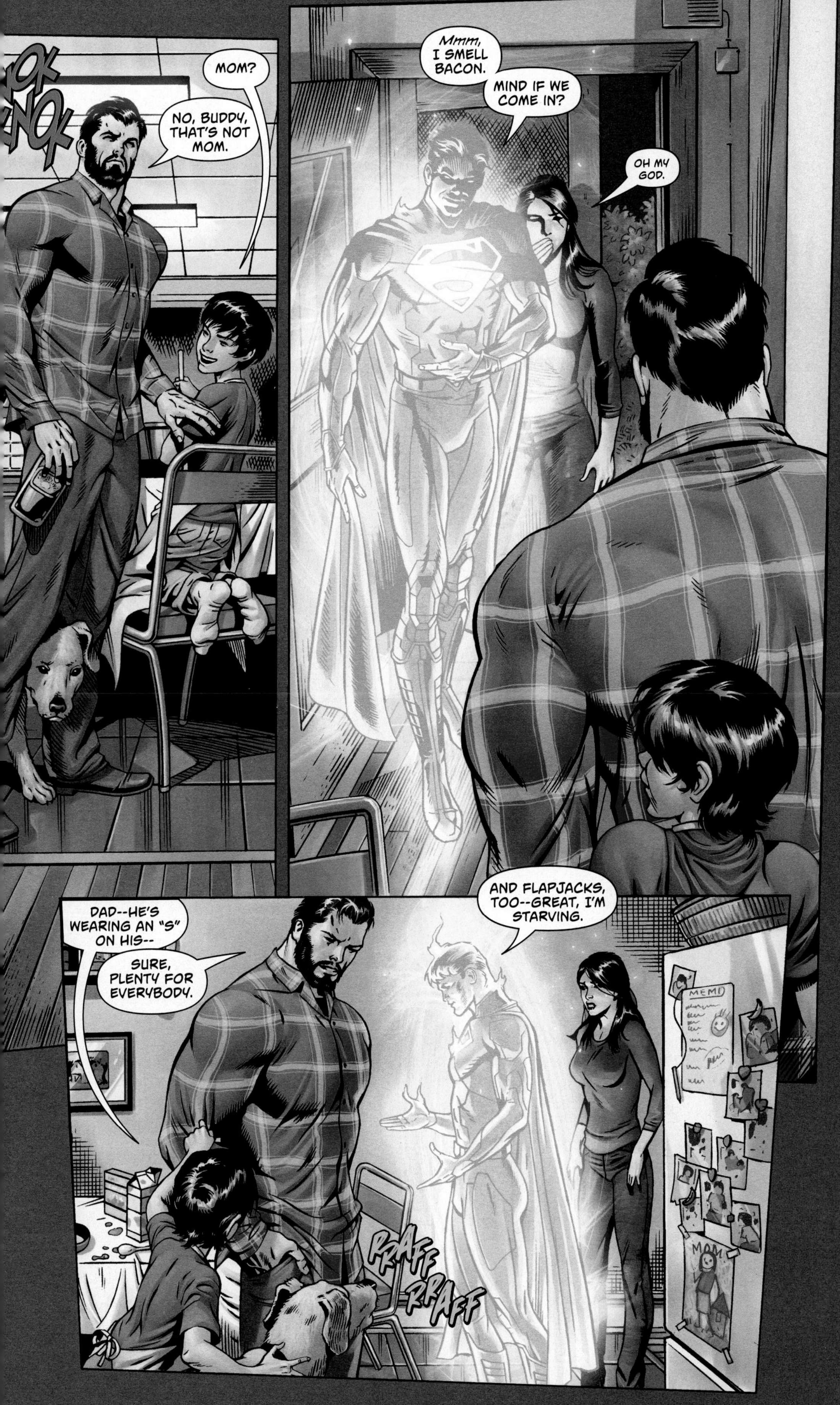
KNOK KNOK
MOM?
NO, BUDDY, THAT'S NOT MOM.
Mmm, I SMELL BACON.
MIND IF WE COME IN?
OH MY GOD.
DAD--HE'S WEARING AN "S" ON HIS--
SURE, PLENTY FOR EVERYBODY.
AND FLAPJACKS, TOO--GREAT, I'M STARVING.
RRAFF RRAFF
MEMO
MOM

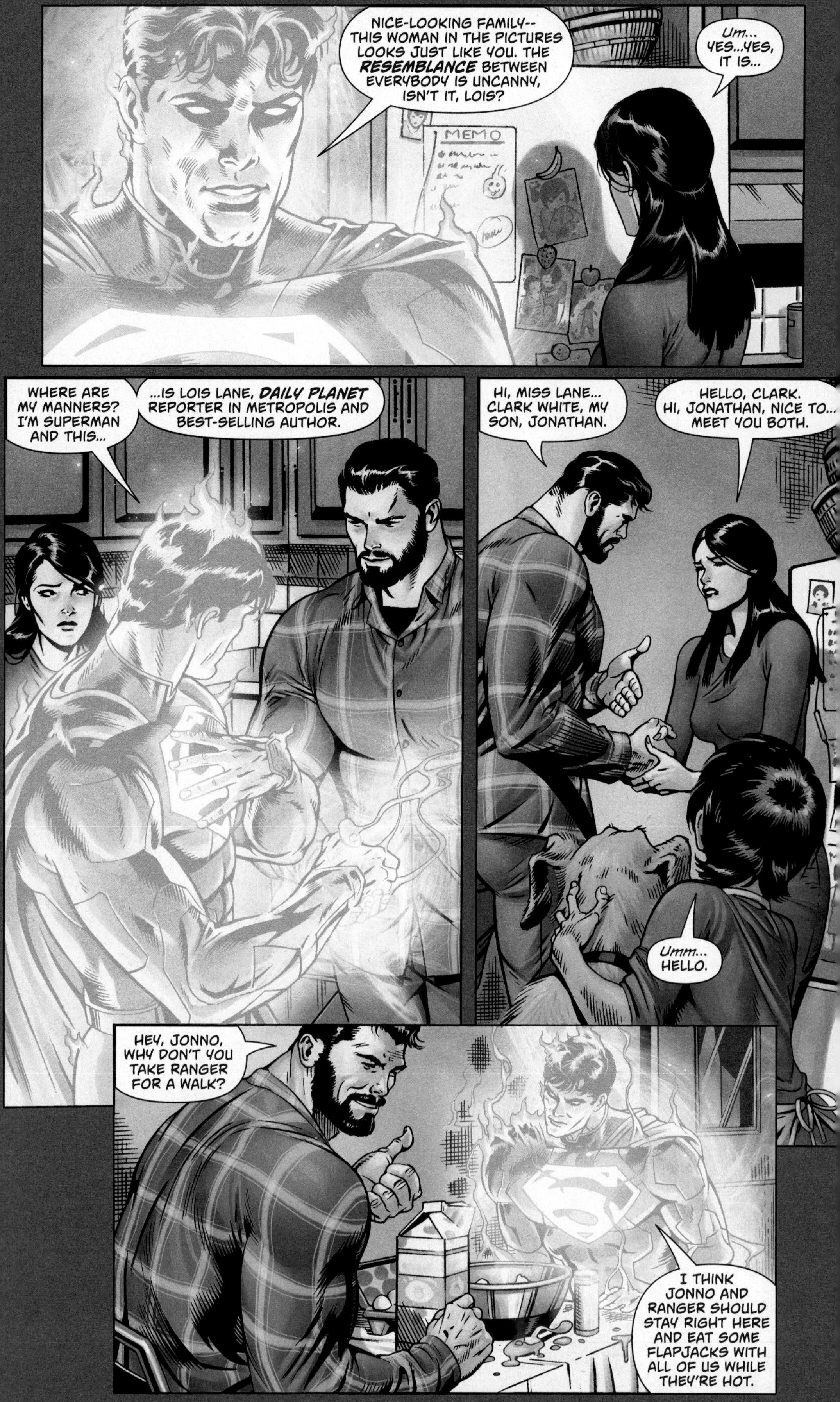
NICE-LOOKING FAMILY-- THIS WOMAN IN THE PICTURES LOOKS JUST LIKE YOU. THE RESEMBLANCE BETWEEN EVERYBODY IS UNCANNY, ISN'T IT, LOIS?
Um... YES...YES, IT IS...
MEMO
WHERE ARE MY MANNERS? I'M SUPERMAN AND THIS...
...IS LOIS LANE, DAILY PLANET REPORTER IN METROPOLIS AND BEST-SELLING AUTHOR.
HI, MISS LANE... CLARK WHITE, MY SON, JONATHAN.
HELLO, CLARK. HI, JONATHAN, NICE TO... MEET YOU BOTH.
Umm... HELLO.
HEY, JONNO, WHY DON'T YOU TAKE RANGER FOR A WALK?
I THINK JONNO AND RANGER SHOULD STAY RIGHT HERE AND EAT SOME FLAPJACKS WITH ALL OF US WHILE THEY'RE HOT.

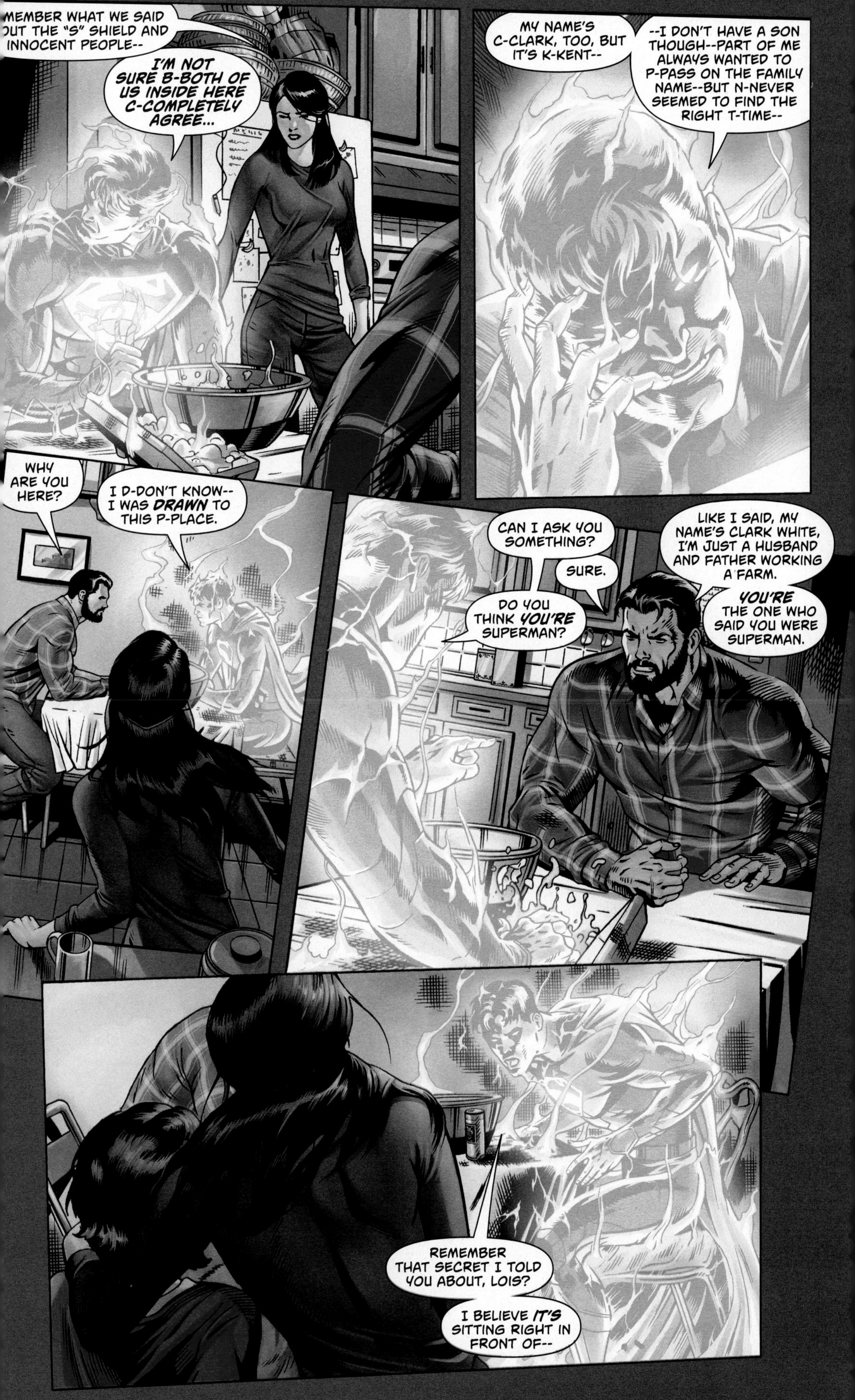
MEMBER WHAT WE SAID
OUT THE "S" SHIELD AND
INNOCENT PEOPLE--
I'M NOT SURE B-BOTH OF US INSIDE HERE C-COMPLETELY AGREE...
MY NAME'S C-CLARK, TOO, BUT IT'S K-KENT--
--I DON'T HAVE A SON THOUGH--PART OF ME ALWAYS WANTED TO P-PASS ON THE FAMILY NAME--BUT N-NEVER SEEMED TO FIND THE RIGHT T-TIME--
WHY ARE YOU HERE?
I D-DON'T KNOW-- I WAS DRAWN TO THIS P-PLACE.
CAN I ASK YOU SOMETHING?
SURE.
DO YOU THINK YOU'RE SUPERMAN?
LIKE I SAID, MY NAME'S CLARK WHITE, I'M JUST A HUSBAND AND FATHER WORKING A FARM.
YOU'RE THE ONE WHO SAID YOU WERE SUPERMAN.
REMEMBER THAT SECRET I TOLD YOU ABOUT, LOIS?
I BELIEVE IT'S SITTING RIGHT IN FRONT OF--

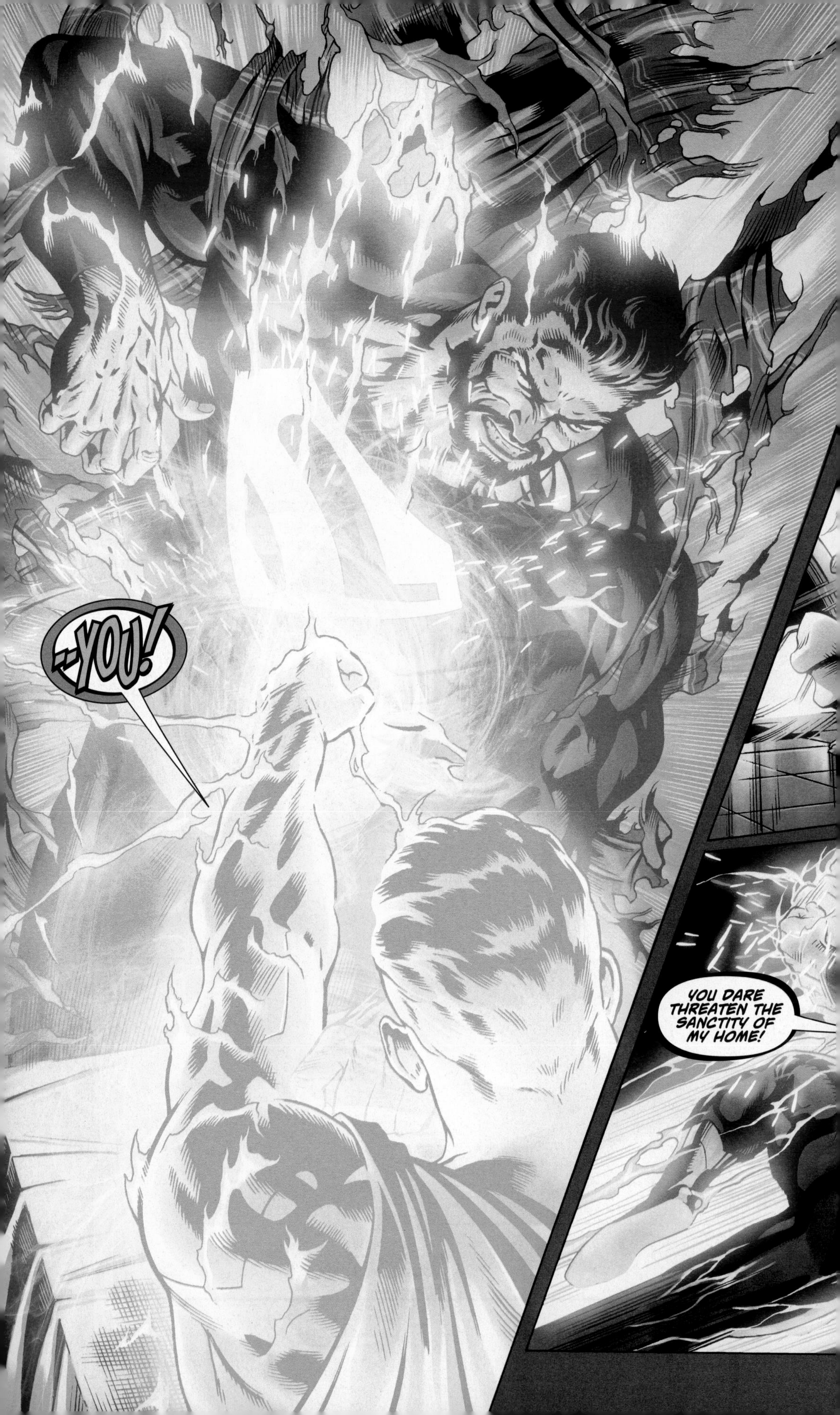

--YOU!
YOU DARE THREATEN THE SANCTITY OF MY HOME!

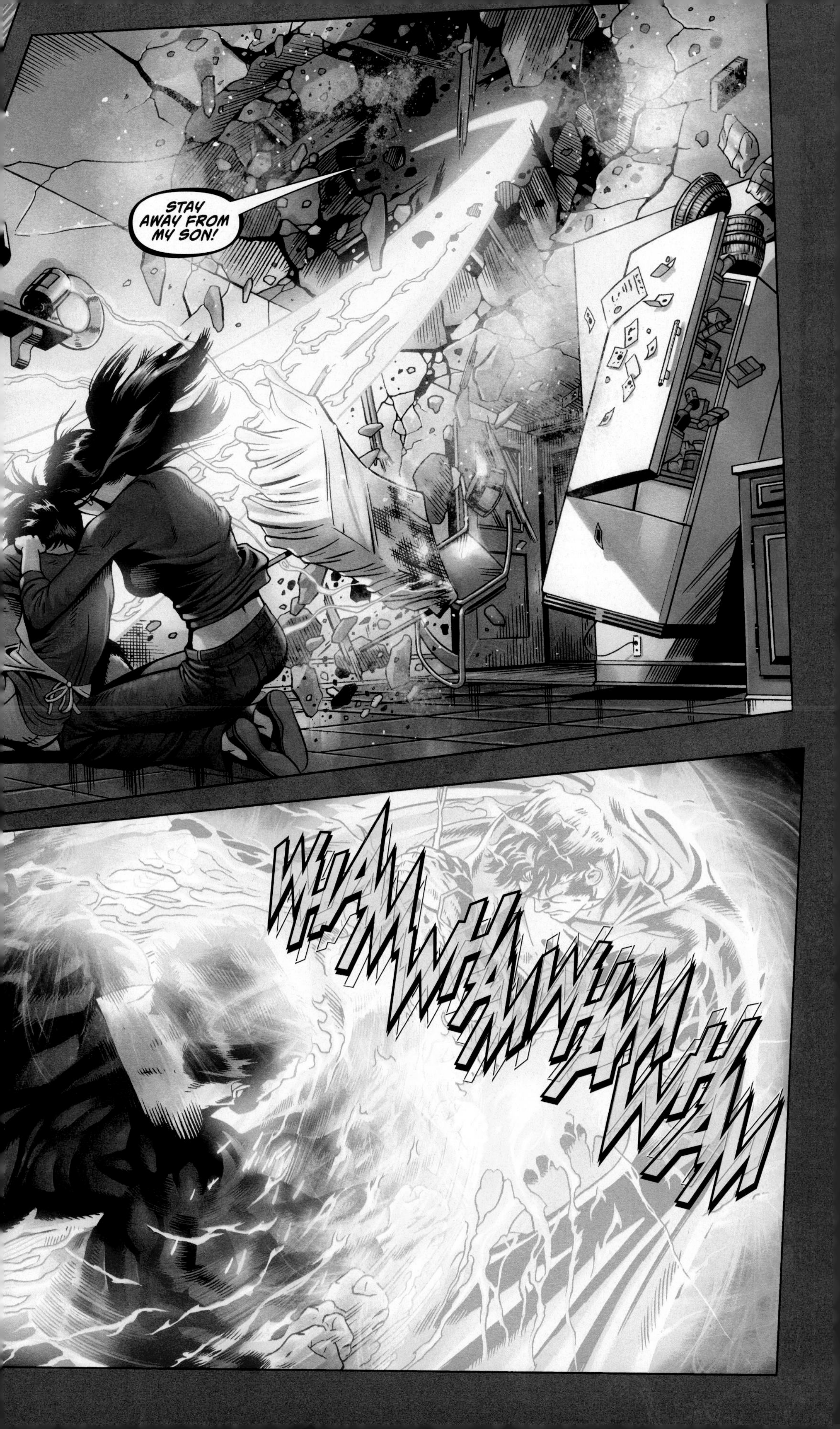
STAY AWAY FROM MY SON!
WHAMWHAMWHAMWHAM

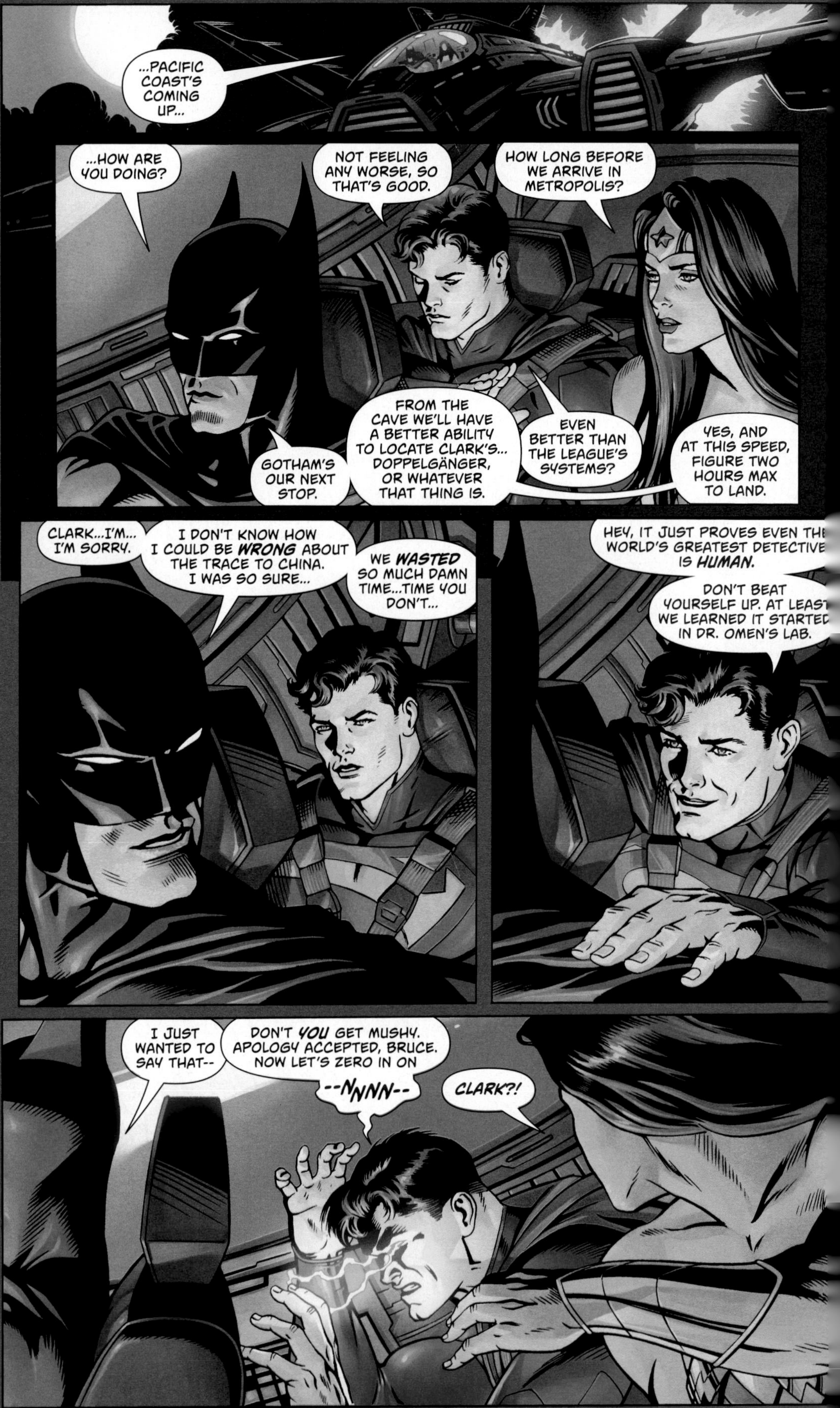
...PACIFIC COAST'S COMING UP...
...HOW ARE YOU DOING?
NOT FEELING ANY WORSE, SO THAT'S GOOD.
HOW LONG BEFORE WE ARRIVE IN METROPOLIS?
YES, AND AT THIS SPEED, FIGURE TWO HOURS MAX TO LAND.
GOTHAM'S OUR NEXT STOP.
FROM THE CAVE WE'LL HAVE A BETTER ABILITY TO LOCATE CLARK'S... DOPPELGÄNGER, OR WHATEVER THAT THING IS.
EVEN BETTER THAN THE LEAGUE'S SYSTEMS?
CLARK...I'M... I'M SORRY.
I DON'T KNOW HOW I COULD BE WRONG ABOUT THE TRACE TO CHINA. I WAS SO SURE...
WE WASTED SO MUCH DAMN TIME...TIME YOU DON'T...
HEY, IT JUST PROVES EVEN THE WORLD'S GREATEST DETECTIVE IS HUMAN.
DON'T BEAT YOURSELF UP. AT LEAST WE LEARNED IT STARTED IN DR. OMEN'S LAB.
I JUST WANTED TO SAY THAT--
DON'T YOU GET MUSHY. APOLOGY ACCEPTED, BRUCE. NOW LET'S ZERO IN ON
--NNNN--
CLARK?!

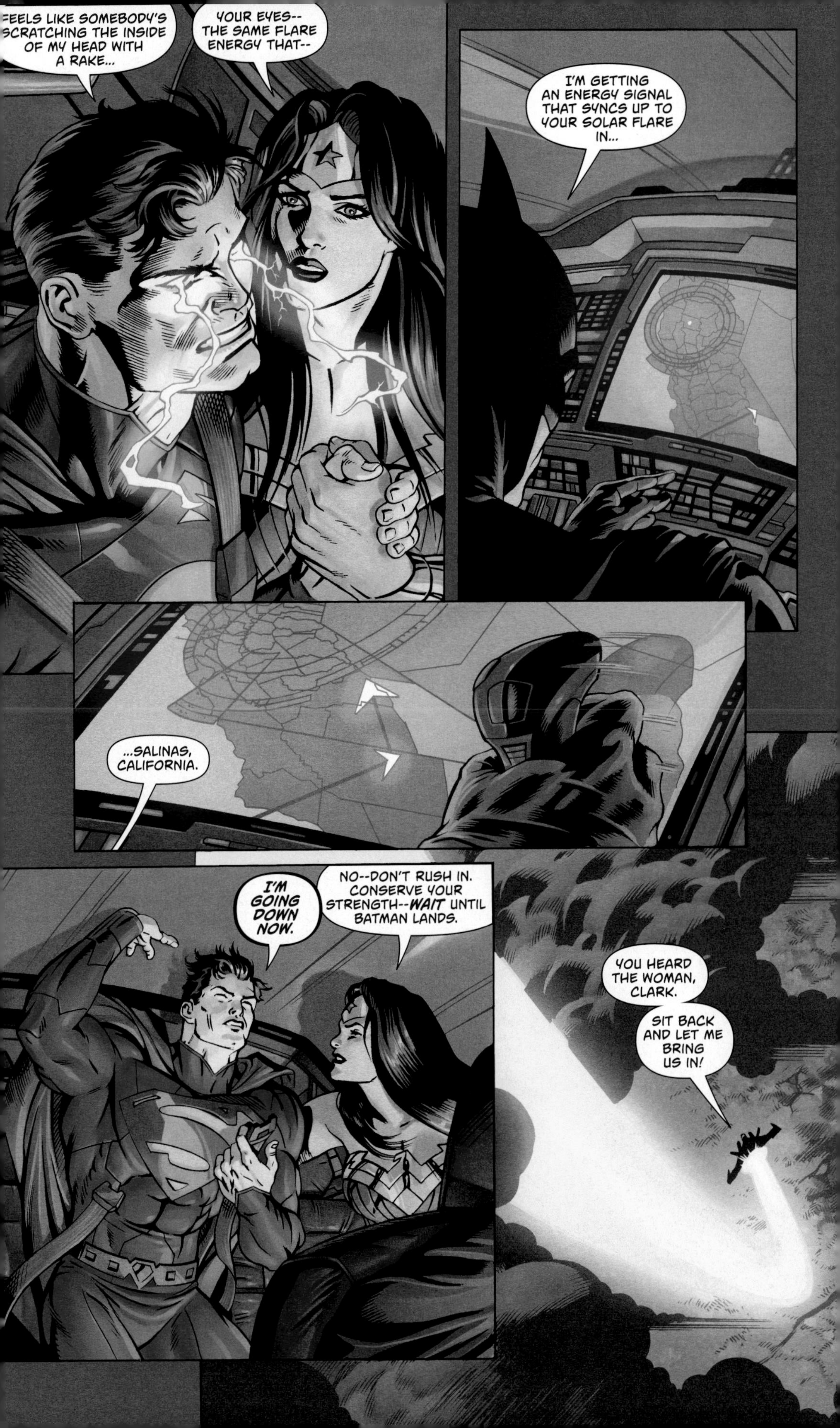
FEELS LIKE SOMEBODY'S SCRATCHING THE INSIDE OF MY HEAD WITH A RAKE...
YOUR EYES-- THE SAME FLARE ENERGY THAT--
I'M GETTING AN ENERGY SIGNAL THAT SYNCS UP TO YOUR SOLAR FLARE IN...
...SALINAS, CALIFORNIA.
I'M GOING DOWN NOW.
NO--DON'T RUSH IN. CONSERVE YOUR STRENGTH--WAIT UNTIL BATMAN LANDS.
YOU HEARD THE WOMAN, CLARK.
SIT BACK AND LET ME BRING US IN!

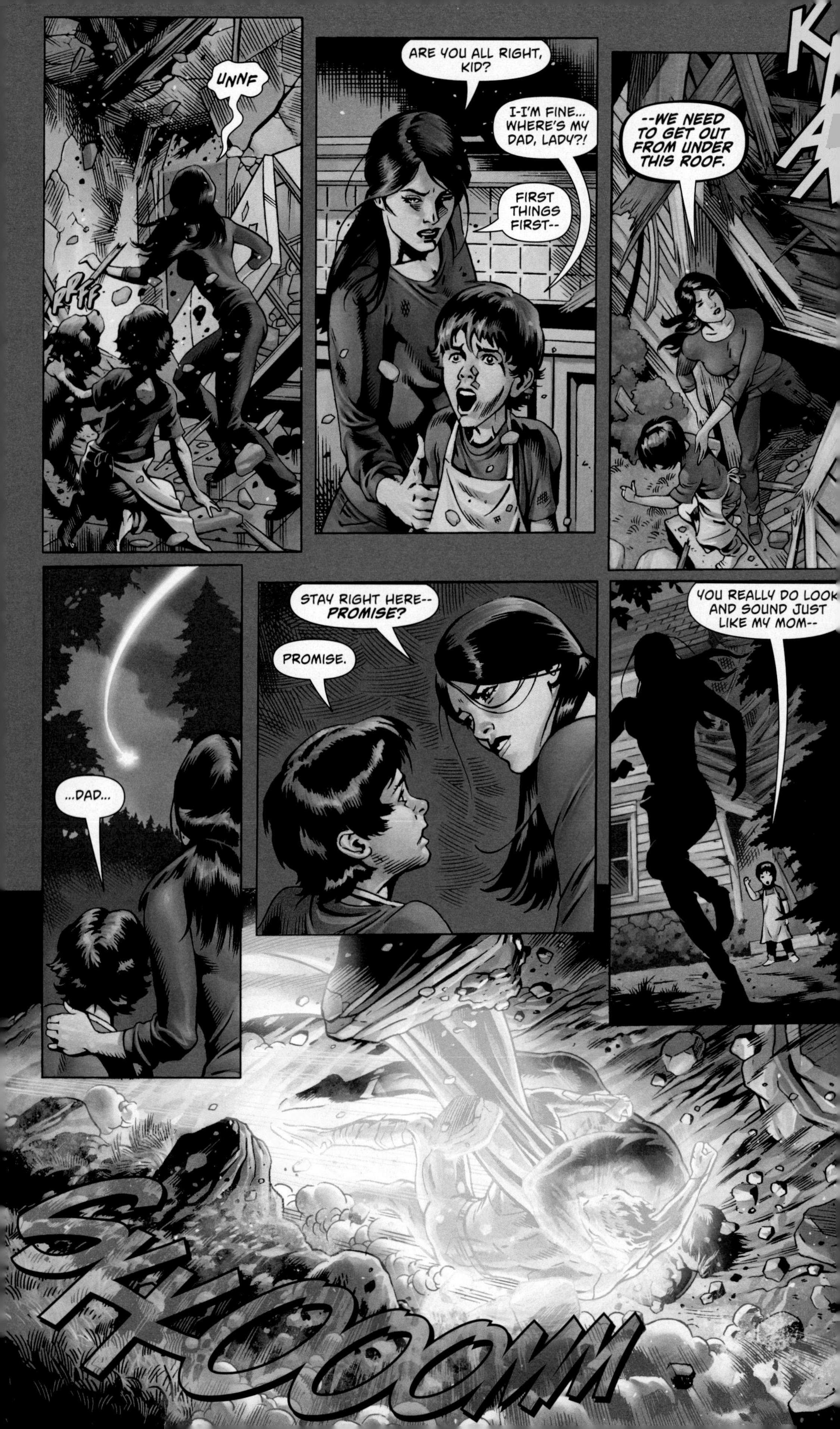
UNNF
KRFF
ARE YOU ALL RIGHT, KID?
I-I'M FINE... WHERE'S MY DAD, LADY?!
FIRST THINGS FIRST--
--WE NEED TO GET OUT FROM UNDER THIS ROOF.
STAY RIGHT HERE-- PROMISE?
PROMISE.
YOU REALLY DO LOOK AND SOUND JUST LIKE MY MOM--
...DAD...
SHWOOOMM

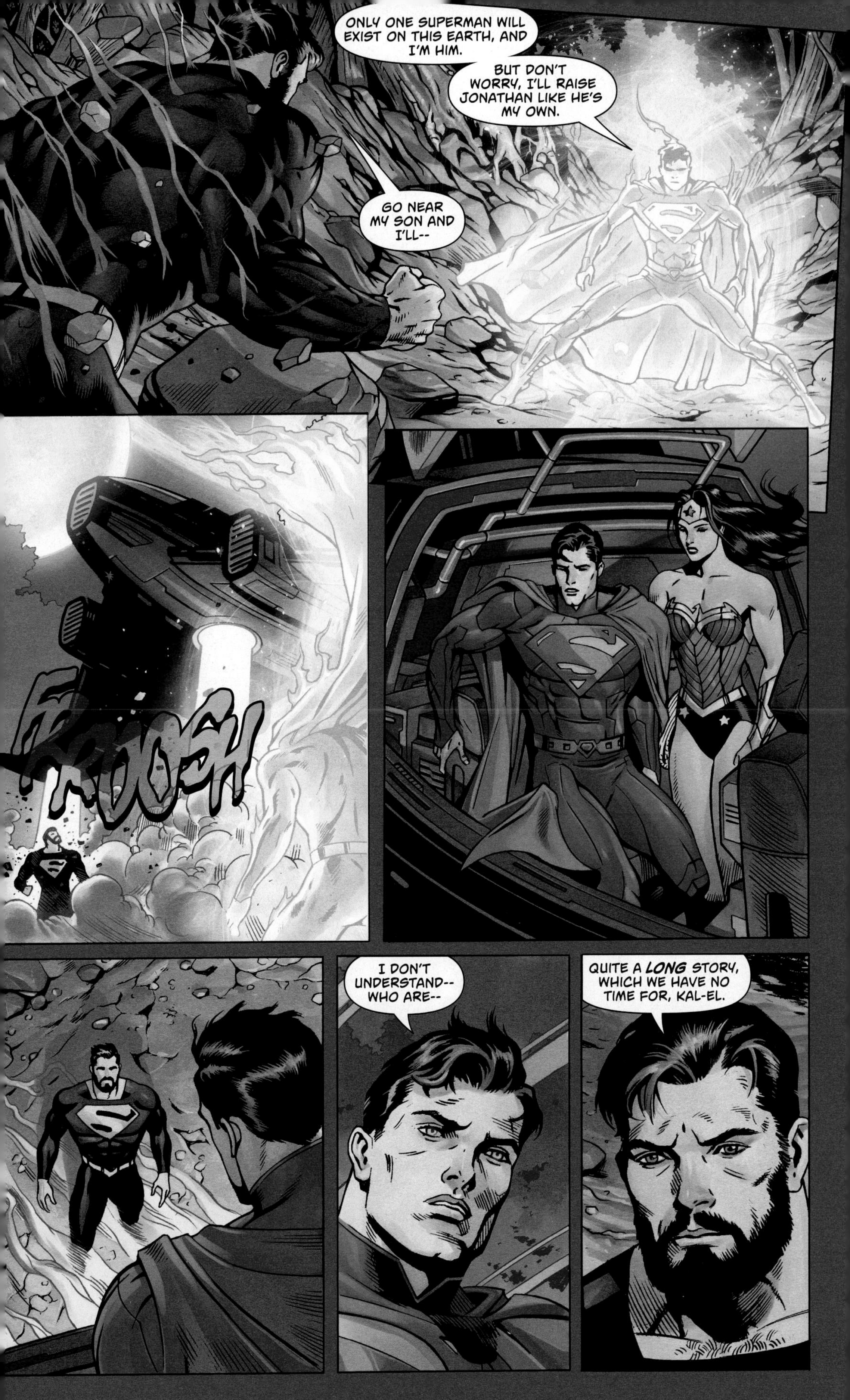
ONLY ONE SUPERMAN WILL EXIST ON THIS EARTH, AND I'M HIM.
BUT DON'T WORRY, I'LL RAISE JONATHAN LIKE HE'S MY OWN.
GO NEAR MY SON AND I'LL--
FROOSH
I DON'T UNDERSTAND-- WHO ARE--
QUITE A LONG STORY, WHICH WE HAVE NO TIME FOR, KAL-EL.

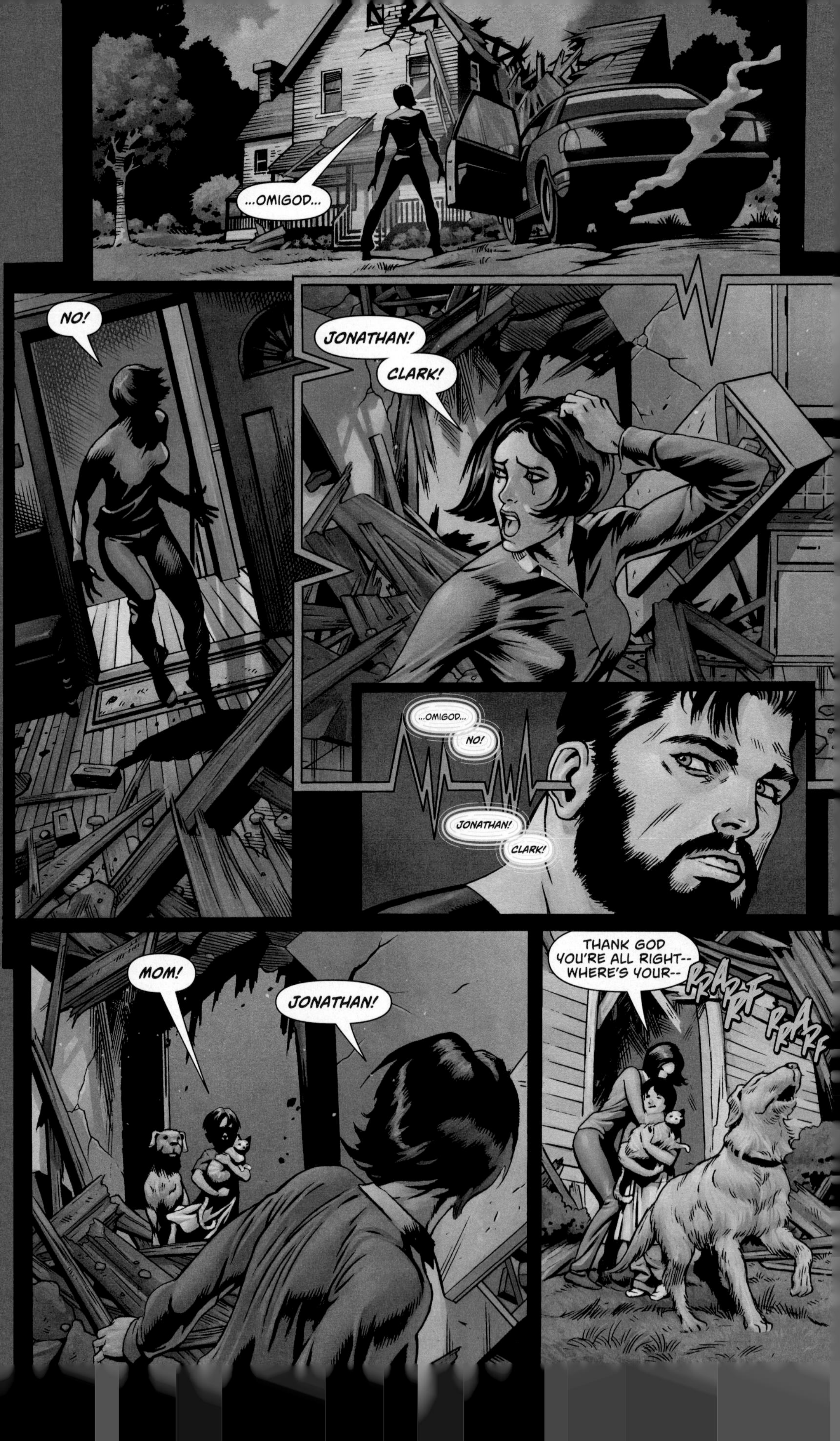
...OMIGOD...
NO!
JONATHAN!
CLARK!
...OMIGOD...
NO!
JONATHAN!
CLARK!
MOM!
JONATHAN!
THANK GOD YOU'RE ALL RIGHT-- WHERE'S YOUR--
RRARF RRARF

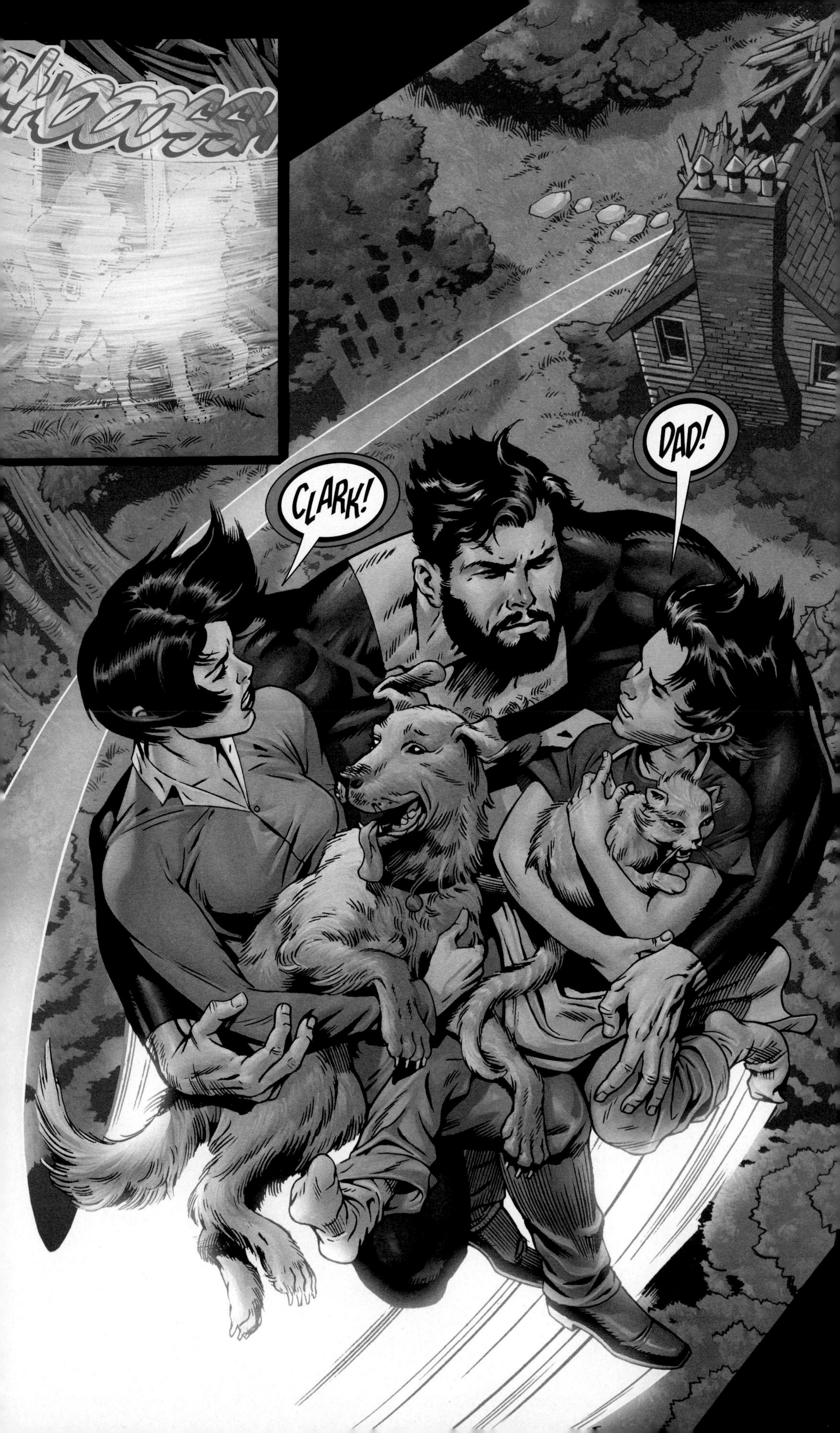
CLARK!
DAD!

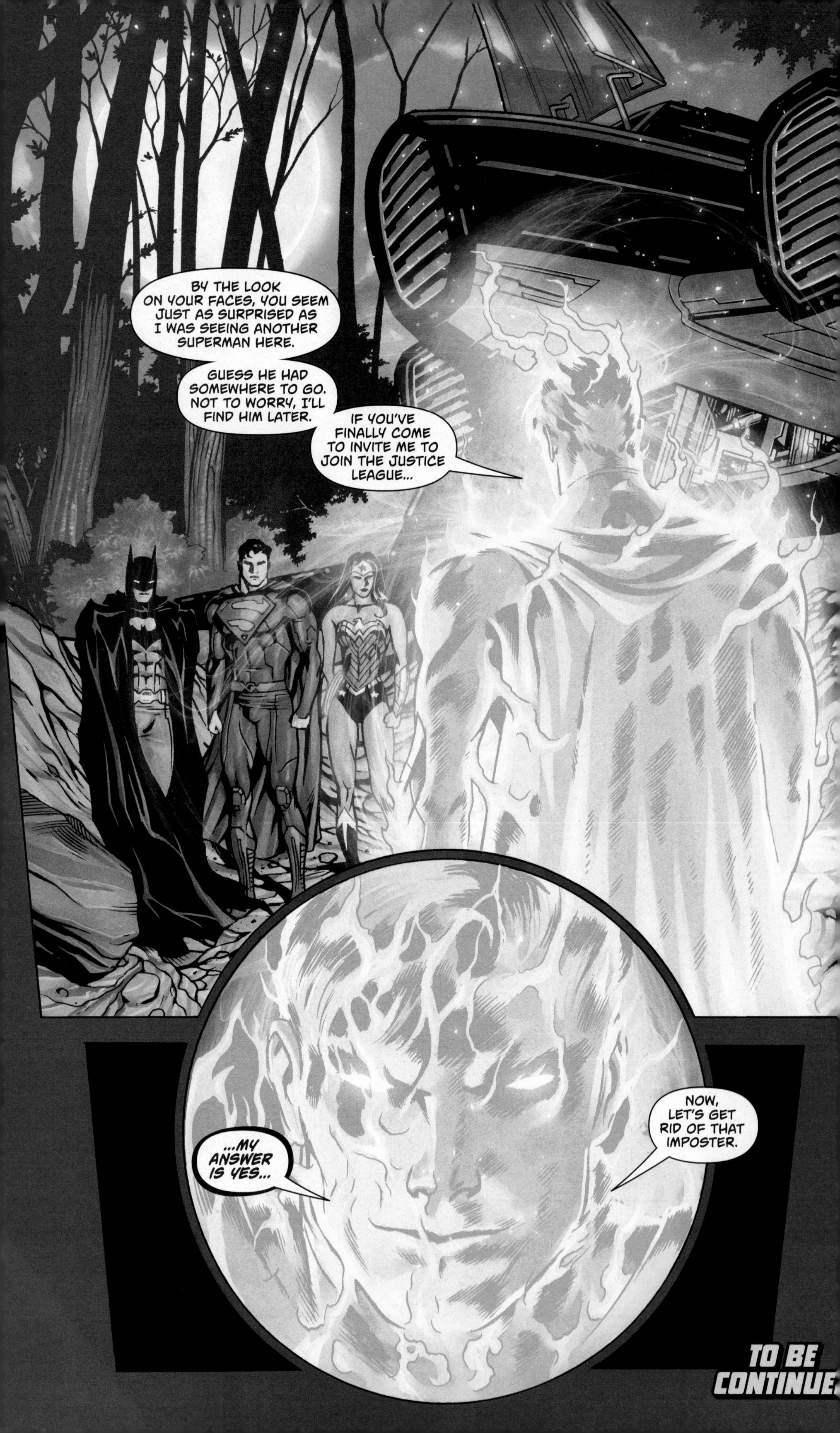
BY THE LOOK ON YOUR FACES, YOU SEEM JUST AS SURPRISED AS I WAS SEEING ANOTHER SUPERMAN HERE.
GUESS HE HAD SOMEWHERE TO GO. NOT TO WORRY, I'LL FIND HIM LATER.
IF YOU'VE FINALLY COME TO INVITE ME TO JOIN THE JUSTICE LEAGUE...
...MY ANSWER IS YES...
NOW, LET'S GET RID OF THAT IMPOSTER.
TO BE CONTINUE

VARIANT COVER GALLERY

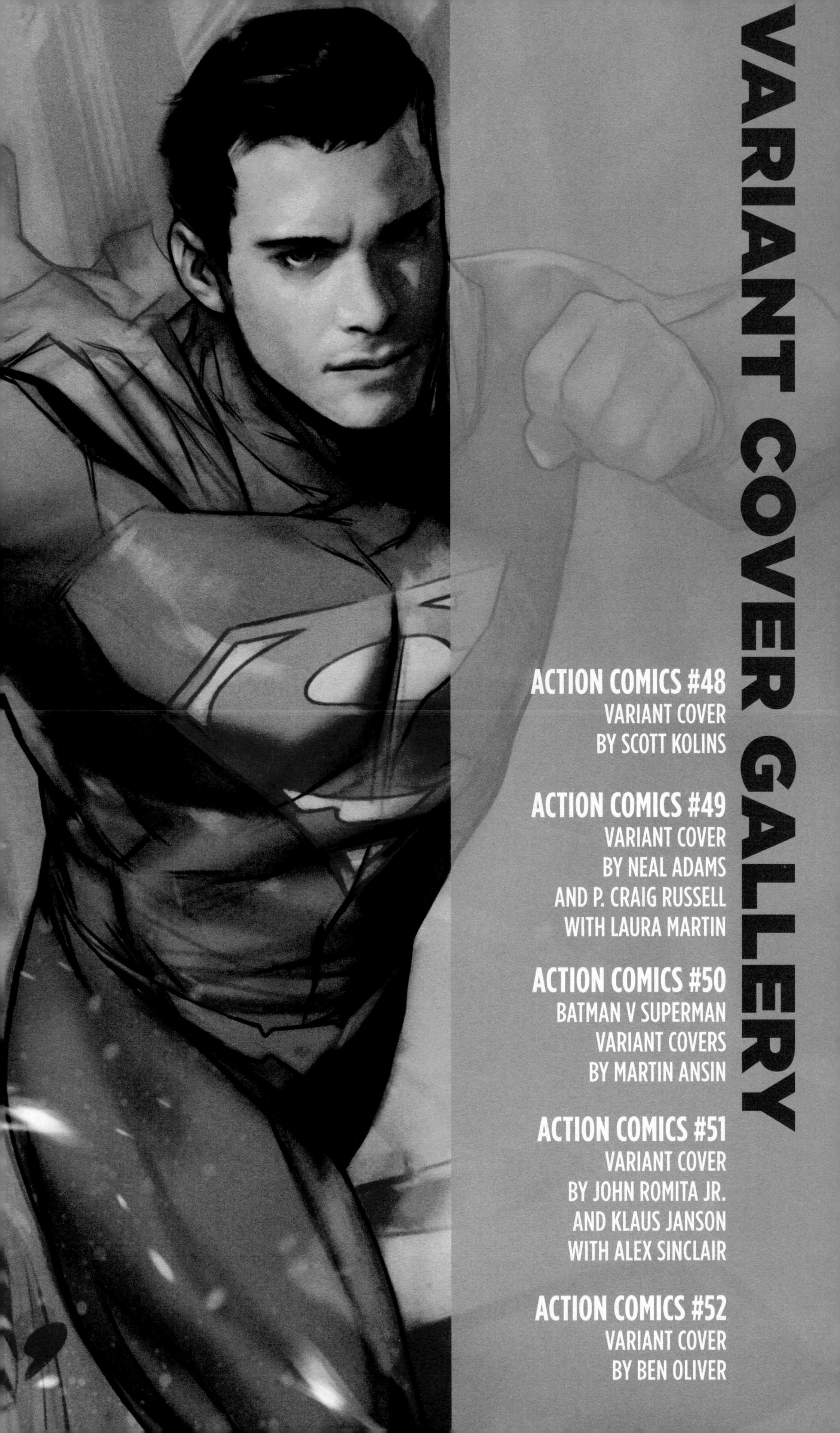

ACTION COMICS #48
VARIANT COVER
BY SCOTT KOLINS

ACTION COMICS #49
VARIANT COVER
BY NEAL ADAMS
AND P. CRAIG RUSSELL
WITH LAURA MARTIN

ACTION COMICS #50
BATMAN V SUPERMAN
VARIANT COVERS
BY MARTIN ANSIN

ACTION COMICS #51
VARIANT COVER
BY JOHN ROMITA JR.
AND KLAUS JANSON
WITH ALEX SINCLAIR

ACTION COMICS #52
VARIANT COVER
BY BEN OLIVER

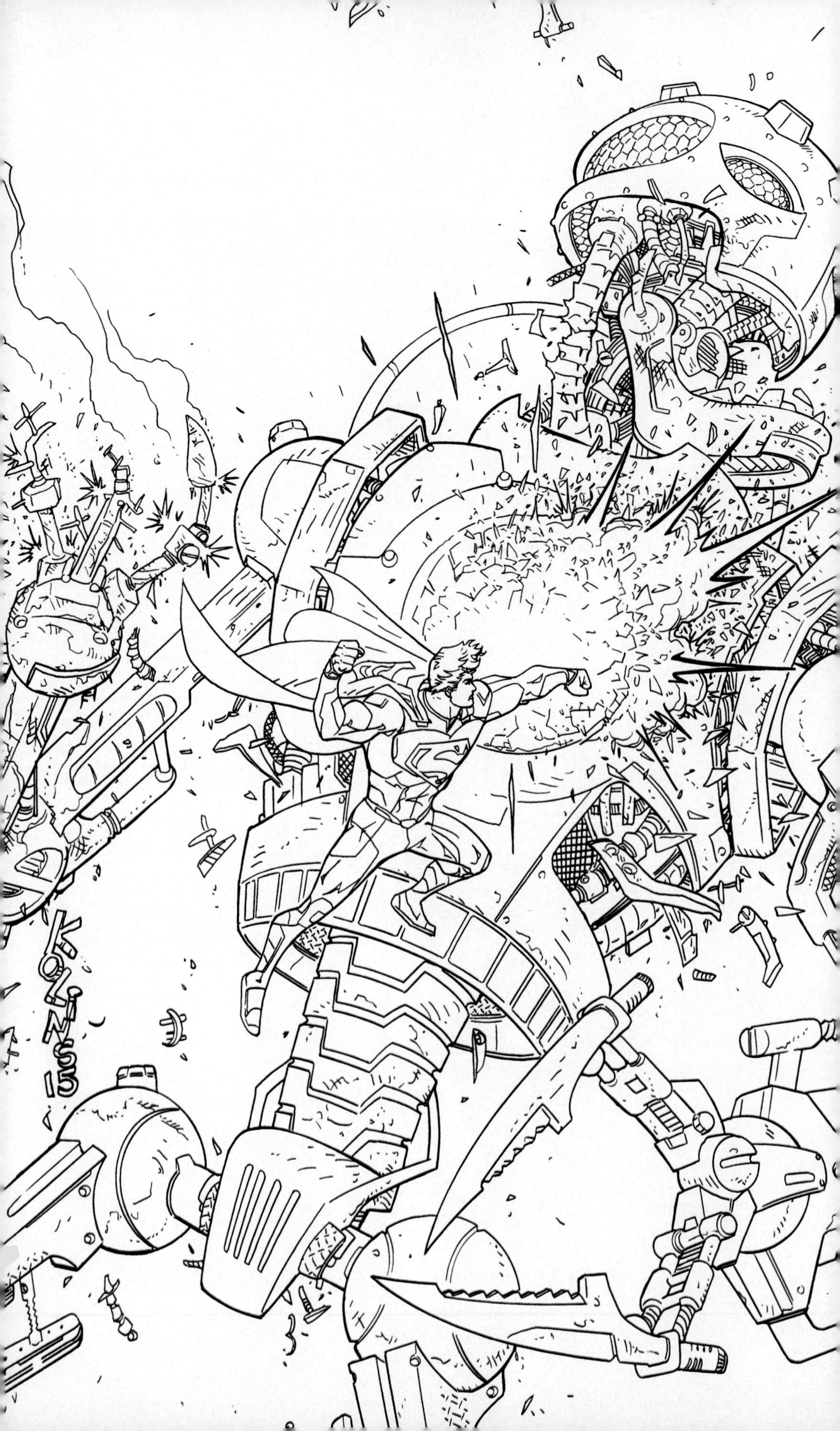

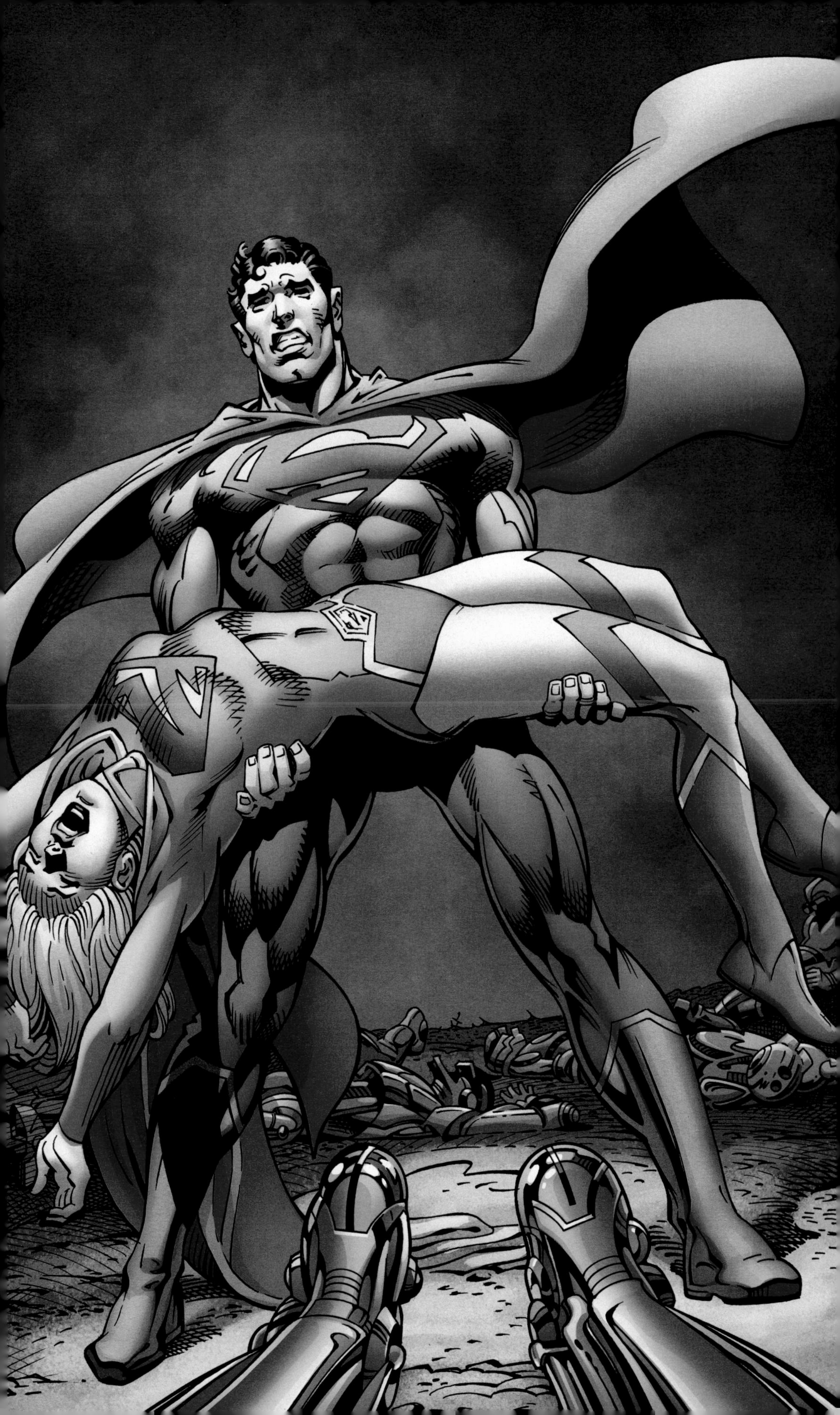

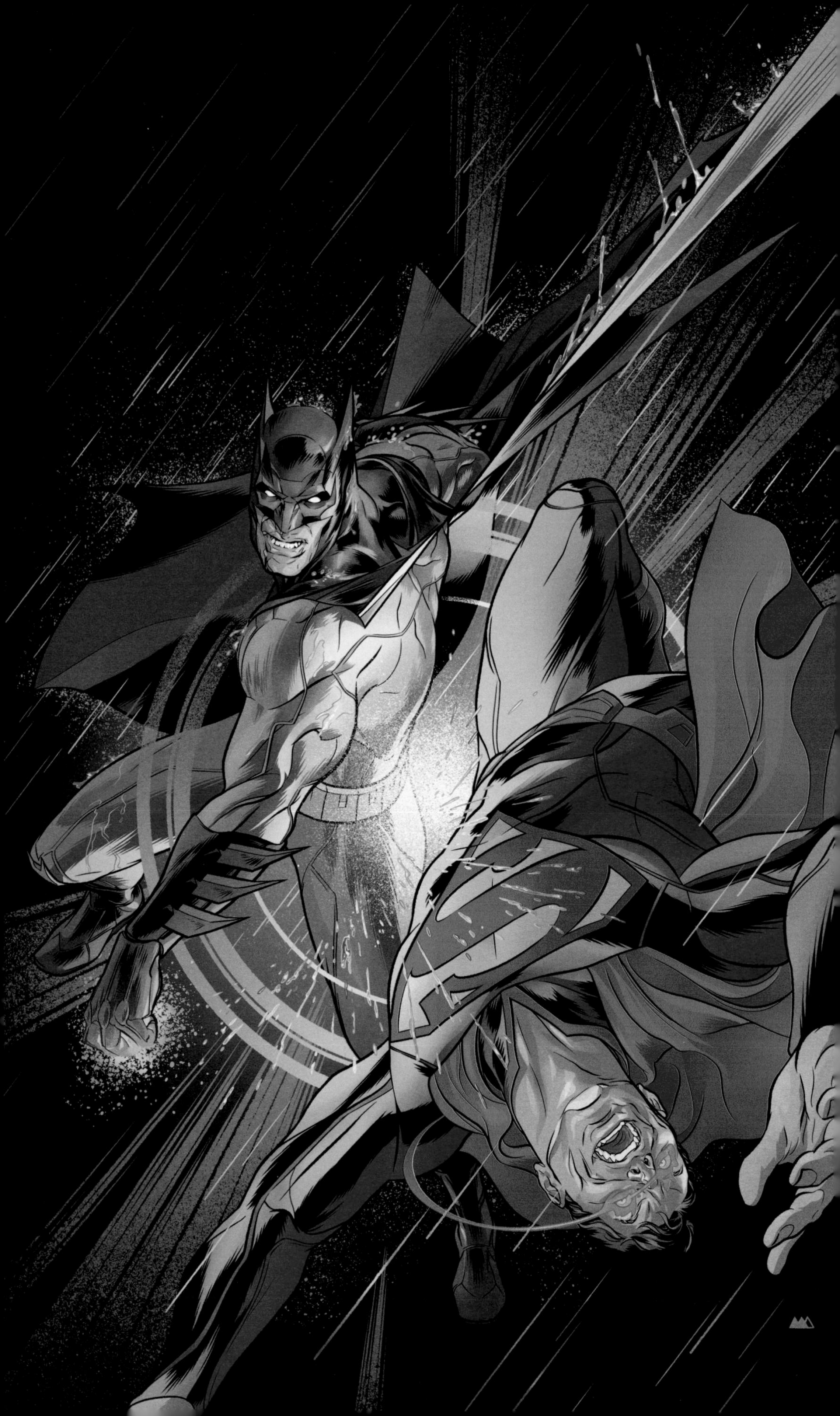

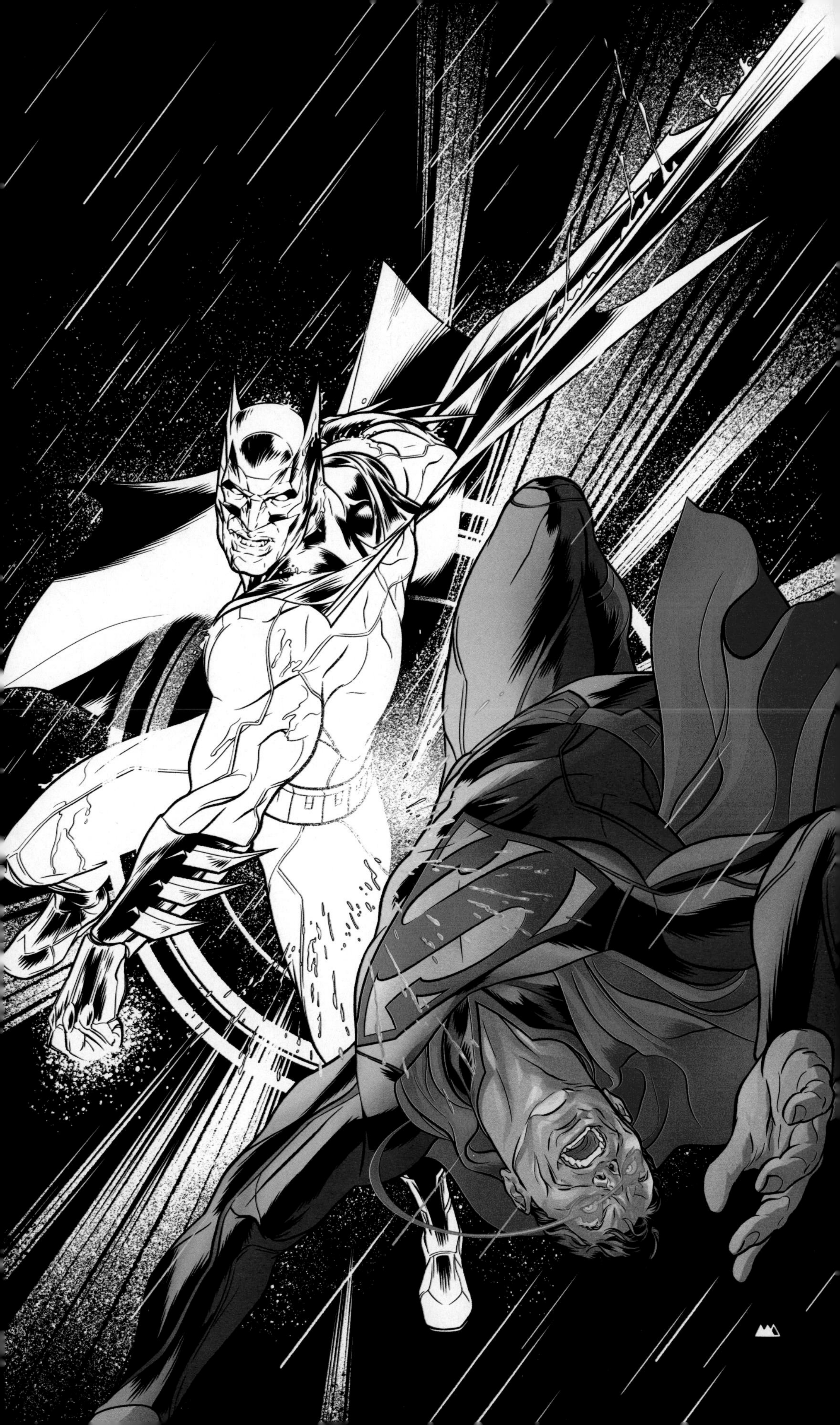

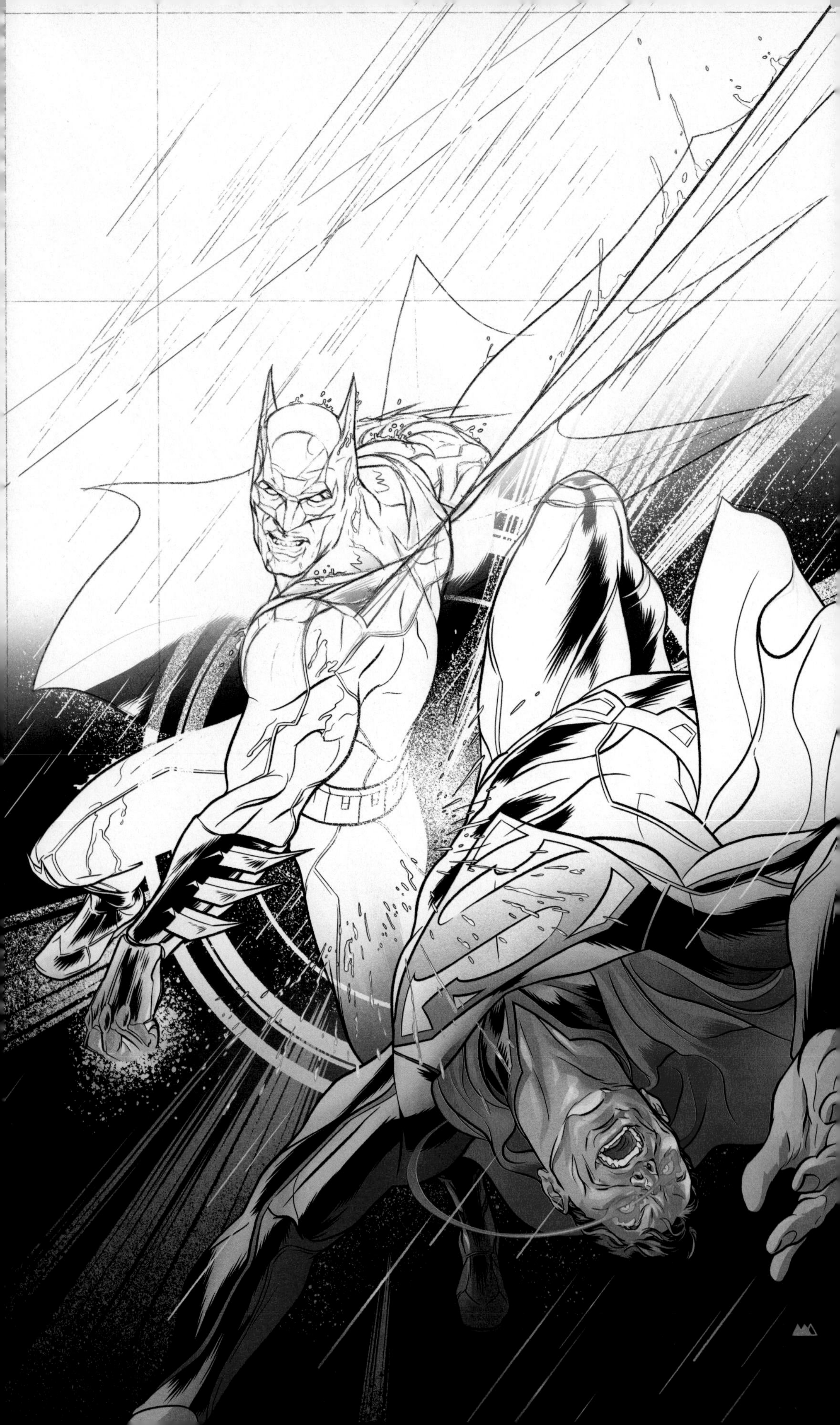

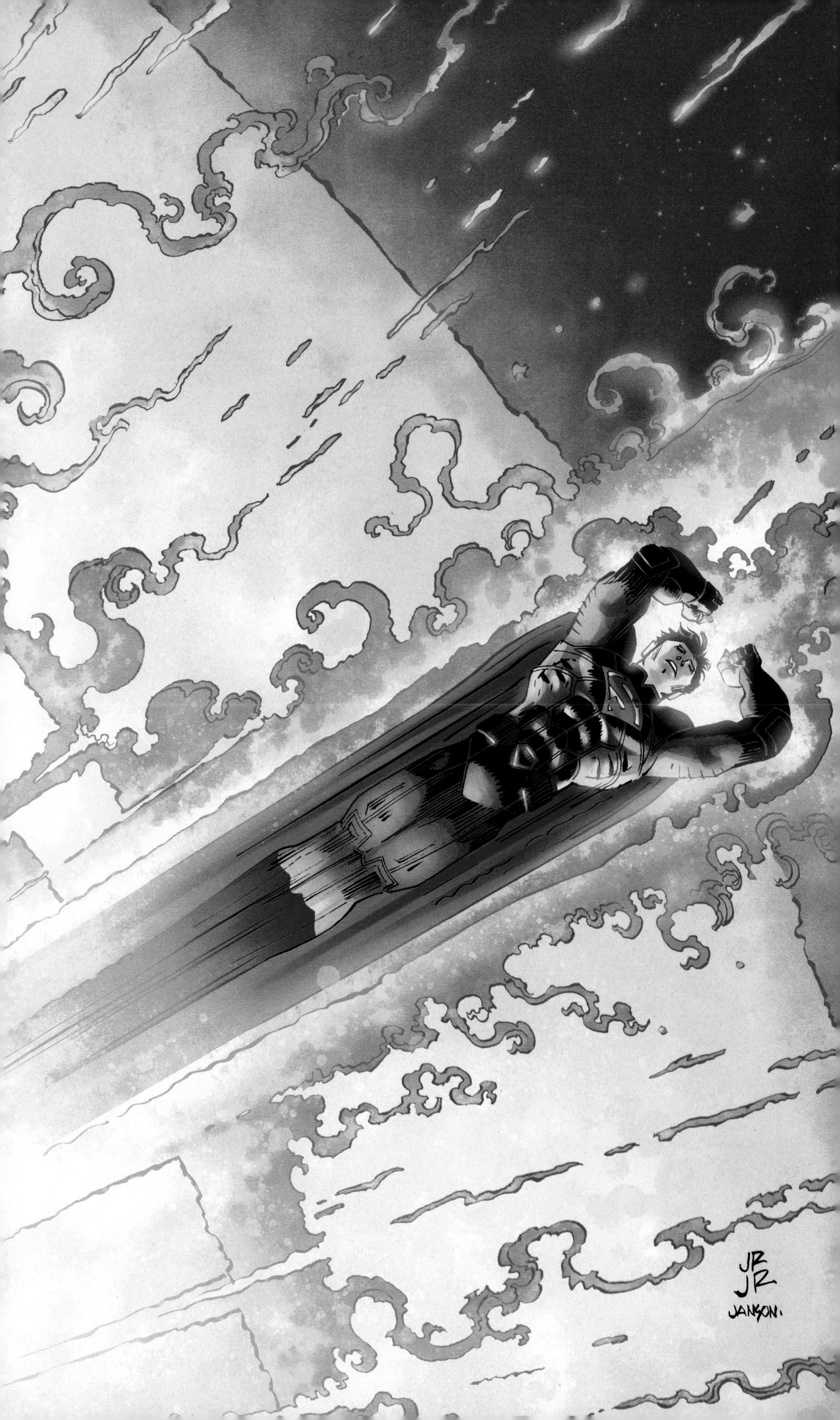
JR JR
JANSON.

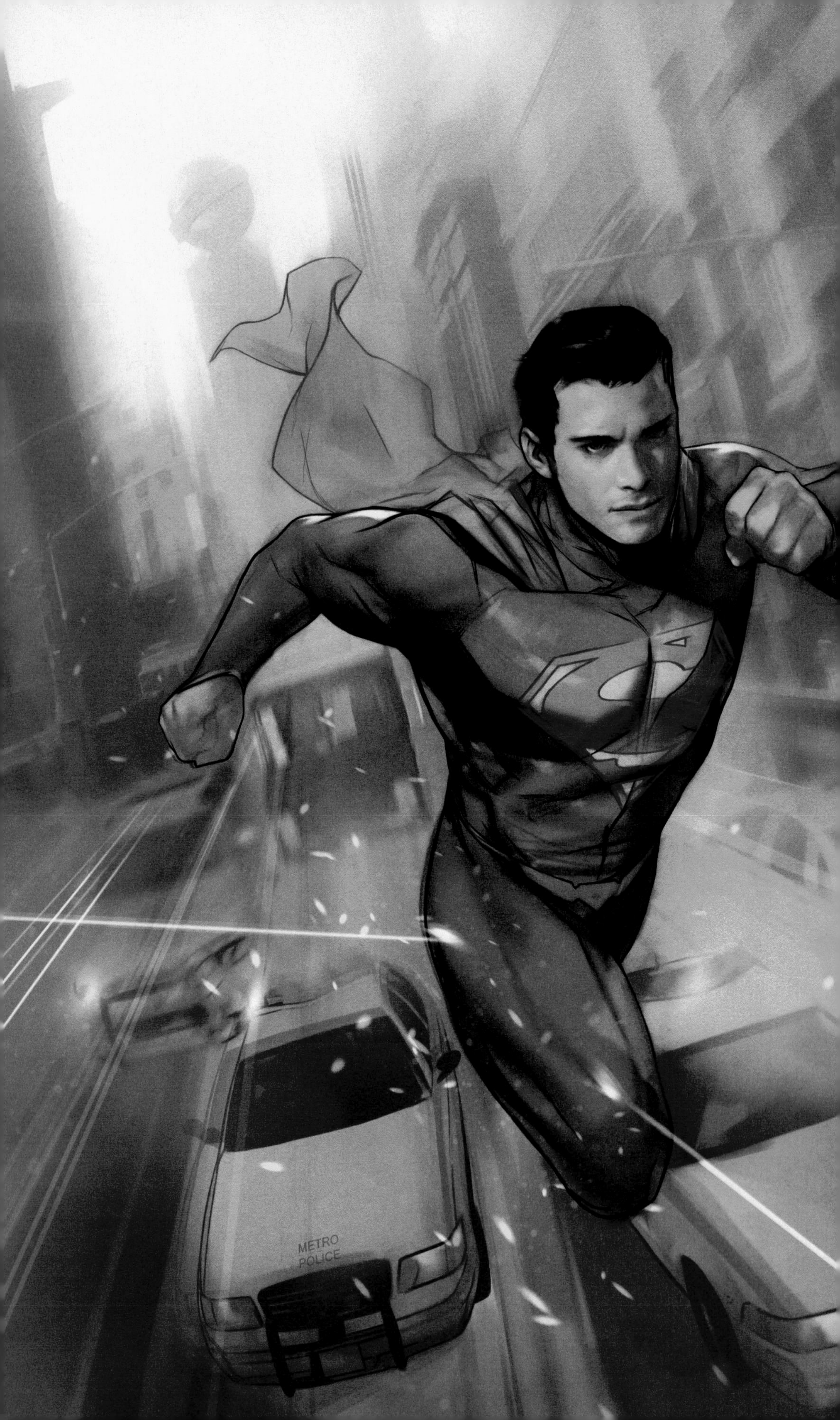
METRO
POLICE

"An invigorating, entertaining and modern take on the Man of Steel."
—VARIETY

"Grade: A-."
—ENTERTAINMENT WEEKLY

FROM THE WRITER OF *JUSTICE LEAGUE* & *GREEN LANTERN*

GEOFF JOHNS
with GARY FRANK

SUPERMAN: THE LAST SON OF KRYPTON

ith RICHARD DONNER & ADAM KUBERT

SUPERMAN & THE LEGION OF SUPER-HEROES

with GARY FRANK

JPERMAN: BRAINIAC

with GARY FRANK

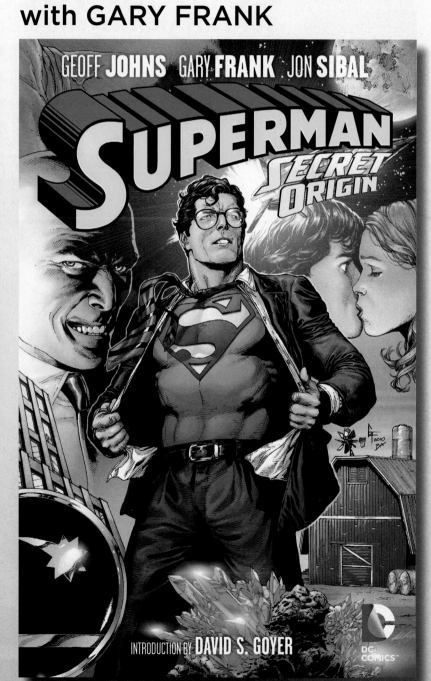

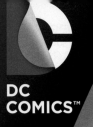

DC COMICS™

"ACTION COMICS has successfully carved
own territory and continued exploring Morriso
familiar themes about heroism and ideas."—

"Casts the character in a new light, opens up fresh storyt
ing possibilities, and pushes it all forward with dynamic R
Morales art. I loved it."—THE ONION/AV CL

START AT THE BEGINNING

SUPERMAN: ACTION COMICS VOLUME 1 SUPERMAN AND THE MEN OF STEE

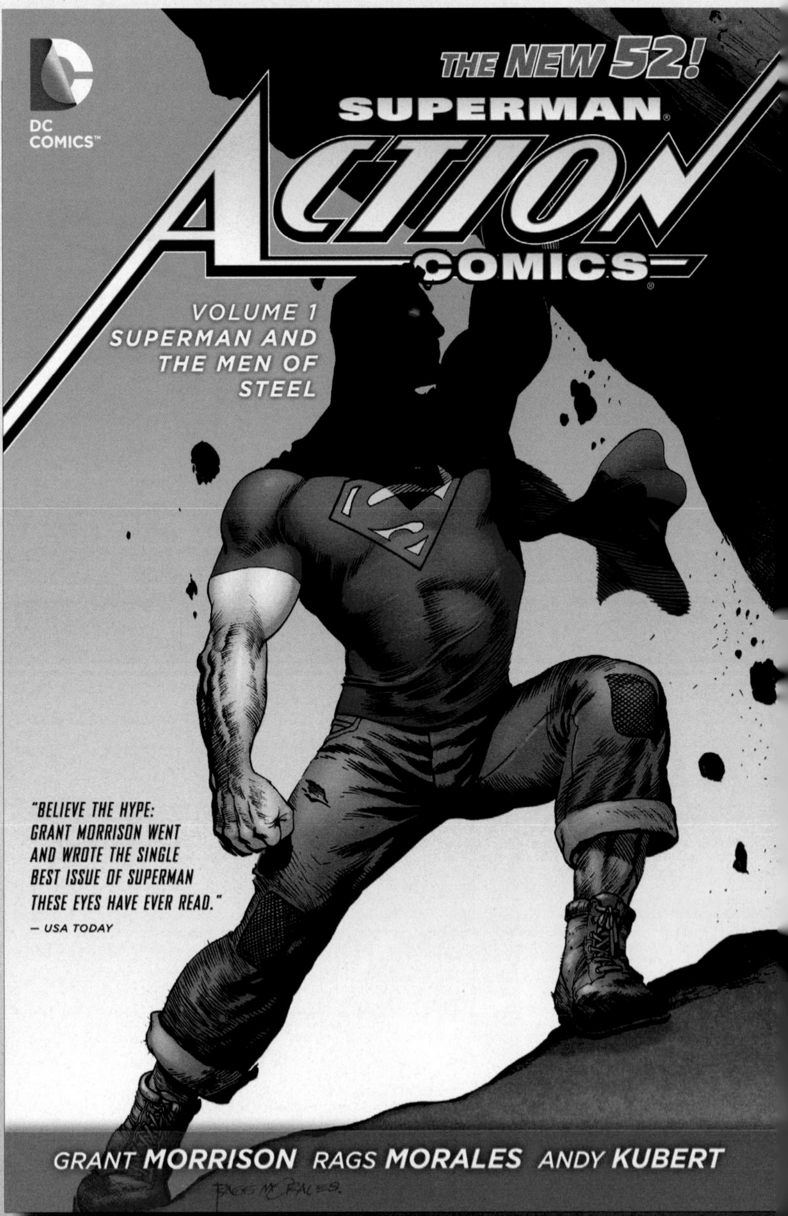
DC COMICS
THE NEW 52!
SUPERMAN
ACTION COMICS
VOLUME 1 SUPERMAN AND THE MEN OF STEEL
"BELIEVE THE HYPE: GRANT MORRISON WENT AND WROTE THE SINGLE BEST ISSUE OF SUPERMAN THESE EYES HAVE EVER READ."
— USA TODAY
GRANT MORRISON RAGS MORALES ANDY KUBERT

SUPERMAN: ACTION COMICS VOL. 2: BULLETPROOF

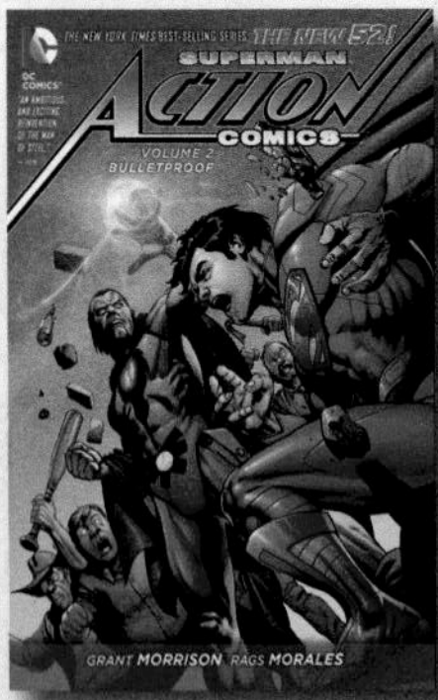
THE NEW 52!
SUPERMAN
ACTION COMICS
GRANT MORRISON RAGS MORALES

with GRANT MORRISON and RAGS MORALES

SUPERMAN: ACTION COMICS VOL. 3: AT THE END OF DAYS

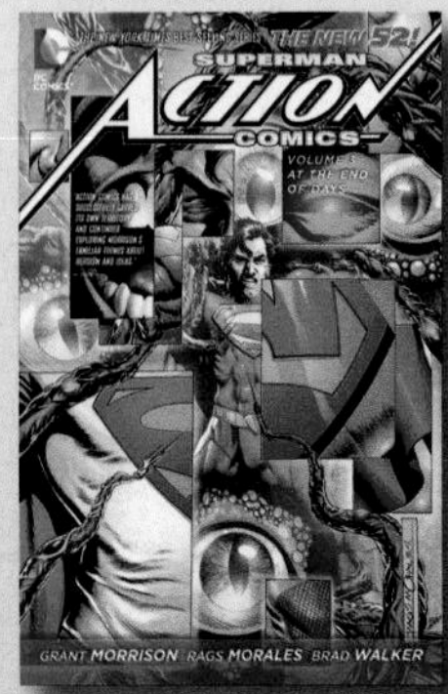
THE NEW 52!
SUPERMAN
ACTION COMICS
GRANT MORRISON RAGS MORALES BRAD WALKER

with GRANT MORRISON and RAGS MORALES

SUPERBOY VOL. 1: INCUBATION

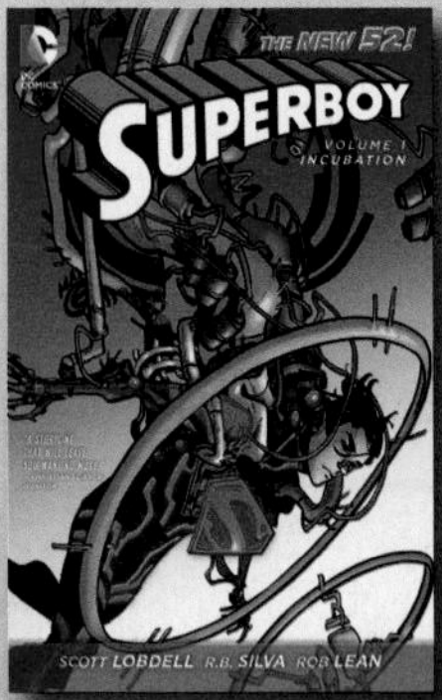
THE NEW 52!
SUPERBOY
SCOTT LOBDELL R.B. SILVA ROB LEAN

"Superman is still super."
—WALL STREET JOURNAL

"The SUPERMAN world is also one now where fans new and old, young and not-so-young, can come to a common ground to talk about the superhero that started it all."
—CRAVE ONLINE

START AT THE BEGINNING!

SUPERMAN VOLUME 1: WHAT PRICE TOMORROW?

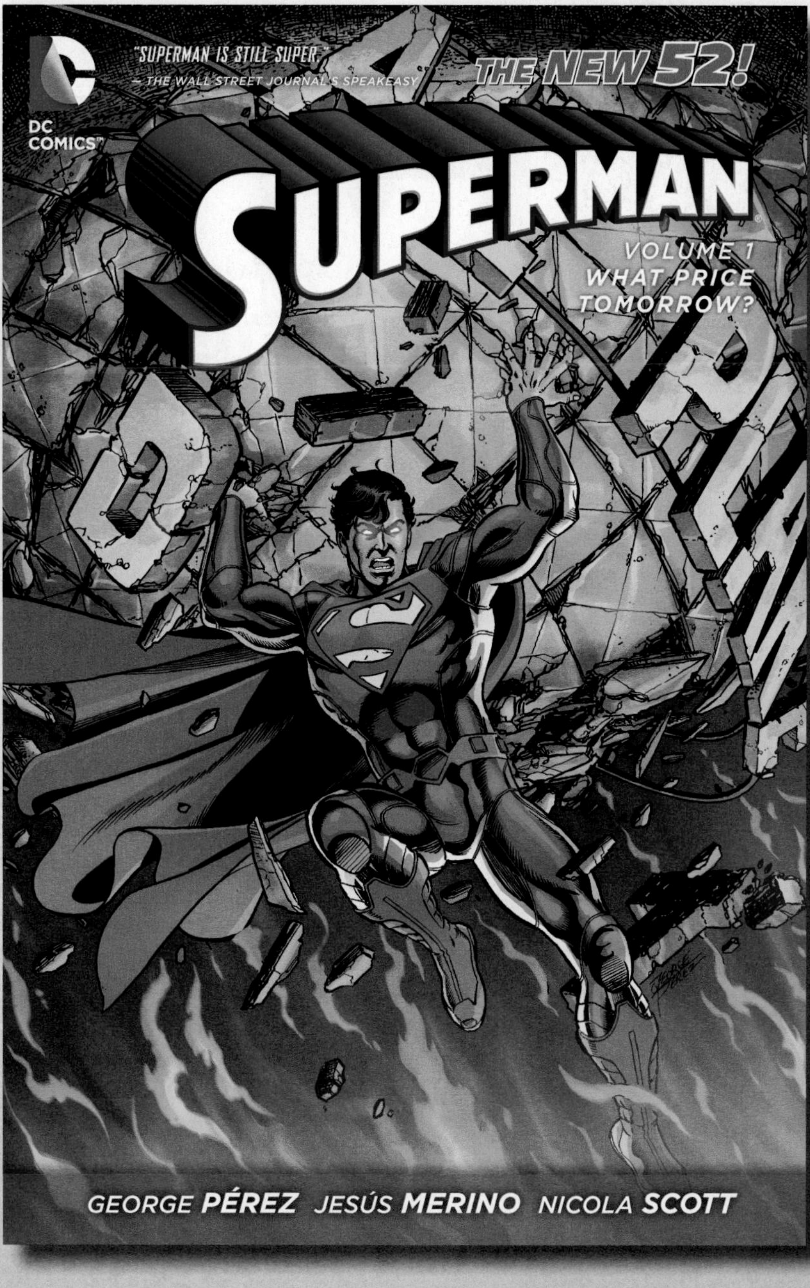

DC COMICS
"SUPERMAN IS STILL SUPER."
— THE WALL STREET JOURNAL'S SPEAKEASY
THE NEW 52!
SUPERMAN
VOLUME 1
WHAT PRICE TOMORROW?
GEORGE PÉREZ JESÚS MERINO NICOLA SCOTT

SUPERMAN VOL. 2: SECRETS & LIES

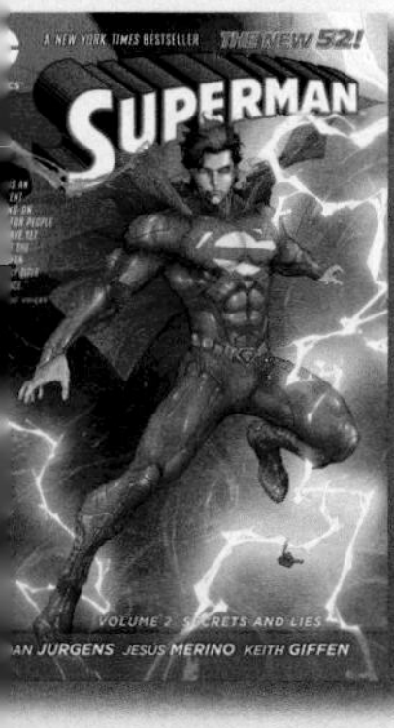

THE NEW 52!
SUPERMAN

SUPERMAN VOL. 3: FURY AT WORLD'S END

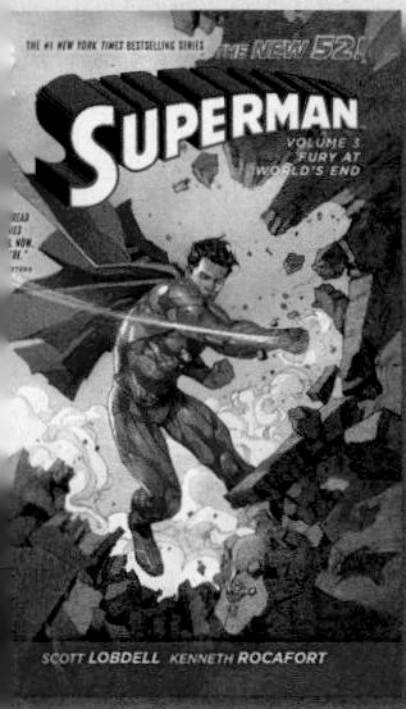

THE NEW 52!
SUPERMAN
SCOTT LOBDELL KENNETH ROCAFORT

SUPERMAN: H'EL ON EARTH

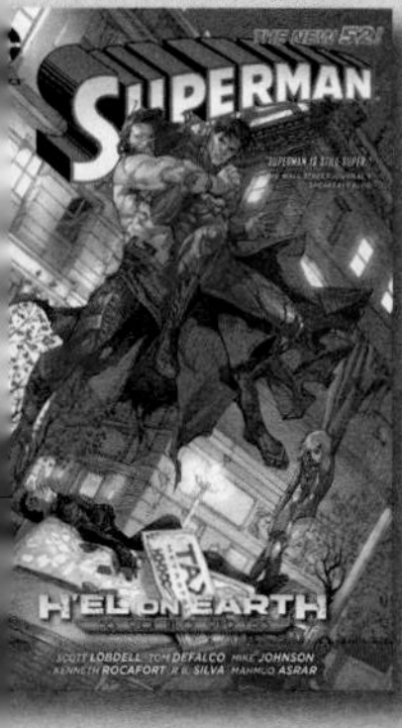

THE NEW 52!
SUPERMAN
H'EL ON EARTH

DC COMICS™

"[A] comic legend." —ROLLING STON[E]

"[Grant Morrison is] comics' high shaman[…]
—WASHINGTON POS[T]

"[Grant Morrison] is probably my favori[te]
writer. That guy has more ideas in his pin[k…]
than most people do in a lifetime[.]"
—Gerard Way from MY CHEMICAL ROMANC[E]

FROM THE WRITER OF *ALL-STAR SUPERMAN* AND *BATMAN & ROBIN*

GRANT MORRISON

with HOWARD PORTER

JLA VOL. 2

with HOWARD PORTER

JLA VOL. 3

with HOWARD PORTER

JLA VOL. 4

with HOWARD PORTER,
MARK WAID, and MARK
PAJARILLO

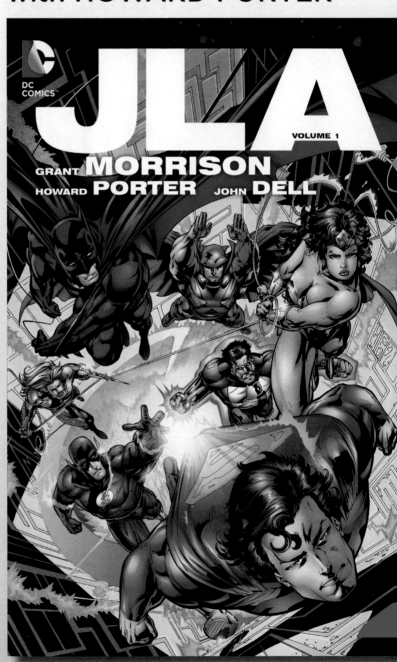